China's Semiconductor Industry Strategy

SpringerBriefs in Economics

SpringerBriefs present concise summaries of cutting-edge research and practical applications across a wide spectrum of fields. Featuring compact volumes of 50 to 125 pages, the series covers a range of content from professional to academic. Typical topics might include:

- A timely report of state-of-the art analytical techniques
- A bridge between new research results, as published in journal articles, and a contextual literature review
- A snapshot of a hot or emerging topic
- An in-depth case study or clinical example
- A presentation of core concepts that students must understand in order to make independent contributions

SpringerBriefs in Economics showcase emerging theory, empirical research, and practical application in microeconomics, macroeconomics, economic policy, public finance, econometrics, regional science, and related fields, from a global author community.

Briefs are characterized by fast, global electronic dissemination, standard publishing contracts, standardized manuscript preparation and formatting guidelines, and expedited production schedules.

Tao Ma • Tiantian Wang • Jian Zhang

China's Semiconductor Industry Strategy

Assessment and Optimization

 Springer

Tao Ma
Harbin Institute of Technology
Harbin, China

Tiantian Wang
Harbin Institute of Technology
Harbin, China

Jian Zhang
Fujian Electronic Information Application
Technology Research Institute Co., Ltd.
Fuzhou, China

ISSN 2191-5504   ISSN 2191-5512   (electronic)
SpringerBriefs in Economics
ISBN 978-981-95-3331-2   ISBN 978-981-95-3332-9   (eBook)
https://doi.org/10.1007/978-981-95-3332-9

Funding: The Major Program of National Social Science Fund of China (Grant No. 23&ZD040).

Dedicated to those who have inspired me to pursue knowledge and persevere in research

Preface

The impetus for writing this book stems from the profound transformation of the global semiconductor industry in recent years. Once characterised by a logic of technology-driven global collaboration, the industry has entered a new phase defined by geopolitical restructuring, regional consolidation, and heightened security concerns. For China, the semiconductor sector is not only a foundation for technological progress but also a strategic linchpin for safeguarding economic stability and industrial competitiveness.

Against this backdrop, this book focuses on two interrelated objectives: assessing the security level of China's semiconductor industry chain and exploring pathways for its optimisation. We approach this challenge by integrating global industry perspectives with detailed empirical analysis of China's current capabilities, vulnerabilities, and opportunities.

The research builds upon a multidimensional indicator system covering import concentration, trade competitiveness, innovation capacity, and policy environment. Using Principal Component Analysis, the Entropy Weight Method, and the TOPSIS model, we conduct both longitudinal (2015–2023) and cross-regional assessments. The study further disaggregates the industry chain into upstream, midstream, and downstream segments to capture structural differences and segment-specific risks. Special attention is given to external shocks—such as US supply chain review policies, international trade frictions, and global industry relocation—and to analysing the pathways through which these shocks influence security via changes in industrial structure, external dependence, and innovation capability.

The book is organised into three main parts. The first part outlines the global semiconductor landscape, the strategic significance of China's industry, and the methodological foundations of the study. The second part presents the empirical assessment of the industry chain's security level, including quantitative measurement and analysis of the transmission channels of external shocks. The third part explores strategies for layout optimisation, from regional coordination to global integration, and from industrial park upgrading to international expansion.

This work is intended for policymakers, industry practitioners, and researchers interested in semiconductor industry security, supply chain resilience, and strategic industrial planning. It is my hope that the insights and analytical tools presented here will contribute to informed decision-making and constructive dialogue among stakeholders.

I would like to express my sincere gratitude to the funding support from the Major Program of the National Social Science Foundation of China (Grant No. 23&ZD040), as well as to Emily Zhang and Nandakini Lahiri of Springer Nature for their professional guidance and editorial assistance throughout the preparation of this manuscript. I am also grateful to my doctoral student Tiantian Wang for her substantial contributions to Chapters 1, 5, 6, and 7, and to Jian Zhang for authoring Chapter 8. Their analytical insights and empirical work have enriched this book greatly.

School of Civil Engineering, Harbin Institute of Technology   Tao Ma
Harbin, China
August 1, 2025

Acknowledgements

This work was supported by the Major Program of the National Social Science Foundation of China (NSSFC) [Grant No. 23&ZD040], Research on Optimizing the Layout of Major Productive Forces in the New Development Stage. The author would like to express sincere gratitude to Emily Zhang and Nandakini Lahiri for their professional guidance, constructive suggestions, and dedicated editorial support throughout the preparation of this manuscript.

About This BookThis book provides a comprehensive examination of the security assessment and layout optimisation of China's semiconductor industry chain, situated within the context of global industrial restructuring and intensifying geopolitical tensions. As a strategic cornerstone of the digital economy and advanced manufacturing, the security of the semiconductor industry is essential not only for technological progress but also for safeguarding economic stability and sustaining industrial competitiveness.

Building on an analysis of global industry trends and the current state of China's semiconductor sector, the book develops a holistic framework that covers the upstream (raw materials and equipment), midstream (manufacturing and packaging/testing), and downstream (end-use applications) segments. Employing a multidimensional indicator system—including import concentration, trade competitiveness, innovation capacity, and policy environment—and applying Principal Component Analysis, the Entropy Weight Method, and the TOPSIS model, it offers both a longitudinal assessment (2015–2023) and a cross-regional comparison of the security of China's semiconductor industry chain. The study also disaggregates risk characteristics and structural differences across different segments of the value chain.

Particular attention is devoted to major external shocks—such as US supply chain review policies, international trade frictions, and global industry relocation—and to analysing the channels through which these shocks influence security via changes in industrial structure, external dependence, and innovation capacity. Based on this analysis, the book proposes practical strategies at the policy, industry, and enterprise levels to strengthen resilience. In the discussion of layout optimisation, it draws on global industrial development patterns and China's regional resource endowments to suggest pathways for regional coordination, integration into global value chains, upgrading of key industrial parks, and international expansion.

With its robust analytical framework, diverse empirical sources, and rigorous methodology, this book serves as a valuable resource for policymakers designing industrial security and development strategies, as well as for scholars and practitioners seeking data-driven insights and analytical tools to understand and enhance the resilience of China's semiconductor industry chain.

Contents

1 Introduction.. 1
Tiantian Wang
  1.1 Research Background and Significance........................ 1
      1.1.1 Global Semiconductor Industry Changes and Challenges ... 1
      1.1.2 Global Strategic Significance of China's Semiconductor
             Industry... 3
  1.2 Definition of Relevant Concepts and Literature Review........... 12
      1.2.1 Industry Chain...................................... 12
      1.2.2 Industrial Chain Security............................. 13
      1.2.3 Semiconductor Industry Chain........................ 16
      1.2.4 Literature Review.................................... 18
  1.3 Research Objectives and Content............................ 20
      1.3.1 Comprehensive Assessment of the Security of China's
             Semiconductor Industry............................. 20
      1.3.2 In-Depth Discussion of Strategies for Optimising the Layout
             of China's Semiconductor Industry.................... 22
  1.4 Research Methods and Data Sources......................... 23
      1.4.1 Research Methods.................................. 23
      1.4.2 Data Sources...................................... 26

2 Global Semiconductor Industry Development Pattern and Trends.... 31
Tao Ma
  2.1 Historical Evolution of the Global Semiconductor Industry......... 31
      2.1.1 Origin and Early Development Stages of the Industry 31
      2.1.2 Industrial Expansion in the Wave of Globalisation 32
      2.1.3 Recent Technological Changes and Industrial Restructuring .. 33
  2.2 Current Global Semiconductor Industry Landscape and Regional
      Characteristics 33
      2.2.1 United States: A Hub of Technological Innovation and
             Global Industry Leader.............................. 33

2.2.2   Europe: Strategic Advantages in Specialised Technologies
        and High-End Applications 35
2.2.3   Japan: Core Competitiveness in Materials and Equipment . . . 36
2.2.4   South Korea: A Dual-Track Approach Combining Memory
        Dominance and Advanced Process Technology 38
2.2.5   Chinese Taiwan: Important Position in Contract
        Manufacturing. 39
2.2.6   Emerging Powers: The Strategic Rise of India and Southeast
        Asia 41
2.3   Future Development Trends of the Global Semiconductor Industry . . . 42
        2.3.1   Technological Innovation-Driven Industrial Upgrading
                Directions 42
        2.3.2   Dynamic Changes in Market Demand and Emerging
                Application Areas 45

3   **Development Environment and Trade Structure of China's**
    Semiconductor Industry During the 15th Five-Year Plan Period 49
    Tao Ma
    3.1   Impact of the Global Policy Environment on China's
          Semiconductor Industry 50
          3.1.1   Analysis of Semiconductor Industry Policies in Major
                  Countries and Regions 50
          3.1.2   China's Response to International Policy Coordination and
                  the Competitive Landscape 52
    3.2   Global Economic Environment and Its Relationship with China's
          Semiconductor Industry 54
          3.2.1   The Interrelationship Between Global Economic Growth
                  and Semiconductor Market Demand 54
          3.2.2   The Impact of International Trade Frictions on China's
                  Semiconductor Industry Chain 55
    3.3   Opportunities and Challenges for China's Semiconductor Industry
          in the Global Technology Environment 56
          3.3.1   Current Status and Trends in International Technical
                  Exchange and Cooperation 56
          3.3.2   Dual Pressures of Technological Barriers and Independent
                  Innovation. 58
    3.4   Trade Structure of China's Semiconductor Industry Chain 59
          3.4.1   Trade Structure in the Upstream Industry Chain 60
          3.4.2   Trade Structure in the Midstream of the Industry Chain 64
          3.4.3   Trade Structure in the Downstream Industry Chain. 66
    3.5   Summary 69

4   **Current Distribution of China's Semiconductor Industry** 73
    Tao Ma
    4.1   Regional Distribution of China's Semiconductor Industry and
          Comparison with the Global Landscape 74

4.1.1   Characteristics and Development Potential of Industrial
        Distribution in the Eastern Coastal, Central and Western
        Regions 74
4.1.2   Spatial Differences Analysis with Major Global
        Semiconductor Industry Clusters 77
4.2 Issues Facing the Current Industrial Layout and Challenges in
     International Competition 78
4.2.1   Insufficient Industrial Synergy and Competitive Disadvantages 78
4.2.2   Risk of Industrial Layout Not Matching Global Industrial
        Development Trends 81
4.2.3   Regional Development Imbalances and Resource Allocation
        Issues 84
4.3 Trends in the Transfer of the Semiconductor Industry and the
     Urgency of Adjusting China's Semiconductor Industry Layout 87
4.3.1   Historical Characteristics and Lessons Learned from the
        Transfer of the Semiconductor Industry 87
4.3.2   New Trends and Underlying Logic in the Current Transfer
        of the Semiconductor Industry 88
4.3.3   Opportunities and Challenges for China in the Global
        Semiconductor Industry Shift. 90

5 **Comprehensive Quantitative Assessment of the Security Level of
   China's Semiconductor Industry Chain** **93**
   Tiantian Wang
   5.1 Safety Level Measurement Based on Indicator System. 93
   5.1.1   Construction of the PCA-Entropy Weight-TOPSIS Model . . . 93
   5.1.2   Vertical Analysis of the Security Level of China's
           Semiconductor Industry Chain 98
   5.1.3   Horizontal Analysis of China's Semiconductor Industry
           Chain Security Level 99
   5.1.4   Security of China's Semiconductor Industry Chain from
           Upstream to Downstream from a Trade Perspective 104
   5.2 Assessing Semiconductor Industry Chain Security Risks from the
        Perspective of Import Concentration 108
   5.2.1   Construction of Import Concentration Indicators 108
   5.2.2   Overall Assessment of the Security Level of the
           Semiconductor Industry Chain 109
   5.2.3   Country (Region) Heterogeneity in the Security Level of the
           Semiconductor Industry Chain 111
   5.2.4   Heterogeneity of the Semiconductor Industry Chain
           Security Level. 113

6 **The Reshaping of the US Supply Chain and the Security Level of
   China's Semiconductor Industry Chain** **117**
   Tiantian Wang
   6.1 Theoretical Mechanisms and Research Hypotheses 118

6.1.1   The Direct Impact of US Supply Chain Review Policies on
the Security Level of Industrial Chains 118
6.1.2   Moderating Effect Mechanism 118
6.2   Empirical Design 120
6.3   Benchmark Regression Analysis 121
6.4   Parallel Trend Test 122
6.5   Endogeneity and Robustness Tests. 123
6.5.1   Endogeneity Test 123
6.5.2   Robustness Tests. 123
6.6   Analysis of Influencing Mechanisms 126
6.7   Policy Implications. 128

7   **Optimisation of China's Semiconductor Industry Layout** **133**
Tiantian Wang
7.1   Optimisation of Semiconductor Industry Layout and Strategic Goal
Setting from a Global Perspective 133
7.1.1   Follow the Development Laws of the Semiconductor
Industry and the Principles of Regional Coordination and
Development 133
7.1.2   Setting Goals for Enhancing Global Competitiveness and
Ensuring Industrial Security 135
7.1.3   Aligning with Global Industrial Development Trends and
Setting Scientific and Forward-Looking Goals 137
7.2   Regional Coordination and Global Industrial Chain Integration
Strategies 139
7.2.1   Strengthen Domestic Regional Industrial Cooperation and
Enhance the Synergistic Effects of the Industrial Chain . . . 139
7.2.2   Accelerate the Integration of Domestic and International
Resources and Optimise the Global Industrial Chain Layout   141
7.2.3   Promote Coordinated Development Among Different
Regions Within the Country and Enhance the Overall
Competitiveness of Industries. 143
7.3   Internationalisation Development Pathways for Key Industrial Parks
and Bases 145
7.3.1   Planning and Construction Benchmarked Against
International Advanced Parks: From Park Construction to
Operation and Management. 145
7.3.2   Pathways for Promoting the Transformation of Industrial
Bases into High-End Manufacturing and R&D Innovation
Centres 148
7.3.3   Challenges and Solutions in the Process of
Internationalisation 150
7.4   Policy and Market-Driven Industrial Layout Optimisation Pathways   152
7.4.1   Policy Guidance: Support the Development of High-Tech
Industrial Parks and the Process of Globalisation 152

7.4.2   Market Demand Changes Drive Industrial Optimisation:
The Dual Role of Technological Progress and Market
Guidance 154

8   **The Development of the Semiconductor Industry in Fujian Province:**
A Regional Sample of China's Semiconductor Industry Chain 159
Jian Zhang
8.1   Current Status of Semiconductor Industry Development in Fujian
Province 160
8.1.1   Overall Situation 160
8.1.2   Overall Status of the Industry 160
8.1.3   Current Status of the Design Industry 161
8.1.4   Current Status of Manufacturing Development 162
8.1.5   Current Status of the Packaging and Testing Industry 163
8.1.6   Current Development Status of the Equipment and
Materials Industry 164
8.2   Advantages and Disadvantages of Fujian Province's Semiconductor
Industry Development 164
8.2.1   Advantages of Industry Development 164
8.2.2   Insufficient Industrial Development 165
8.3   Key Directions and Main Tasks 166
8.3.1   Key Directions for Industrial Development 166
8.3.2   Main Tasks for Industrial Development 167
8.4   Insights into the Development of Fujian Province's Semiconductor
Industry 170
8.4.1   Accelerate the Development of the Upstream Industry Chain
and Leverage the Industrial Foundation to Develop the
Semiconductor Materials Segment 171
8.4.2   Addressing Development Bottlenecks to Accelerate the
High-Quality Development of the Semiconductor Materials
Industry 173

Chapter 1
Introduction

Tiantian Wang

Abstract Chapter 1 introduces the background and research significance of China's semiconductor industry chain within the context of global industrial transformation. It focuses on structural challenges including technological paradigm shifts, evolving collaboration models, and supply chain reconfigurations. The chapter highlights China's strategic role as a key player in the global semiconductor ecosystem, while acknowledging enduring constraints in critical technological domains. It defines core concepts—industry chain, supply chain security, and the semiconductor value chain—and reviews relevant academic literature. Furthermore, it identifies principal factors affecting industrial chain security and outlines the research objectives and indicator framework, thereby laying the theoretical and methodological groundwork for the ensuing empirical analysis.

Keywords Semiconductor Industry Chain • Supply Chain Security • Technological Self-Reliance • Import Dependence • Industrial Chain Resilience

1.1 Research Background and Significance

1.1.1 Global Semiconductor Industry Changes and Challenges

Semiconductors are hailed as the 'industrial grain' of the modern information society. The evolution of the semiconductor industry not only reflects the continuous leap in technological paradigms, but is also deeply embedded in geopolitics, the global economy and security games. Entering the third decade of the twenty-first century, the global semiconductor industry is shifting from a logic system of 'technology-driven global collaboration' to a new pattern of 'political restructuring and regional embedding.' This transformation brings three core challenges:

1.1.1.1 Approaching Technical Bottlenecks and Paradigm Shifts

As Moore's Law gradually slows down and transistor sizes approach physical limits, advanced processes (such as those below 3 nanometres) face multiple challenges, including yield control, thermal management, and manufacturing costs. To break through the limitations of traditional processes, the industry is accelerating the adoption of next-generation chip architectures such as Chiplet heterogeneous integration, 3D packaging, and system-level optimisation (SoIC), reshaping the technical boundaries between design, manufacturing, and packaging. According to Siemens EDA, multi-chip system-level packaging (SiP) will grow rapidly, with heterogeneous integration becoming the mainstream trend. Additionally, emerging technologies such as quantum computing and photonic chips, though still in their early stages, already hint at structural transformations in the 'post-Moore era.' McKinsey highlights that quantum computing holds the earliest potential for economic impact in sectors such as chemicals, life sciences, financial services, and transportation. Despite current technical challenges, the development trajectory of quantum computing has already drawn significant global attention from the tech community.

1.1.1.2 Systematic Increase in Geopolitical Risks

The Sino-US technology friction has expanded from the corporate level to institutional 'technology decoupling.' The United States passed the CHIPS and Science Act, allocating $52.7 billion to support domestic manufacturing, while the European Union and Japan have also established localisation subsidy mechanisms aimed at enhancing the competitiveness of their semiconductor industries. Key countries such as the Netherlands, South Korea, and India have been incorporated into 'technology alliances' or 'de-Chinaisation' strategic chains, making semiconductors the core vehicle for the new round of international rules and national security. Brookings points out that semiconductor industry cooperation between Japan, the United States, and South Korea will primarily be driven by the private sector, and commercial competition may weaken the effectiveness of policy coordination. This trend is leading to the fragmentation and reduced efficiency of global supply chains, increasing uncertainty in the industry.

1.1.1.3 Reconstructing Supply Chain Security Logic

The logic of global division of labour has been deeply questioned in the face of the pandemic, war, and technological blockades. Countries have successively proposed 'friend-shoring' and 'China+1' strategies to reduce their reliance on a single region. Companies such as TSMC are accelerating their expansion in the United States, Japan, and Germany to achieve both regional redundancy and political security. Meanwhile, control over critical resources and equipment such as rare earths, photoresist, and neon gas has emerged as a new focal point of global competition. The Centre for Strategic and International Studies (CSIS) noted that Russia and Ukraine previously accounted for 40–50% of global neon gas supply, and the war has disrupted supply chains, highlighting the risks of reliance on a single source.

In summary, the global semiconductor industry is transitioning from efficiency-driven to security-driven, and from unipolar hegemony to multipolar competition. Against this complex backdrop, China's semiconductor industry faces not only the challenge of catching up technologically but also the dual exposure of external dependency and systemic vulnerabilities. How to break through 'chokepoint' technologies in the regional competitive landscape and achieve global integration has become an urgent strategic imperative.

1.1.2   Global Strategic Significance of China's Semiconductor Industry

The rise of China's semiconductor industry is not only an inevitable demand for technological independence, but also a core strategic pillar for reshaping the global technological power structure, ensuring the security of the digital economy, and supporting competition among major countries. Its global significance is reflected in the following four dimensions.

1.1.2.1   Global Economic Stabiliser: Dual Drivers of Demand and Supply Capacity

With the rapid development of the global digital economy, semiconductors, as a strategic foundation industry, have a profound impact on the stability and resilience of the world economy through their supply and demand structure and regional layout. China's semiconductor industry, through a three-pronged structure of 'terminal market scale, manufacturing capacity layout, and material and process support,' is becoming an important stabiliser in the global semiconductor system, as reflected in the following two aspects:

1.1.2.1.1   Demand Side: Strategic Leverage of the World's Largest End Market

According to IC Insights (2023), China has consistently accounted for over 40% of global semiconductor total consumption since 2013, making it the world's largest market for chip demand. In core end-market sectors such as smartphones, new energy vehicles, and industrial automation, China boasts the world's largest application market scale. For example, in 2022, China's smartphone shipments exceeded 270 million units, accounting for approximately 35% of the global total; new energy vehicle sales reached 6.887 million units, accounting for 60% of global total sales (EV Volumes, 2023); and annual installations of industrial robots reached 268,000 units, accounting for 52% of the global total (IFR, 2023). Such terminal devices drive diverse customisation demands for System-on-Chip (SoC), high-speed interconnect chips, and automotive-grade power devices, accelerating the global transition of chip design and manufacturing models toward application-driven and scenario-customised approaches.

Taking new energy vehicles as an example, the trends toward vehicle intelligence and electrification significantly enhance the structural demand for power semiconductors and control chips. In 2023, the domestic production rate of IGBT modules installed in BYD's new energy vehicles exceeded 70% (Omdia), creating a reverse pressure effect on international giants such as Infineon and ON Semiconductor to invest and localise their technologies in China. In the field of intelligent computing, China is gradually deploying autonomous AI chip platforms such as Huawei Ascend, Cambricon's ShenYuan series, to support high-performance computing centres like the 'Tianhe-3' and industry-specific AI infrastructure. This has effectively established a closed-loop ecosystem encompassing 'data-algorithms-computing power-chips,' reducing systemic reliance on foreign high-end GPU resources like NVIDIA's A100/H100.

1.1.2.1.2 Supply Side: The 'Ballast Stone' Role of Mature Manufacturing Processes and Material Systems

In addition to the strong demand from the consumer end, China's foundational production capacity in wafer manufacturing, packaging and testing, and the supply of key materials also plays a crucial role in maintaining the stability of the global semiconductor supply chain. According to TrendForce (2023) data, China's production capacity for wafers in the 28-nanometre and above mature process nodes accounts for approximately 29% of the global total, and is projected to grow to 33% by 2027. Representative companies such as SMIC expanded their production lines in Beijing, Shanghai, and Shenzhen in 2023, adding an annual capacity of 150,000 wafers per month for 28-nanometre and above processes, effectively alleviating global capacity bottlenecks in areas such as analogue circuits and automotive electronics.

Additionally, in the field of semiconductor key materials, China has demonstrated strategic catch-up capabilities. The Russia-Ukraine conflict in 2022 disrupted global neon gas supply (Ukraine accounted for approximately 70% of global neon gas supply), directly threatening the stable operation of global lithography processes. Domestic companies such as China's Kaimeite Gas have rapidly achieved the conversion of industrial-grade neon gas to semiconductor-grade neon gas through independent purification and plasma separation technologies, covering approximately 40% of global replacement supply in the short term. This has significantly alleviated the manufacturing disruption risks caused by the global neon gas shortage and strengthened China's global role in the 'stable supply chain for materials.'

In summary, China's semiconductor industry has established a new strategic position of 'bidirectional integration and structural coupling' within the global semiconductor supply chain through the spillover effects of domestic demand and external supply chain supplementation mechanisms. This provides structural stability support for the global economy amid fluctuations in semiconductor technology and geopolitical risks.

1.1.2.2   The Battle for Technological Sovereignty: Breaking the 'Centre-Periphery' Division of Labour System

1.1.2.2.1   Break Through the Bottom of the 'Smile Curve': Leap from Packaging and Testing to Core Processes

For a long time, China's semiconductor industry has primarily focused on low-value-added segments such as packaging and testing, placing it at the bottom of the global 'smile curve' (IC Insights, 2023). To address this situation, China has invested over 500 billion yuan through two phases of the National Integrated Circuit Industry Investment Fund (the 'Big Fund') to extend the industrial chain upstream into design and materials, challenging the US-dominated 'design-manufacturing-equipment' triangle (National Integrated Circuit Industry Investment Fund Announcement, 2023).

In chip design, Huawei HiSilicon's Ascend 910B AI chip, manufactured using SMIC's 7-nanometre process (N+2 technology), has achieved 80% of the performance of NVIDIA's A100, supporting the training needs of large language models such as Baidu's 'Wenxin Yiyuan' and Alibaba Cloud's 'Tongyi Qianwen' (Huawei Technologies Co., Ltd. Press Conference, 2023). In the materials field, as one of the first domestic manufacturers to achieve large-scale production of 12-inch silicon wafers, Shanghai Xinsheng's products have been certified by domestic wafer foundries such as SMIC and Huali, marking a significant advancement in China's high-end silicon wafer manufacturing capabilities (TSMC Annual Report, 2023). In equipment manufacturing, Northern HuaChuang has made significant progress in the field of domestically produced ICP and CCP etching equipment, with cumulative shipments exceeding 3,500 chambers in 2023, establishing a solid application foundation in logic and memory chip manufacturing (Northern HuaChuang Technology Group Co., Ltd. Announcement, 2023).

1.1.2.2.2   Building an Open Technology Ecosystem

China has made significant progress in building an open technology ecosystem. As of 2023, the Xuanji C910 processor launched by Alibaba's PingTouGe company has shipped over 2 billion units, widely used for energy efficiency optimisation in Alibaba Cloud data centres (Alibaba Group Annual Report, 2023). Within the international RISC-V Foundation, the Institute of Computing Technology of the Chinese Academy of Sciences and Huawei, along with other Chinese institutions, have been actively contributing to multiple technical working groups involved in the development of the RISC-V international standard, challenging the dominant position of the ARM architecture (RISC-V International Annual Report, 2023).

In terms of packaging technology, the 'Chip-to-Chip Interconnect Interface Specification' has accelerated the standardisation process for Chiplet technology. Changjiang Microelectronics Technology's XDFOI™ packaging technology enables multi-chip heterogeneous integration, enhancing performance and reducing costs, with technical specifications comparable to Intel's EMIB technology.

The establishment of an independent and controllable ecosystem based on the RISC-V architecture and chiplet heterogeneous integration standards is breaking the closed systems of ARM and x86, providing a 'Chinese solution' for the diversification of global semiconductor technology.

1.1.2.3 The Cornerstone of National Security: Comprehensive Defence from Supply Chain Security to Digital Sovereignty

1.1.2.3.1 Defence and Critical Infrastructure Self-Reliance

Against the backdrop of the current complex international geopolitical landscape, enhancing the self-reliance and control over national defence and critical infrastructure has become a core element of national security strategy. Take aerospace and strategic weapon systems as an example: the active electronically scanned array (AESA) radar chips on the J-20 fighter jet and the inertial navigation modules on the Dongfeng-41 intercontinental ballistic missile have both achieved 100% domestic production, significantly enhancing the equipment's independent R&D capabilities and system interference resistance (China Electronics Technology Group Corporation, 14th Research Institute, publicly available technical report, 2023). At the same time, in the field of civilian infrastructure, as of 2023, the domestic production rate of chips used in the State Grid's new generation of smart meters has exceeded 95% (State Grid Corporation of China tender platform data), effectively avoiding the risks of foreign control-type cyber attacks revealed by incidents such as 'Stuxnet.'

To standardise and strengthen the security protection mechanisms for critical information infrastructure (CII), the State Council promulgated the Regulations on the Security Protection of Critical Information Infrastructure in 2022, clearly requiring that core information technology components used in strategic industries such as energy, finance, and communications must undergo national security reviews, and emphasising the priority procurement of domestically produced chips and systems that have passed certification.

1.1.2.3.2   Building Data Sovereignty and Cyber Defence Capabilities

Against the backdrop of increasingly intense global data flows and competition in cyberspace, the issue of national data sovereignty has become increasingly prominent. In 2018, the United States enacted the Clarifying Lawful Overseas Use of Data Act (CLOUD Act), which authorises the US government to access data stored in third countries without notifying the government of the data's location. In response, China has accelerated the domestic substitution of AI chips and servers to strengthen the technological independence of its domestic infrastructure.

For example, the Cambricon 'Thunder' series of AI chips have been deployed in multiple financial and government data centres, establishing localised high-performance computing capabilities and enhancing data processing security in critical scenarios. Huawei's 'Kunpeng 920' server CPU, based on the ARM v8 architecture with permanent development authorisation, is widely used in China Mobile's 5G core network environment, achieving a systematic replacement of the previously relied-upon Intel 'Xeon' processors. The FT-2000 series of high-performance CPU chips launched by Feiteng Company have been successfully deployed on the 'Tianhe-3' supercomputing platform, marking China's advancement toward high-level autonomous control in the supercomputing field.

1.1.2.4   Participation in Global Governance: From Rule Follower to Co-Governor

1.1.2.4.1   Increased Influence in International Standard-Setting

In recent years, Chinese companies have significantly enhanced their influence in the global standard-setting process, marking a transition from being 'rule followers' to 'rule co-creators.' In the field of fifth-generation mobile communication (5G) standard-setting, according to a statistical report released by IPlytics in 2023, Chinese companies dominate the total number of standard-essential patent (SEP) applications, with Huawei and ZTE collectively contributing 39%, far exceeding the combined share of major European and American telecommunications equipment suppliers. This shift in the patent structure means that China has gained strong technical influence in key 5G technology areas such as millimetre-wave communication and base station radio frequency front-ends, and is leading the standard-setting process through its patent layout.

During the development of the IEEE 802.11ax (Wi-Fi 6) standard, Huawei's contributions accounted for approximately 12% of the total, ranking second among all companies, trailing only Qualcomm. Its contributions in key technical areas such as PHY and OFDMA were particularly notable (as documented in IEEE meeting records and publicly available technical committee materials). This demonstrates its breakthrough in the traditionally US-dominated landscape led by Qualcomm and Broadcom, driving the restructuring of global wireless communication chip design paradigms. Additionally, in the semiconductor sector, Huawei and ZTE have steadily increased their voting shares in international standard-setting organisations such as JEDEC and ISO, indicating that Chinese companies have transitioned from 'participants' to 'key players' in the competition for critical technological standards.

Through the 'Digital Silk Road' initiative, China is further integrating its standard influence with technology transfer mechanisms to build a new global digital production collaboration network. For example, Chinese companies have transferred 65-nanometre process technology to Saudi Arabia and are promoting the construction of a wafer fab in the China-Saudi Jizan Industrial Park. Meanwhile, semiconductor packaging and testing companies such as Tongfu Microelectronics are expanding local packaging and testing capacity through joint ventures with Malaysian companies. This integrated 'technology-capacity-market' output model not only enhances the local manufacturing capabilities of countries along the route but also substantially weakens the control of traditional semiconductor technology alliances over the global industrial chain.

1.1.2.4.2 Technological Multipolarisation Drives the Rebalancing of the Global Industrial Structure

Against the backdrop of an increasingly multi-polar global technology competition, China's strategic breakthroughs in several cutting-edge technology fields are driving a profound restructuring of the global industrial landscape. Take third-generation semiconductors as an example: Chinese companies are steadily increasing their market share in the silicon carbide (SiC) materials sector. According to TrendForce's 2023 industry analysis, Chinese suppliers such as Tianke Heda and Tianyue Advanced are rapidly emerging in the global silicon carbide substrate market, with the two companies accounting for approximately 17–18% of the market share each, collectively contributing approximately 30–35% of the global market share. TrendForce also noted that China is accelerating its integration across the entire value chain, from materials to epitaxy to devices. The US Department of Commerce added 8-inch silicon carbide wafers to its semiconductor export control list in 2022 (effective October 2022), which to some extent indirectly validates that China has posed a substantial technical challenge in this field.

In the field of quantum communication, China has also taken the lead in deploying a 'space-ground integrated' network. The quantum communication system, centred on the 'Micius' quantum science experiment satellite and the 'Beijing-Shanghai quantum trunk line,' has built the world's first wide-area quantum key distribution network, laying the foundation for the commercialisation of quantum encryption technology. The construction of this system not only demonstrates China's leading position in the field of quantum information science but also foreshadows a fundamental transformation in the future global network security governance structure.

In summary, China's enhanced technological capabilities in 5G, semiconductors, and quantum communication are challenging traditional technological hegemony, driving a transition in global governance structures from unilateral dominance to multilateral cooperation, and providing practical examples and institutional models for building a new global science and technology governance system centred on consultation, cooperation, and shared benefits.

1.1.2.5   The Impact of China's Semiconductor Industry on the Restructuring of the Global Industrial Landscape

1.1.2.5.1   Technological Multipolarisation: A Strategic Shift from Unilateral Dominance to Regional Coexistence

As the global technology governance system evolves towards a multipolar landscape, China's continuous breakthroughs in semiconductor technology are becoming an important driving force in reshaping the global industrial landscape. In particular, concentrated investment and capacity expansion in mature process nodes (28 nanometres and above) and third-generation semiconductor materials (such as silicon carbide SiC and gallium nitride GaN) have prompted structural adjustments in the industrial policies of the United States and European countries.

According to the 2023 annual reports released by SEMI and TrendForce, China's share of global silicon carbide substrate shipments has reached approximately 25%, with companies such as Tianke Heda and Sanan Optoelectronics currently establishing 8-inch silicon carbide production lines to meet the growing demand for electric vehicles and industrial-grade power devices.

At the same time, China is rapidly catching up in GaN RF and power devices, which are widely used in 5G base stations, electric vehicles, and photovoltaic inverters. This capacity expansion trend has broken the linear logic that 'advanced technology equals competitive advantage,' forcing technology-leading countries such as the United States to re-evaluate their industrial strategies.

A notable example is the US Department of Defense's 2022 funding of Sky-Water to expand its 90-nanometre process factory, emphasising self-reliance and supply chain resilience in 'non-advanced process' areas. This policy shift marks the transition of global semiconductor industry strategy from 'comprehensive high-end development' to 'node diversification,' signifying the gradual formation of a multi-polar technological landscape.

1.1.2.5.2   Supply Chain Redundancy: Global Risk Hedging and the Solid Position of Chinese Manufacturing

Against the backdrop of intensifying Sino-US technological competition and geopolitical uncertainty, global technology companies are generally pursuing a 'decentralisation' strategy, forming a so-called 'China + 1' production model, with the aim of establishing additional manufacturing redundancy without completely severing ties with China. Although Southeast Asia and India have emerged as new destinations, practice has shown that Chinese manufacturing still has irreplaceable advantages in terms of economies of scale, process stability and labour quality.

Take Apple Inc. as an example. The company plans to transfer approximately 30% of its global iPhone production capacity to India by the end of 2023, primarily relying on Foxconn's new factory complex in Chennai, Tamil Nadu. However, according to Bloomberg's on-site investigation in October 2023, the yield rate for the metal frames of the iPhone 15 series produced at this factory was only around 50%, lower than the yield rate at Foxconn's factory in Zhengzhou, China. This significant gap reflects China's global leadership in manufacturing coordination, process accumulation, and ecosystem completeness in the high-precision consumer electronics manufacturing sector.

Additionally, according to IC Insights and relevant industry statistics, by 2023, China's share of global chip packaging and testing (ATP) capacity had exceeded 37%, forming a group of large OSAT companies represented by Changjiang Microelectronics Technology, Huada Semiconductor, and Tongfu Microelectronics, making it one of the largest regions in the global back-end manufacturing sector. Beyond the front-end wafer manufacturing system dominated by TSMC, China's chip packaging and testing industry chain has become an indispensable pillar of the global semiconductor ecosystem. Even with some foundry capacity relocating overseas, China's comprehensive industrial system in packaging and testing, materials, components, and technical services continues to provide strong support for its core position in the global semiconductor supply chain.

In summary, China's semiconductor industry has become a key factor in reshaping the global industrial structure and promoting the diversification of the technological landscape through its three-pronged strategic approach of 'mature process leadership, cutting-edge technology catch-up, and a stable manufacturing ecosystem.' This enhanced influence is not only reflected in market share expansion but also in systemic competitive advantages in technical standards, manufacturing capabilities, and supply chain resilience.

1.1.2.6 Dual Strategic Significance

China's semiconductor industry exhibits a typical 'dual nature' in its strategic position within the global value chain, achieving a complex unity of contradictions between being a 'driver of technological multipolarisation' and a 'vulnerable entity dependent on high-end segments.' This dual nature not only reflects the current evolution of global technological governance but also provides a theoretical starting point for understanding China's strategy of technological self-reliance.

On the one hand, the development of China's semiconductor industry has benefited from multiple structural advantages, including its massive market size, intensive policy support, and a multilateral open ecosystem. According to IC Insights (2023), China's domestic chip market accounts for over 35% of global consumption, making it the world's largest semiconductor application market. Under the national '14th Five-Year Plan,' the semiconductor industry has been designated as a core strategic technology sector, with fiscal subsidies, tax breaks, and fund-guided investments totaling tens of billions of yuan. Additionally, through participation in international technical standards organisations, open-source architectures (such as RISC-V), and technology transfer and collaboration under the 'Belt and Road' framework, China has gradually built an open-technology ecosystem centred on 'technology co-construction,' emerging as a key driving force behind global 'technological multipolarisation.'

However, at the same time, China's semiconductor system still faces 'choke-point' technology bottlenecks in several key areas, and its highly dependent structure constitutes a critical vulnerability in the current 'dual circulation' strategic system. A typical example is extreme ultraviolet (EUV) lithography equipment, where China's domestic production rate is less than 1%, and core equipment still heavily relies on Dutch ASML and its supply chain system. Although Shanghai Microelectronics is developing China's first 28-nanometre lithography machine, it still lags significantly behind the 7-nanometre and below nodes supported by EUV technology. In terms of chip architecture, the ARM architecture, as the de facto standard for general-purpose processors (CPUs) and mobile device chips, poses systemic risks due to its reliance on IP licensing. Although Chinese domestic companies have actively expanded into the RISC-V open-source architecture in recent years and promoted the research, development, and application of indigenous CPU architectures such as Loongson and Feiteng, from the perspective of ecosystem development, achieving commercial-scale application and the maturity of the software ecosystem is still expected to require a 5 to 10-year timeline. This process involves operating system adaptation, developer community building, application compatibility optimisation, and collaboration across the entire supply chain. In the short term, it is unlikely to fully replace x86 or Arm architectures.

This dual characteristic of 'constraints embedded in progress' means that the development path of China's semiconductor industry will no longer follow a linear growth logic, but will gradually move towards a strategic rebalancing between openness and security, efficiency and resilience. Building a dynamic equilibrium between internal self-reliance and external cooperation systems will be the decisive factor in whether China can transition from a 'technology rule follower' to a 'technology rule shaper.' This duality not only has theoretical strategic significance but also provides a systematic logical anchor for the subsequent chapters on 'China's semiconductor vulnerability assessment' and 'industrial layout optimisation path design.'

In the context of an increasingly fragmented global governance system and intensifying geopolitical technological competition, only by effectively managing the tensions within this dual structure can China avoid the two-pronged trap of 'security isolation' or 'efficiency illusions' and achieve sustainable leapfrogging on the path to technological self-reliance.

1.2 Definition of Relevant Concepts and Literature Review

1.2.1 Industry Chain

The concept of the industrial chain can be traced back to classical economics, with Adam Smith's theory of the division of labour and David Ricardo's theory of comparative advantage laying the foundation. The Industrial Revolution drove the division of labour and collaboration in production processes. In the early twentieth century, scientific management and assembly line production further optimised the industrial chain. In the mid-twentieth century, Michael E. Porter was the first economist to adopt a systematic 'chain' perspective to examine economic activities and proposed the concept of the value chain (Porter 1985). With the continuous refinement of trade specialisation and the deepening of theoretical research, concepts such as industrial chains and supply chains emerged. Industrial chains and supply chains are two closely related but distinct concepts. Industrial chains encompass the entire production process from raw materials to final products, emphasising collaborative cooperation between upstream and downstream enterprises; supply chains, on the other hand, focus on the entire process from raw material procurement to product delivery, prioritising efficient coordination between all links (Song & Yang 2022). The industrial chain has a broader scope, spanning multiple industries, while the supply chain has a narrower scope, primarily focusing on the production and delivery of a single enterprise or product. Both aim to enhance efficiency and competitiveness, meet market demands, and are interdependent and synergistic.

Although the concept of industrial chains originated in the West, foreign scholars have focused more on derivative fields such as value chains and supply chains, while domestic scholars have placed greater emphasis on industrial chains and their application in manufacturing. As a result, the concept of industrial chains has undergone more in-depth localisation and development in China. The 'structure-process-element' framework proposed by Lambert and Cooper (1998) provided a theoretical foundation for related analyses . At the beginning of the twenty-first century, a number of studies on industrial chains emerged in China. Wu and Shao (2006) proposed that an industrial chain is a comprehensive chain formed by the integration and organic connection of four dimensions: the supply chain, the enterprise chain, the spatial chain, and the value chain, spanning all links from the upstream to the downstream of an industry. Based on existing research, an industrial chain is defined as an economic activity network comprising diverse entities such as upstream, midstream, and downstream enterprises and research institutions that collaborate vertically and horizontally through industrial linkages in time and space, with the core objective of achieving value-added growth and overall structural optimisation. It not only encompasses economic activities such as raw material supply, production manufacturing, logistics distribution, and market sales but also emphasises, in the context of globalisation, ensuring the stable supply of critical resources, technological self-reliance, and the risk-resilience of the industrial system through trade cooperation and security management, thereby balancing economic efficiency and national security objectives.

1.2.2 Industrial Chain Security

In the face of the wave of economic globalisation, industrial development is confronted with numerous complex challenges, and supply chain security has emerged as a focal point of academic attention. According to relevant statistical data from China National Knowledge Infrastructure (CNKI), the number of studies focusing on supply chain security has surged since 2021, becoming a key research issue in fields such as economic system reform, industrial economy, trade economy, and corporate economy. Supply chain security and supply chain resilience are two related yet distinct concepts. Supply chain security focuses on ensuring autonomy and control over critical links to prevent disruptions caused by external threats, while supply chain resilience emphasises the system's ability to rapidly recover and adapt after suffering shocks. Both aim to ensure the stable operation of supply chains and minimise the impact of external shocks. Industrial chain security is the foundation of resilience, ensuring that critical links are not threatened; resilience complements security by enhancing the system's ability to recover after shocks.

Current research on industrial chain security has transcended the traditional focus on protecting the physical facilities and inventory assets of industrial chains. The focus of research has expanded from purely material-level protection to more comprehensive and forward-looking risk management strategies. Sharma and Vasant (2015) argue that industrial chain security should be viewed as collaborative efforts between entities within and outside the industrial chain, through the continuous design, implementation, and optimisation of regulations, policies, and technical measures, with the aim of protecting the industrial chain from various risks and shocks, preventing damage to its functions, and ensuring that the supply chain can resume normal operations in the shortest possible time and at the lowest economic cost globally. Optimisation and stability are precise summaries of industrial chain security. Li and Zhao (2022) starts from the network structure characteristics of industrial chains and divides industrial chain security into two aspects: 'entity security' and 'structural security,' i.e., the security of nodes and the stability of the connections between nodes. Sheng (2021) emphasised that a country's ability to control risks and maintain international competitiveness in critical links of the industrial chain is the core of industrial chain security. Based on the above analysis, this book defines industrial chain security as the ability to ensure the continuity and stability of the industrial chain, reduce the negative impact of external shocks on the industrial chain, and protect industries from potential threats.

Key industries: Current research on industrial chain security primarily focuses on core industries such as critical minerals and high-tech manufacturing. In terms of mineral resources, Zhang and Fu (2024) found that the overall level of supply chain security for China's strategic key mineral resources has shown a fluctuating upward trend, reflecting the continuous improvement of China's industrial strength and security assurance capabilities in the field of strategic key mineral resources. Fu et al. (2024) analysed the impact of price fluctuations on the supply chain security of strategic key mineral resources using iron, manganese, and chromium as examples. Zheng and Liu (2025) studied the international supply chain security of the tungsten industry and found that in the global tungsten supply chain risk propagation, China, Germany, and the United States have the largest influence scope. In the high-tech manufacturing sector, Li and Long (2024) conducted research on the resilience and security of China's semiconductor supply chain, analysed its evolution trends and major risks, and proposed countermeasures. Wang and Wang (2024) predicted the production layout trends of Chinese Taiwan's semiconductor industry from a supply chain security perspective. Hu and Dou (2023) conducted research and analysis on the cultivation and identification of specialised, refined, and innovative enterprises in China from a supply chain security perspective.

Key factors influencing supply chain security: Due to the complexity of economic development, numerous factors influence supply chain security. Additionally, risks faced by a single entity within the supply chain can rapidly spread to other entities through technological and economic interconnections, thereby impacting value creation activities across the entire supply chain (Baqaee 2018). Current research on factors affecting supply chain security primarily focuses on geopolitics and war, transportation, policy, and technological innovation. Sielker and Dannenberg (2024) analysed supply chain security risks arising from military and armed conflict risks as well as broader geopolitical challenges. Li and Niu (2023) analysed the characteristics and mechanisms of industrial risk contagion under geopolitical events. Cai et al. (2024) found that the US 'de-risking' policy impacts China's industrial chain security by controlling core technologies, intermediate goods exports, key resources, and reshaping the global industrial spatial layout. Ghassibe (2021) analysed the impact of monetary policy shocks on US downstream consumption and their subsequent effects on the entire production network. Belzer and Swan (2011) analysed the impact of the transportation sector on industrial chain security from the perspectives of the labour market and labour-management relations. Shi (2024) found that artificial intelligence (AI) plays a significant role in promoting industrial chain and supply chain security, with new productive forces serving as an important transmission channel for AI's influence on industrial chain and supply chain security.

Risk response strategies and improvement pathways: Many studies have proposed supply chain security risk response strategies based on theoretical analysis, conducting in-depth analyses at the macro, meso, and micro levels. In a globalised and complex economic environment, these three levels of strategies complement each other and form a synergistic effect, playing a crucial role in enhancing supply chain security. Shi and Lu (2023) pointed out that at the micro level, enterprises should give full play to their leading role in innovation, improve risk response speed and risk management capabilities, and become 'chain leader' enterprises in the value chain; at the meso level, industries should accelerate the implementation of projects to address shortcomings in industrial chains and supply chains, and accelerate the digital transformation of industrial chains and supply chains; at the macro level, countries should accelerate the construction of a dynamic evaluation mechanism for industrial chains and supply chains, and actively participate in the regulatory restructuring of global industrial chains and supply chains. Cicerelli and Ravetti (2024) analysed the complexity of supply chains from a micro-level enterprise perspective, combining the specific circumstances of electronic device enterprises, and pointed out that complex production systems with multi-level and multi-product value chains can enhance supply chain resilience and promote innovation. Sun et al. (2024) proposed measures to enhance the security of industrial chains and supply chains from a meso-level perspective, combining the specific circumstances of the semiconductor and large-capacity battery industries. Li (2023) and other scholars mainly analysed from a macro perspective and proposed policy recommendations based on China's new development pattern, the comprehensive promotion of high-quality development, and the global value chain.

In terms of the construction of an evaluation system theory, China's evaluation index system for industrial security is mainly based on the research of He (2001) and covers four categories of first-level indicators: industrial domestic environment evaluation indicators, industrial international competitiveness evaluation indicators, industrial external dependence evaluation indicators, and industrial control evaluation indicators. Zhang (2021) pointed out that the main factors affecting industrial chain security include foreign investment, international trade, competitiveness, and external policies, and constructed a three-level evaluation system comprising industrial chain competitiveness, industrial chain control power, and industrial chain development environment. Xiao et al. (2024) systematically reviewed supply chain resilience evaluation methods represented by the core variable method, comprehensive evaluation method, and input-output method, providing diverse and robust methodological support for measuring and enhancing supply chain resilience. Currently, quantitative measurements for supply chain security assessment and analysis are relatively scarce. However, based on the continuous improvement of theoretical frameworks, some scholars have begun to explore quantitative measurements of supply chain security.

Macro-level industrial chain security: Ma et al. (2023) analysed the formation, measurement, and influencing factors of global industrial chain security and resilience using a multi-regional input-output dataset from 1990 to 2021. Baldwin and Freeman (2022) analysed and measured supply chain security from the perspective of supply chain risk exposure, calculating the risk exposure of a specific sector in the importing country, the risk exposure of a specific sector in the exporting country, and the risk exposure of inputs sold by a specific country/region to its trading partners through direct and indirect trade links. Ni et al. (2024) developed a new system for measuring supply chain risk exposure from the perspectives of production chain length and risk-return trade-offs. The study found that traditional GVC participation methods underestimate China's supply chain risk exposure, that risk exposure varies significantly across industries and technological levels, and that supply chain risk exposure across national sectors generally serves as a monitoring and early warning mechanism. Ding and Ge (2024) systematically examined the evolution of China's external risk exposure in industrial chains from 1995 to 2018 and the potential impact of global industrial chain restructuring on China's external risk exposure, based on input-output data.

Supply chain security in specific industries: Guo and Xu (2023) constructed an indicator system for measuring the security of China's pharmaceutical supply chain. They used the import-export concentration index to reflect the 'health' of the supply chain, the trade competitiveness index and the revealed comparative advantage index to reflect the "health" of the supply chain, and the ratio of import and export prices as well as the export price relative advantage index to reflect the 'health' of the value chain. Sun et al. (2024) constructed an indicator system and calculation method for assessing industrial chain security from three dimensions: dependency degree, controllability and resilience, and autonomy. They then analysed and assessed the supply chain security of China's semiconductor and large-capacity battery industries based on these dimensions. Feng et al. (2023) constructed an evaluation indicator system for industrial chain security from four dimensions: control capability, innovation capability, structural security, and development environment, and further analysed China's solar photovoltaic industry. Guo et al. (2023) constructed an evaluation indicator system for industrial chain security based on four dimensions: completeness, stability, control, and competitiveness, and further measured and assessed the industrial chains of electrical machinery and equipment manufacturing and chemical raw materials and chemical products in China. Jing and Li (2024) evaluated the security of China's indium industrial chain from a full life cycle material flow perspective.

Evaluation Methods: Currently, in related evaluations within the field of economics, the most widely applied analytical methods for indicator evaluation systems include the Analytic Hierarchy Process (AHP, also known as the expert scoring method), Principal Component Analysis (PCA), and Entropy Weight Method. With the deepening integration of statistics, mathematics, and economics research, indicator evaluation methods are also continuously evolving. Based on their advantages of strong objectivity and comprehensiveness, the PCA-Entropy Weight-TOPSIS method is selected for the evaluation analysis of indicators.

1.2.3 Semiconductor Industry Chain

The semiconductor industry is a critical strategic sector of the national economy. The survival and development of the semiconductor industry rely on a complex and sophisticated supply chain. A complete semiconductor supply chain can be divided into three main segments: upstream semiconductor support, midstream semiconductor manufacturing, and downstream end-application segments (Upton et al. 2022; Cui et al. 2022) . The upstream semiconductor support segment primarily includes foundational industries such as semiconductor processing equipment and semiconductor raw materials. Materials used in semiconductors include silicon wafers, sputtering targets, and photoresists; semiconductor processing equipment includes single crystal furnaces, lithography machines, and testing equipment.

The midstream manufacturing segment can be divided into three major industries: design, manufacturing, and testing and packaging. Among these, the design industry has high added value and a high degree of innovation, requiring design based on mature architectural foundations and related software tools, such as EDA software, CAD, core IP, and patents. After product design is completed, the design layout is handed over to the front-end manufacturing segment of the midstream industry, i.e., wafer foundries, for production. The wafer manufacturing process is relatively complex and can be divided into seven main production stages: diffusion, thin film growth, lithography, etching, ion implantation, polishing, and metallisation. During wafer manufacturing, specialised precision equipment and materials are required. Core equipment includes lithography machines, etching machines, and thin film deposition equipment; manufacturing materials include silicon wafers, photoresist, and polishing solutions. After the front-end manufacturing process, the wafer is cut into individual circuits, known as die. These must pass testing at a wafer test facility before proceeding to the packaging stage. Semiconductor packaging refers to the process of processing tested wafers into independent chips according to product models and functional requirements, which belongs to the back-end manufacturing process. To confirm that the wafers are functioning normally, each packaged wafer must undergo testing, and wafers that pass the final test can be shipped to downstream terminal application industries, where the packaged chips are installed in various application equipment and products.

The downstream end-use market spans numerous sectors of the electronics industry, including automotive electronics, consumer electronics, computers, healthcare, communications, and defence. Each link in the semiconductor supply chain is highly integrated technologically, forming a complex and interdependent composite system through extensive information flow, material exchange, and value transfer, fully demonstrating the supply chain's deep integration and efficient coordination characteristics (Li & Han 2024).

The semiconductor industry is critical to national security and economic prosperity, and countries around the world are striving to enhance their semiconductor industry capabilities. Against this backdrop, many scholars have conducted research on industrial policies. Bown CP et al. (2024) conducted research on modern industrial policies in the semiconductor industry, pointing out the different strategies adopted by governments worldwide in global competition. They specifically analysed the competitive strategies of Japan and South Korea in the 1980s, the rise of China's semiconductor industry, and the US CHIPS Act, revealing the profound impact of geopolitics on the semiconductor industry (Bown & Wang 2024). Goldberg and Juhász (2024) conducted an in-depth analysis of industrial policies in the global semiconductor industry, revealing the importance of subsidies in industry development and their complex economic impacts. Although China has made significant investments in subsidies, its efforts are not particularly notable compared to other countries.

When discussing the core factors and constraints of semiconductor industry development, scholars generally agree on three key constraints: the shortage of highly skilled talent, the difficulty of obtaining sufficient funds, and the challenge of technological barriers. For China, the failure to form a closely coordinated industrial chain structure has become another important factor constraining the breakthrough of its domestic semiconductor industry. McClean (2015) explicitly pointed out that for a country to achieve significant success in the semiconductor field, it must possess a high-quality talent pool and adequate fiscal support. These two factors are precisely the challenges that developing countries commonly face in the development of their semiconductor industries. Sun and Liu (2023) further emphasised that China's semiconductor industrial chain has not yet achieved effective coordination, which is also one of the key factors hindering the sustained progress of the domestic industry. Song and Wen (2023) and Tong and Wan (2023) discussed the impact of policies on semiconductor industry innovation, finding that fiscal subsidies inhibit technological innovation in the semiconductor industry, and tax incentives have a relatively weak promotional effect, while national semiconductor industry investment funds significantly promote industrial technological innovation.

Research on semiconductor supply chain security has generally focused on the impacts of Sino-US trade frictions and conducted theoretical analyses of related risks. Li Hongbing et al. (2023) noted that the global semiconductor supply chain is accelerating its restructuring, gradually exhibiting characteristics of shortening, nearshoring, and localisation. The principles guiding semiconductor supply chain construction have shifted from pursuing efficiency and cost optimisation to a secondary optimisation principle prioritising supply security (Li et al. 2023). Li and Long (2024) identified the main risks facing China's semiconductor supply chain as the decoupling policy led by the United States, the high volatility and intensified competition in the semiconductor industry, significant technological gaps, and the resulting heightened risks of distrust. Sun et al. (2024) compared the semiconductor supply chain security of China with that of developed countries and found that there is an asymmetric dependency relationship between China's semiconductor industry and that of developed countries. Bown and Wang (2024) noted that the US CHIPS Act and related export control measures have significantly constrained China's semiconductor industry development but have also prompted China to accelerate technological innovation and market diversification.

1.2.4 Literature Review

With the deepening development of economic globalisation, supply chain security has increasingly become a focal point of attention for academia and policymakers, with a rapid increase in related research and an expanding scope of application. Among these, key industries such as energy and mineral resources, high-tech manufacturing, and others have become priority areas of study for scholars. The core objective of research on supply chain security lies in enhancing the stability of supply chains and their ability to respond to risks. Existing research primarily relies on theoretical analysis, proposing strategies at three levels: macro, meso, and micro. In the context of globalisation and a complex and ever-changing economic environment, strategies at these three levels complement and reinforce one another, collectively providing important safeguards for enhancing supply chain security. However, to effectively enhance supply chain security, it is first necessary to conduct an in-depth analysis of its influencing factors. The complexity of economic development means that these factors are diverse and may interact in complex ways. Currently, research on the factors affecting industrial chain security mainly focuses on the following areas: geopolitical conflicts and wars, the stability of transportation networks, changes in the policy environment, and the speed and direction of technological innovation. These factors not only have individual impacts on industrial chains but may also intertwine, further exacerbating the vulnerability of industrial chains. Therefore, comprehensively identifying and analysing these influencing factors is the foundation for formulating scientific strategies and enhancing industrial chain security.

Although a large number of studies have explored the factors affecting industrial chain security and corresponding strategies, there are still obvious shortcomings in the quantitative measurement of industrial chain security, which means that many studies remain at the theoretical level with little quantitative analysis. Currently, the indicator systems and methods for assessing industrial chain security can be broadly categorised into two types: for macro-level assessments of a nation's overall industrial chain security, calculations are typically based on input-output tables; for meso-level assessments of specific industries, however, input-output tables are often insufficient due to their coarse product classification, making them unsuitable for detailed analysis. As a result, such assessments often rely more heavily on import-export trade data. A common approach is to directly use import concentration as a measure of industrial chain security, or to comprehensively evaluate using indicators such as import concentration, export concentration, and trade competitive advantage. However, these methods have not yet formed a unified and systematic evaluation system. Although some scholars have conducted research on the industrial chain security assessment of key industries such as pharmaceuticals, photovoltaics, and batteries, quantitative measurement of semiconductor industrial chain security remains relatively scarce. This research gap not only limits our comprehensive understanding of the current state of China's semiconductor industrial chain security, but also constrains the scientific formulation and effective implementation of relevant policies. Therefore, establishing a set of quantitative assessment methods applicable to semiconductor industrial chain security is not only an urgent academic need, but also an important support for policy practice.

As a core area of national security and economic prosperity, the semiconductor industry chain has received high attention from countries around the world in recent years, and related research has become increasingly in-depth. The role of industrial policies and the factors influencing industrial development are the focus of research. At the policy level, the current competitive landscape of the global semiconductor industry is being profoundly influenced by geopolitics, with countries adopting different industrial policies and strategic measures to gain a competitive edge in global competition. Existing research indicates that different fiscal, monetary, and industrial policies may have vastly different impacts, making it crucial to select appropriate policies based on a country's specific development needs. In terms of influencing factors, scholars generally agree that the development of the semiconductor industry is constrained by multiple factors, including shortages of highly skilled talent, difficulties in accessing capital, technological barriers, and supply chain coordination. Particularly in developing countries, the lack of high-quality talent and adequate fiscal support has become a key bottleneck hindering industrial breakthroughs. Overall, the global semiconductor supply chain is undergoing profound adjustments, with supply chains becoming shorter, nearshoring and localisation becoming more prevalent, and the principles of supply chain construction shifting from pursuing efficiency and cost optimisation to secondary optimisation with a focus on supply security. This shift reflects the increased awareness of global supply chain security, but it also brings new challenges, such as widening technological gaps, intensified competition and increased trust risks.

In summary, supply chain security, especially semiconductor supply chain security, has become a key focus of research and holds critical significance for China's development. However, systematic assessments of China's semiconductor supply chain security remain inadequate, making it difficult to comprehensively evaluate its current security status and potential risks. By establishing a scientific and reasonable evaluation indicator system to measure China's semiconductor supply chain security, this study lays the foundation for better understanding the current state and influencing factors of China's semiconductor supply chain security. This not only helps enhance China's semiconductor supply chain security but also provides an important safeguard for the sustainable development of the national economy.

1.3   Research Objectives and Content

1.3.1   Comprehensive Assessment of the Security of China's Semiconductor Industry

Against the backdrop of the current global restructuring of industrial chains and escalating geopolitical risks, semiconductors, as a strategic emerging industry, have become a critical issue for China's economic security and technological self-reliance. This book aims to establish a scientific and systematic analytical framework to quantitatively measure and diagnose the overall security level of China's semiconductor supply chain, with the goal of comprehensively identifying risk sources, clarifying structural weaknesses, and proposing systematic improvement pathways. This research provides theoretical support and empirical evidence for national science and technology security strategies and policy formulation. The specific research is conducted from the following aspects:

First, based on global value chain and complex network theory, a comprehensive map covering the upstream (raw materials and equipment), midstream (wafer manufacturing and packaging and testing), and downstream (end-use products) segments of the industrial chain is constructed to identify key intermediate products and technological nodes, and systematically analyse the structural characteristics and key dependency pathways of the semiconductor industrial chain. On this basis, relying on six-digit customs import and export data from 2015 to 2024, we will systematically sort out the evolution trend of China's semiconductor industry chain trade structure, conduct comparative analysis according to three major categories of major trading partners, namely G7 countries, 'Belt and Road' countries, and East Asian countries, and reveal changes in import concentration, export dependence, and market restructuring trends in different links.

Second, we construct a multi-dimensional evaluation indicator system centred on import concentration, export concentration, trade competitive advantage, self-reliance capability, and policy environment. Combining principal component analysis (PCA), entropy weight method, and TOPSIS comprehensive evaluation models, we conduct a dynamic measurement of the security level of China's semiconductor industry chain. From a longitudinal perspective, this study analyses the trends in the security level of the industrial chain from 2015 to 2023, identifies critical years of risk inflection points and influencing factors; from a horizontal perspective, it assesses the differences in the security of the industrial chain among provinces and cities in China in 2024, and characterises the heterogeneous performance of different regions in terms of external dependence and self-reliance capabilities.

Third, we further divide the supply chain into upstream, midstream, and downstream segments to measure their security levels, identify structural differences in security performance across different segments, and point out the main issues, such as the high concentration of imports of upstream high-end equipment and key materials, the midstream manufacturing segment being constrained by technological limitations, and the relatively high security level of the downstream segment. At the same time, we construct an import concentration index system based on the Herfindahl-Hirschman Index (HHI) to describe the concentration trajectory of the import network from the product-country-month perspective and reveal in detail the disturbance effects of external shocks such as Sino-US trade frictions, the COVID-19 pandemic, and geopolitical conflicts on the risks of the semiconductor industrial chain.

Finally, based on the above empirical results, this book proposes a systematic path for improving security: at the policy level, a supply chain security governance system covering early warning and monitoring, risk classification and response, and emergency response should be established; at the industry level, the resilience and autonomy of the semiconductor supply chain should be enhanced by building a diversified international procurement network, accelerating domestic substitution and breakthroughs in key technologies, and optimising regional industrial layout and coordination mechanisms; At the enterprise level, companies should enhance their innovation capabilities and supply chain management levels, and proactively build internal and external coordination and linkage mechanisms.

In summary, this book constructs a comprehensive analytical framework and a multi-level evaluation system, striving to form a closed loop in terms of theoretical logic and data support, systematically depicting the current status and trends of China's semiconductor industry chain security, and providing strategic support for achieving high-level scientific and technological self-reliance and strength.

1.3.2   In-Depth Discussion of Strategies for Optimising the Layout of China's Semiconductor Industry

Against the backdrop of intensifying global technological competition and rising geopolitical risks, China's semiconductor industry is facing unprecedented strategic pressures and development opportunities. This book aims to systematically explore the strategic path and implementation mechanisms for optimising the layout of China's semiconductor industry, with the core objectives of enhancing global competitiveness and ensuring industrial security. Through the setting of scientific and forward-looking goals, it seeks to promote regional coordination and global resource integration.

First, based on the development patterns and technological evolution trends of the global semiconductor industry, this book analyses China's shortcomings and advantages in key areas such as chip design, manufacturing, and materials, and proposes that the industry layout should adhere to the principles of self-reliance, complementary advantages, and international cooperation. Second, from the perspective of national security, it emphasises the importance of building a diversified and stable supply chain system and a technology self-reliance system for industrial security. At the same time, this book conducts an in-depth analysis of the differences in resource endowments and industrial foundations among China's eastern, central, and western regions, proposing a regional coordinated development strategy with the eastern region as the core for R&D and high-end manufacturing, and the central and western regions as the support for manufacturing and packaging and testing, to enhance the overall resilience and efficiency of the industrial chain. At the international level, centring on open platforms such as the Belt and Road Initiative, it explores how Chinese enterprises can achieve globalisation and value chain upgrading through cross-border mergers and acquisitions, technological cooperation, and industrial chain restructuring. In addition, this book focuses on the transformation and upgrading of key industrial parks, emphasising the transformation of parks from traditional manufacturing bases to 'high-end manufacturing + R&D innovation centres' and improving the international competitiveness of parks by drawing on international park management experience. Finally, it systematically analyses the role of the dual-drive mechanism of policy guidance and market demand in industrial optimisation, and clarifies the necessity of supporting the construction of an innovation ecosystem and guiding industrial upgrading through market trends.

Through the in-depth exploration of the above content, this book aims to provide systematic insights and practical pathways for optimising the layout of China's semiconductor industry, thereby assisting China in building a stable, self-reliant, and high-quality industrial system within the global semiconductor landscape.

1.4 Research Methods and Data Sources

1.4.1 Research Methods

1.4.1.1 Principles for Constructing the Indicator System

When establishing a security indicator system for China's semiconductor industry chain, it is essential to adhere to a series of scientific, systematic, and practical principles to ensure its effectiveness and applicability. (1) The selection of indicators must be based on solid scientific evidence to ensure that the chosen indicators accurately reflect the security status of the industry chain. A thorough understanding of the characteristics of the semiconductor industry and its related influencing factors is necessary to identify key elements during indicator selection and avoid one-sidedness. (2) The indicator system should be systematic, with each indicator organically linked to form a comprehensive assessment framework. All links in the industrial chain are interconnected, and changes in the external environment can also affect its security. Therefore, when designing indicators, attention should be paid to both internal process security and the impact of external market and policy environments to ensure the comprehensiveness and adaptability of the indicator system. (3) The operability of indicators is crucial. Selected indicators should be quantifiable and measurable, and relevant data should be easily accessible to facilitate practical application and analysis. Only indicators that provide effective guidance in actual operations can truly fulfil their intended purpose. (4) Given the complexity of the semiconductor industry chain, the indicator system should follow the principle of simplification, avoiding redundancy and complexity to ensure ease of understanding and use by managers and policymakers. (5) Given the dynamic nature of the supply chain, the indicator system must possess flexibility and adaptability, enabling adjustments in response to industry development and changes in the external environment. This dynamic characteristic will ensure that the indicator system remains cutting-edge, capable of promptly reflecting the security status of the supply chain, and providing robust support for decision-making.

1.4.1.2 Construction of a Security Indicator System for the Semiconductor Circuit Industry Chain

This book establishes a semiconductor industry chain security evaluation indicator system (Table 1.1) based on the core concepts of semiconductor industry chain security, as well as the common concerns of national economic security theory and

Table 1.1 Index system and calculation method

Primary Indicator	Secondary Indicators		Computational Method
External Dependence	Import concentration	Upstream x1	$\sum\limits_{j=1}^{N}\left(\frac{import_{jn}}{import_n}\right)^2 \frac{import_{jn}}{import_n}$ indicates the share of China's N product imports from country (region) J to the proportion of China's total N product imports.
		Midstream x2	
		Downstream x3	
		Semiconductor products x4	
	Exports concentration	Upstream x5	$\sum\limits_{j=1}^{N}\left(\frac{export_{jn}}{export_n}\right)^2 \frac{export_{jn}}{export_n}$ indicates the proportion of China's N product exports from country (region) J to China's total N product exports.
		Midstream x6	
		Downstream x7	
		Semiconductor products x8	
Self-reliance	Trade competitive advantage	Upstream x9	$\frac{export_n - import_n}{export_n + import_n}$, $export_n - import_n$ indicates the net export value of China's n products. $export_n + import_n$ indicates the total value of imports and exports of n products.
		Midstream x10	
		Downstream x11	
		Semiconductor products, x12	
	number of the enterprise	x13	Number of enterprises related to the semiconductor industry
	self-dependent innovation	x14	Semiconductor layout design certificate number
Policy Environment	Global policy uncertainty	x15	Global economic policy uncertainty index
	China's policy uncertainty	x16	China's economic policy uncertainty index
	Government subsidies	x17	Average government subsidies for a-share enterprises related to the listed semiconductor industry

Table 1.1 shows the security evaluation index system and calculation method of China's semiconductor industry chain constructed in this book, in which x9 to x14 and x17 are positive indicators, that is, the larger the value, the safer the industrial chain, and the rest are negative indicators, that is, the smaller the value, the safer the industrial chain.

industrial security theory, such as independence, stability, and the international economic environment. It fully considers the relevance of dimensions, the distinction and accessibility of data, and constructs an evaluation framework tailored to the semiconductor industry chain. Semiconductor supply chain security encompasses multiple critical dimensions, including the industry's ability to develop independently without excessive external constraints, as well as national policy support and guidance for the industry. Based on this, three primary indicators—external dependency, self-reliance capability, and policy environment—are selected to form the evaluation framework.

The external dependence primary indicator includes two secondary indicators: import concentration and export concentration. Import concentration reflects

China's reliance on a few countries or regions for semiconductor imports. If imports are overly concentrated among a few suppliers, any disruption in supply due to political or economic factors could severely impact China's semiconductor industry and disrupt its normal operations. Export concentration reflects the degree of concentration of China's semiconductor product sales in international markets. Excessively high export concentration means that the industry is overly reliant on specific overseas markets. If these markets encounter trade barriers or a sudden decline in demand, it will have a negative impact on the domestic industry's revenue and development. Therefore, through these two secondary indicators, one can clearly understand the supply and demand dependency of China's semiconductor industry in the international market, providing an important basis for assessing supply chain security.

The primary indicator of self-reliance includes three secondary indicators: trade competitiveness, number of enterprises, and independent innovation. The trade competitive advantage indicator comprehensively evaluates the competitiveness of China's semiconductor industry in international markets. A strong trade competitive advantage indicates that the industry holds significant influence in international markets, enabling it to withstand external competitive pressures and reduce risks to industrial security caused by external shocks. The number of enterprises is a key factor in measuring the completeness and development potential of the industrial chain. A larger number of enterprises typically indicates a more diversified range of participants in the industrial chain, which can form a more comprehensive collaborative network and enhance the industrial chain's autonomy and controllability. In addition, a larger number of enterprises also indicates active market competition, which helps to promote technological innovation and efficiency improvements, further strengthening autonomous capabilities. Autonomous innovation capabilities are primarily reflected through the number of semiconductor layout design certificates issued, which directly demonstrate China's scientific and technological innovation capabilities and intellectual property reserves in the semiconductor field. Abundant intellectual property reserves not only help to drive industrial technological upgrades but also form technological barriers in international competition, protecting domestic industries from infringement and unfair competition. In addition to the above three indicators, the semiconductor industry ecosystem is also a key indicator for measuring self-reliance, such as the degree of industrial cluster development and the intensity of inter-enterprise collaboration. However, due to limitations in data availability, these indicators are not currently included in the indicator system.

The policy environment first-level indicator includes three second-level indicators: global policy uncertainty, Chinese policy uncertainty, and government subsidies. The indicator of global economic policy uncertainty reflects the potential impact of changes in the international political and economic situation on China's semiconductor industry. In the context of globalisation, factors such as adjustments to economic policies in various countries, intensified trade frictions, and geopolitical conflicts may bring about numerous uncertainties for the semiconductor industry, affecting the stability of the industry's supply chain and market expectations. China's economic policy uncertainty focuses on the impact of domestic policy adjustments on the industry. Policy changes in areas such as taxation, subsidies, and industrial planning directly guide the allocation of industrial resources and the development strategies of enterprises. Increased policy uncertainty can also have adverse effects on enterprise investment, technological innovation, market confidence, and supply chain stability. Government subsidies and grants are important tools for economic regulation, primarily including tax incentives, fiscal subsidies, and non-monetary asset transfers. The intensity of these measures reflects the extent of government support for industrial development. A reasonable grasp of these three indicators can help to promptly identify the impact of internal and external policy environment changes on the security of the semiconductor industry chain and provide forward-looking guidance for industrial development.

Table 1.1 shows the evaluation indicator system and calculation method for the security of China's semiconductor industry chain. Among them, x9 to x14 and x17 are positive indicators, i.e., the higher the value, the more secure the industry chain; the remaining indicators are negative indicators, i.e., the lower the value, the more secure the industry chain.

1.4.2 Data Sources

Data sources include the following databases: the General Administration of Customs of the People's Republic of China, the National Intellectual Property Administration, the Forward Industry Research Institute, Qichacha, and the Economic Policy Uncertainty Database, covering the time period from 2015 to 2024; and the CNRDS Database, covering the time period from 2015 to 2023.

For trade-related data, based on the six-digit customs codes obtained by mapping the industrial chain, the customs database was used to retrieve information on the import and export values, trading partners, and registered locations of importers and exporters for products across the upstream, midstream, and downstream segments of the industrial chain, as well as semiconductor products. This information was further analysed to calculate the import concentration, export concentration, and trade competitiveness indicators for the upstream, midstream, and downstream segments of the industrial chain, as well as for semiconductor products.

Semiconductor industry-related enterprises are sourced from the Forward-Looking Industry Research Institute, which includes nearly 23,000 enterprises, mainly involved in the upstream and midstream of the industrial chain and with strong relevance to the semiconductor industry. Further information such as the date of establishment and the province of origin is obtained from Qichacha based on the list of enterprise names, and their industry affiliation and relevance to the semiconductor industry is further verified.

Data on independent innovation was selected from the National Intellectual Property Administration database statistics on the number of semiconductor layout design certificates issued in China. Semiconductor layout design plays a crucial role in enhancing chip performance, achieving functional integration and innovation, and promoting technological iteration and breakthroughs, thereby reflecting independent innovation capabilities.

The Economic Policy Uncertainty Index is sourced from the Economic Policy Uncertainty Index website, with the index calculated based on the Economic Policy Uncertainty Index (EPU) proposed by Baker et al. (2016). The monthly global economic policy uncertainty index (GEPU) is the GDP-weighted average of the national EPU indices of 21 countries/regions. The Chinese economic policy uncertainty index is a monthly index calculated by Steven J. Davis and Xuguang S. Sheng based on mainland newspapers, and the annual index is calculated based on the monthly index.

Government subsidy data is sourced from the CNRDS database. First, A-share listed companies in the semiconductor industry were screened to obtain 339 companies with a total of 3,544 observation data points. Then, the average fiscal subsidies received by listed companies in the semiconductor industry for the year were calculated to obtain the annual fiscal subsidy data for the semiconductor industry.

References

Baldwin, R., & Freeman, R. (2022). Risks and global supply chains: What we know and what we need to know. *Annual Review of Economics*, 14, 153–180.

Baqaee, D. R. (2018). Cascading failures in production networks. *Econometrica*, (5), 1819–1838.

Belzer, M. H., & Swan, P. F. (2011). Supply chain security: Agency theory and port drayage drivers. *The Economic and Labour Relations Review*, 22, 41–63.

Bown, C. P., & Wang, D. (2024). Semiconductors and modern industrial policy. *Journal of Economic Perspectives*, 38, 81–110.

Cai, H., Zheng, H., & Yu, T. (2024). The impact of the United States' 'deregulation' on the security of China's industrial chain and supply chain and countermeasures. *Research on Financial Issues*, (1), 33–43. https://doi.org/10.19654/j.cnki.cjwtyj.2024.01.004

Cicerelli, F., & Ravetti, C. (2024). Sustainability, resilience and innovation in industrial electronics: A case study of internal, supply chain and external complexity. *Journal of Economic Interaction and Coordination*, 19(2), 343–372.

Cui, X., Xiong, W., Yang, P., et al. (2022). Measurement of global supply chain vulnerability: An analysis based on trade network methods. *Statistical Research*, 39(8), 38–52. https://doi.org/10.19343/j.cnki.11-1302/c.2022.08.003

Ding, X., & Ge, H. (2024). Dynamic changes in China's industrial chain's external risk exposure, international comparison, and counterfactual simulation. *Journal of Quantitative Economics and Technical Economics*, 41(10), 26–45.

Feng, G., Liu, Q., Zhu, J., et al. (2023). Assessment and response strategies for industrial chain and supply chain security. *Journal of Xi'an Jiaotong University (Social Sciences Edition)*, 43(6), 106–116.

Fu, J., Zhang, H., & Song, M. (2024). The impact of price fluctuations on the security of the industrial chain of strategic key mineral resources: A case study of iron, manganese, and chromium. *Academic Exploration*, (5), 101–110.

Ghassibe, M. (2021). Monetary policy and production networks: An empirical investigation. *Journal of Monetary Economics*, 119, 21–39.

Goldberg, P. K., & Juhász, R. (2024). Industrial policy in the global semiconductor sector. *National Bureau of Economic Research*.

Guo, H., Lun, R., & Sun, W. (2023). Research on the measurement of China's industrial chain security level. *Asia-Pacific Economy*, (2), 114–124.

Guo, Z., & Xu, T. (2023). Research on the resilience and safety level of China's pharmaceutical industry chain and supply chain. *Economy and Management*, 37(3), 82–93.

He, W. (2001). Industrial security issues and countermeasures following China's entry into the World Trade Organisation. *Economic Dynamics*, (11), 41–44.

Hu, H., & Dou, B. (2023). Current status, challenges and countermeasures for the cultivation of specialised, refined, unique and innovative enterprises from the perspective of industrial chain security. *Zhongzhou Academic Journal*, (2), 31–36.

Jing, L., & Li, X. (2024). Security evaluation of China's indium industrial chain: Perspective on substance flow throughout the whole life cycle. *Sustainable Production and Consumption*, 47, 557–569.

Lambert, D. M., & Cooper, M. C. (1998). Supply chain management: Implementation issues and research opportunities. *The International Journal of Logistics Management*.

Li, H., Zhao, L., & Zhai, R. (2023). New developments in the global chip supply chain adjustment and China's response. *International Trade*, (2), 19–27.

Li, T., & Zhao, X. (2022). China's exploration of ensuring the security of industrial chains and supply chains. *Management World*, 38(9), 31–41.

Li, W., & Han, M. (2024). Evolution of the global wind power industry chain trade pattern and simulation of risk transmission. *Resources Science*, 46(9), 1822–1835.

Li, X., & Long, X. (2024). Resilience and security of China's integrated circuit industry chain under new circumstances: Evolutionary trends, major risks, and policy recommendations. *Technology and Economy*, 43(7), 18–27.

Li, Y. (2023). Improving the resilience and security of China's industrial chains and supply chains in accelerating the construction of a new development pattern. *Economic Horizons*, (11), 51–58.

Li, Y., & Niu, T. (2023). Exploration of industrial risk contagion characteristics and mechanism under geopolitical events: Evidence from China. *Applied Economics*, 56, 3582–3599.

Ma, L., Li, X., & Pan, Y. (2023). Global industrial chain resilience research: Theory and measurement. *Systems*, 11(9).

McClean, B. (2015). IC product categories to exceed total IC market growth in 2015. *IC Insights*, 15(3).

Ni, H., Zhong, D., & Fan, Z. (2024). Measurement, structure, and international comparison of China's industrial chain risk exposure: A perspective based on production chain length. *Management World*, 40(4), 1–26+46+27–45.

Porter, M. (1985). *The competitive advantage: Creating and sustaining superior performance*. New York: Free Press.

Sharma, S. K., & Vasant, B. S. (2015). Developing a framework for analyzing global supply chain security. *Social Science Research Network*, 12(3), 7.

Sheng, C. X. (2021). Strategies and approaches for promoting the safe and stable development of industrial chains and supply chains under the new development pattern. *Reform*, (2), 1–13.

Shi, J., & Lu, D. (2023). Research on enhancing the resilience and security of industrial chains and supply chains. *Research on Financial and Economic Issues*, (2), 3–13.

Shi, M. (2024). Artificial intelligence, new productive forces, and industrial chain and supply chain security. *Xinjiang Social Sciences*, (6), 54–64+183.

Sielker, F., & Dannenberg, P. (2024). New economic geographies of war: Risks and disruptions in Eurasian transport routes and supply chains through the military conflict in Ukraine. *ZFW – Advances in Economic Geography*, (59).

Song, H., & Yang, Y. (2022). An exploration of the connotation and development pathways of modernisation of China's industrial chain and supply chain. *Abstracts of Social Sciences*, (2), 48–50.

Song, L., & Wen, Y. (2023). Financial subsidies, tax incentives and technological innovation in China's integrated circuit industry. *Journal of Innovation & Knowledge*, 8.

Sun, Q., & Liu, J. (2023). Integrated circuit industry 'three chains' integration and coordinated development: Mechanism analysis and empirical research. *China Science and Technology Forum*, (7), 63–73.

Sun, T., Zhang, Q., & Yang, D. (2024). Assessment and improvement measures for the security of key industrial chains and supply chains in China. *Economist*, (6), 86–94.

Tong, X., & Wan, X. (2023). National industrial investment fund and China's integrated circuit industry technology innovation. *Journal of Innovation & Knowledge*, 8.

Upton, J., et al. (2022). Caveat utilitor: A comparative assessment of resilience measurement approaches. *Journal of Development Economics*, 157, 102873.

Wang, H., & Wang, L. (2024). Global layout trends of Chinese Taiwan's semiconductor industry from the perspective of industrial chain security. *Asia-Pacific Economy*, (4), 129–139.

Wu, J., & Shao, C. (2006). Research on the formation mechanism of industrial chains: The '4+4+4' model. *China Industrial Economics*, (4), 36–43.

Xiao, X., Wang, Z., & Li, S. (2024). Research progress on methods for measuring industrial chain resilience. *Journal of Economics*, (4), 144–160.

Zhang, H., & Fu, J. (2024). Strategies for the construction of a monitoring and early warning system for the security of China's strategic key mineral resources industry chain. *Journal of Yunnan University (Social Sciences Edition)*, 23(6), 105–117.

Zhang, Y. (2021). The concept and evaluation system of industrial chain security. *China Trade and Economy Guide*, (10), 55–59.

Zheng, X., & Liu, X. (2025). Supply risk propagation in international trade networks of the tungsten industry chain. *Humanities and Social Sciences Communications*, 12.

Chapter 2
Global Semiconductor Industry Development Pattern and Trends

Tao Ma

Abstract Chapter 2 offers a comprehensive overview of the evolution and regional configuration of the global semiconductor industry. It charts the transition from vertically integrated systems, historically led by the United States, to today's globally fragmented yet interconnected value chains. The chapter compares the industrial roles, technological capabilities, and policy approaches of key regions—namely the United States, Europe, Japan, South Korea, and Chinese Taiwan—while also highlighting the emerging roles of India and Southeast Asia within the global supply network. It further explores contemporary challenges, such as the deceleration of Moore's Law and the growing demand for AI-driven applications, which are accelerating the shift towards advanced packaging, heterogeneous integration, and system-level innovation. The chapter concludes by identifying critical future trends, including technological diversification, market restructuring, and increasing regional competition.

Keywords Global Semiconductor Industry • Regional Industrial Structure • Technological Innovation • Advanced Manufacturing • Post-Moore Era • Supply Chain Realignment

2.1 Historical Evolution of the Global Semiconductor Industry

2.1.1 Origin and Early Development Stages of the Industry

The origins of the global semiconductor industry can be traced back to the mid-twentieth century. In 1947, John Bardeen, Walter Brattain, and William Shockley of Bell Laboratories in the United States successfully developed the world's first point-contact transistor. This groundbreaking invention not only ushered in a new era of solid-state electronic devices but also marked humanity's official entry into the electronic information age. In 1958, Jack Kilby, an engineer at Texas Instruments, designed and manufactured the first integrated circuit (IC) prototype, laying the foundation for the large-scale and systematic development of the semiconductor industry.

During the 1960s and 1970s, the United States dominated the global semiconductor industry landscape thanks to its leading scientific research capabilities and strong capital investment. Technology companies such as Fairchild Semiconductor and Intel, which was established later, not only achieved key breakthroughs in the miniaturisation and mass production of integrated circuits, but also established an industry model centred on vertical integration from design to manufacturing and testing, driving Silicon Valley to become a global hub for semiconductor innovation.

During this period, technological progress was concentrated in the maturation of core processes such as single-crystal silicon material purification, photolithography mask technology, ion implantation doping, and chemical vapour deposition (CVD), driving an exponential increase in chip integration. The US Department of Defense funded numerous cutting-edge research projects through agencies such as the Defence Advanced Research Projects Agency (DARPA), fostering a 'military-academic-industrial' tripartite innovation ecosystem that provided institutional safeguards for the sustained evolution of the semiconductor industry.

2.1.2   Industrial Expansion in the Wave of Globalisation

In the 1980s, with the acceleration of global industrial capital flows and the widespread adoption of communication technologies, the semiconductor industry gradually shifted from being dominated by a single country to a model of cross-border collaboration and division of labour. Japan rapidly emerged through its 'Very Large Scale Integration (VLSI) Programme,' challenging the United States' dominance in the memory chip sector. Meanwhile, South Korea's Samsung and Hynix, along with Taiwan Semiconductor Manufacturing Company (TSMC) in Chinese Taiwan, leveraged government support and overseas technology transfers to gain a foothold in manufacturing, establishing East Asia's core position in global semiconductor manufacturing.

From the 1990s to the early 2000s, the rapid development of personal computers, mobile communications, and the internet led to a surge in global demand for semiconductors, driving the deepening of the global industrial value chain. The United States continued to dominate in EDA tools, core IP, and advanced design, while East Asian countries focused on capital- and labour-intensive segments such as wafer manufacturing and packaging/testing. Europe and Japan, meanwhile, established technological barriers in high-end equipment and materials.

During this period, the industrial division of labour became highly institutionalised, forming a stable pattern where the United States dominated upstream design, East Asia handled midstream manufacturing, and Europe and Japan specialised in equipment and materials. This also gave rise to a manufacturing ecosystem dominated by oligopolistic firms such as TSMC and Samsung, further strengthening global collaboration and the standardisation of technologies.

2.1.3 Recent Technological Changes and Industrial Restructuring

As we enter the second decade of the twenty-first century, the semiconductor industry faces multiple structural challenges and transformation pressures. First, Moore's Law is gradually slowing down, transistor sizes are approaching physical limits, and the cost of improving unit performance is rising significantly, prompting the industry to shift to new paradigms such as chiplets, 3D packaging, and heterogeneous integration. Second, geopolitical risks are rising significantly, especially with the intensification of Sino-US technological competition, making the security and autonomy of global supply chains a policy focus.

Additionally, emerging applications such as AI, IoT, 5G, edge computing, and electric vehicles are driving chip demand from 'single computing power' to 'multi-dimensional collaboration,' imposing higher requirements on low-power, high-bandwidth, and customised technology routes. Against this backdrop, the semiconductor industry is transitioning from traditional 'scale-driven growth' to 'system integration-driven collaborative innovation.'

At the policy level, the United States has enacted the CHIPS and Science Act to rebuild its domestic manufacturing capabilities, while the European Union and Japan have also launched localisation plans to enhance supply chain resilience. Emerging economies like India and Vietnam are accelerating their integration into the packaging, testing, and manufacturing segments, with initial signs of a 'de-Chinaisation' trend emerging. However, global companies remain highly dependent on the Chinese market and its production capacity. Overall, the global semiconductor industry landscape is shifting from 'efficiency-driven' to 'security-driven,' with future trends likely to include 'regional collaboration and multi-polar competition.'

2.2 Current Global Semiconductor Industry Landscape and Regional Characteristics

2.2.1 United States: A Hub of Technological Innovation and Global Industry Leader

The United States has long played a dual role as both the 'technological engine' and 'paradigm setter' in the global semiconductor industry. Its industrial structure is highly concentrated in upstream segments, particularly in chip design, electronic design automation (EDA) software, processor architecture, and core intellectual property (IP), establishing a globally leading technological system and ecosystem advantage.

Under the backdrop of global division of labour, US companies have gradually outsourced capital-intensive segments such as wafer manufacturing and packaging/testing to control costs and focus on R&D, heavily relying on Chinese Taiwan and South Korea's wafer foundry systems. However, US companies maintain significant technological advantages in design and system architecture. NVIDIA is a typical example. With its deep accumulation in GPU architecture and parallel computing technology, it dominates the global AI chip market, especially in application scenarios such as data centres, autonomous driving, and generative AI, where its GPU market share exceeds 80%, making it the core computing power provider in the AI era.

Intel, the historical leader in x86 architecture processors, faced pressure from advanced process competition and changes in the chip design ecosystem. In 2021, it officially launched the 'IDM 2.0' strategy, attempting to regain its technological leadership in manufacturing through the restructuring of manufacturing capabilities and the expansion of foundry services. This strategy aims to integrate the entire process from chip design, wafer manufacturing to advanced packaging, enhancing its control over process nodes, supply chain security, and cost management. Qualcomm has established a global competitive advantage in the mobile SoC (System on Chip) sector. Its Snapdragon platform is widely adopted in Android smart devices, driving the rapid expansion of the global mobile communications ecosystem.

In the field of EDA tools, US companies have almost achieved global monopoly. The three major EDA vendors—Cadence, Synopsys, and Mentor Graphics—collectively hold over 95% of the global market share, providing a full-stack toolchain for chip design processes, from RTL-level modelling, verification, and simulation to back-end physical design and layout. Their technical capabilities directly determine chip design efficiency, energy consumption control, and tape-out success rates, making them the infrastructure of global semiconductor design.

To address the risks of manufacturing capability hollowing out and geopolitical challenges, the United States formally passed the CHIPS and Science Act in 2022, with a total investment of US$52.7 billion covering manufacturing subsidies, research funding, and industrial incentives, among other areas, with the aim of rebuilding domestic manufacturing capabilities and technological autonomy. This policy has attracted foreign companies such as TSMC and Samsung to invest in the construction of 7 nm and below process wafer fabs in the United States, while also driving domestic companies (such as Intel) to expand their advanced process production lines.

Although the United States holds an overwhelming technological advantage in chip architecture, design, and IP development, its manufacturing capabilities lag significantly behind TSMC and Samsung in terms of yield control, cost structure, and process node breakthroughs. Particularly in the large-scale mass production of 5-nanometre and below nodes, US companies are constrained by technical accumulation and supply chain coordination, making it difficult to form a complete alternative in the short term. This structural imbalance of 'strong design but weak manufacturing' has become an important bottleneck constraining the strategic security and supply chain resilience of the US semiconductor industry.

2.2.2 Europe: Strategic Advantages in Specialised Technologies and High-End Applications

Compared to the two major semiconductor industry hubs in the United States and Asia, Europe lacks the full-process scale advantages but has built a semiconductor ecosystem with significant technological barriers and differentiated competitiveness, leveraging its deep expertise in manufacturing equipment, materials and processes, and specialised application chips. Its industrial structure is characterised by a technology-driven focus on 'heavy equipment, strong materials, and superior applications,' particularly in high-value-added fields such as automotive electronics, industrial automation, new energy, and communication infrastructure, where it holds significant international influence.

ASML, a Dutch company, is a prime example of Europe's semiconductor technology prowess. Its exclusively produced extreme ultraviolet (EUV) lithography machines are the core equipment required for achieving advanced manufacturing processes at 7 nanometres and below. EUV equipment integrates multidisciplinary cutting-edge technologies such as optical engineering, precision mechanics, vacuum systems, and materials science, and is considered one of the most complex systems in modern manufacturing processes. As of 2024, ASML holds over 90% of the global market share, and its 'unique' position in the industrial chain grants it strategic resource attributes and technological influence. Recent analysis by the National Institute of Standards and Technology provides a detailed review of both the current deployment of EUV lithography and its future technical challenges, highlighting its critical role in enabling sub-7 nm manufacturing (National Institute of Standards and Technology 2023).

Infineon Technologies of Germany is a global leader in power semiconductors, particularly in automotive-grade insulated gate bipolar transistors (IGBTs) and silicon carbide (SiC) devices, where it holds a leading global market share. Its products are widely used in new energy vehicle drive modules, rail transit traction systems, and integrated wind, solar, storage, and power generation devices, making it a key technological pillar for Europe's green energy transition and intelligent transportation strategies.

STMicroelectronics, a typical 'national team' enterprise jointly established by France and Italy, has deep roots in the fields of analogue circuits, sensors and industrial-grade microcontrollers (MCUs). Its chip solutions are widely used in industrial control systems, building automation, sensor networks and energy equipment, and are particularly well-suited and technically compatible with industrial automation and IoT platforms. ST's ecosystem aligns with Europe's industrial demands for 'high reliability, long lifespan, and customisation.'

In terms of policy, the European Union officially adopted the European Chips Act in 2023, planning a total investment of 43 billion euros to strengthen the resilience of the local industrial chain through a three-pronged mechanism of financial subsidies, R&D support, and policy incentives. The bill sets the following goals: by 2030, increase the EU's share of global chip manufacturing capacity from less than 10% to 20%, and establish several 'European Centres of Excellence' to promote the development and application of next-generation semiconductor technologies. The bill also emphasises green manufacturing, carbon-neutral processes, and the construction of a circular materials system, seeking to shape the image of a 'responsible technology powerhouse' under a sustainable development paradigm.

Although Europe has structural advantages in high-end equipment, industrial chips, and green manufacturing, it remains relatively weak in key technologies such as advanced logic chip manufacturing (e.g., 5 nm and below processes), EDA software development, and IP licensing. The design ecosystem is relatively fragmented, and technical synergy is not as effective as in mature industrial clusters in the United States and Asia. European local foundry companies have limited scale, with wafer production capacity concentrated in mature processes, lacking systematic support capabilities for large-scale markets such as general computing and mobile communications. Therefore, their strategic focus is shifting toward 'selective investment and deepening in specific areas,' aiming to enhance their influence in global semiconductor technology governance through technological depth in specific fields and policy guidance.

2.2.3   Japan: Core Competitiveness in Materials and Equipment

Japan has undergone a profound transformation in the global semiconductor industry landscape, transitioning from a 'manufacturing powerhouse' to a 'key player in critical segments.' Since the late 1990s, with the emergence of new manufacturing giants such as TSMC and Samsung, Japan's domestic wafer manufacturing capabilities have gradually declined. However, through sustained R&D investments and technological advancements in upstream materials and equipment sectors, Japan has successfully established a highly irreplaceable competitive edge in critical supply chain nodes. It now serves as the primary supplier of key raw materials and core equipment within the global semiconductor manufacturing ecosystem.

In the semiconductor materials sector, Japanese companies hold global supply chain control over multiple foundational product categories, including silicon wafers, photoresists, electronic gases, and high-purity chemical reagents. Among these, Shin-Etsu Chemical Co., Ltd. and SUMCO Corporation together account for over 60% of the global market share for high-purity silicon wafers, providing a range of products from 300 mm wafers to special epitaxial wafers, serving as the upstream foundation for the wafer foundry process. In the field of advanced lithography materials, companies such as JSR Corporation and Tokyo Ohka Kogyo Co., Ltd. (TOK) have long focused on the development of high-resolution photoresists and EUV resist materials, establishing robust technological barriers and global customer networks. Especially in the field of extreme ultraviolet (EUV) photoresists, the performance of these materials directly impacts the yield and resolution of advanced process technologies, making them of extremely high strategic value.

In terms of equipment manufacturing, Tokyo Electron Limited (TEL) is one of the top three semiconductor equipment suppliers globally, forming a 'duopoly' with Applied Materials in the United States in core processes such as coating and developing, dry etching, and thin film deposition. Its products are widely deployed in leading international foundries such as TSMC, Samsung, and Intel, covering various process platforms including logic chips, memory chips, and sensor manufacturing. TEL has long-term advantages in equipment performance stability, process adaptability, and customer service systems, making it a critical equipment support for global advanced process systems.

Although Japan's manufacturing sector as a whole is in decline, it still holds core competitiveness in the automotive-grade microcontroller (MCU) market. Renesas Electronics, as the representative of Japan's 'national team' in semiconductors, continues to innovate in product lines such as power MCUs, mixed-signal chips, and automotive SoCs, providing high-reliability embedded chip solutions to major automakers like Toyota and Honda, as well as Tier 1 suppliers.

At the policy level, the Japanese government has proposed three strategic objectives since 2021: strengthening domestic manufacturing capabilities, ensuring technological autonomy, and enhancing international cooperation. Specific measures include providing financial subsidies to support TSMC and Sony in jointly establishing a factory in Kumamoto to build local wafer production lines covering 28 nm processes, and promoting the Rapidus programme to jointly develop advanced processes below 2 nm with a number of leading companies in an attempt to catch up with cutting-edge process technologies and 'return to the forefront.'

Overall, Japan's core advantages in the semiconductor industry lie in its irreplaceable upstream materials and key equipment segments, which underpin its technological irreplaceability in the global supply chain. However, it remains relatively weak in advanced logic chip mass production, system-level chip design, and software-hardware integration, with insufficient vertical integration capabilities and ecosystem flexibility, limiting its ability to quickly respond to emerging computing paradigms such as AI chips and RISC-V architecture. In the future, its industrial competitiveness will increasingly rely on a dual strategy of 'technological depth and international collaboration,' namely, maintaining its global leadership in core materials and equipment while leveraging international cooperation to expand process capabilities and ecosystem stickiness, thereby enhancing the systemic resilience of the industry.

2.2.4 South Korea: A Dual-Track Approach Combining Memory Dominance and Advanced Process Technology

South Korea holds a pivotal position in the global semiconductor industry, particularly in the memory chip sector. Leveraging its deep integration of technology, production capacity, and supply chain management, the country has established a robust and leading global market dominance. The country's semiconductor industry system follows a dual-track development model, with memory as the core and manufacturing processes as the wings. It continues to expand into system integration and cutting-edge design in the high-end manufacturing segment, gradually transitioning from a 'manufacturing powerhouse' to a 'technology powerhouse.'

Samsung Electronics and SK hynix are the two core companies in South Korea's semiconductor industry, dominating the DRAM and NAND Flash memory markets with a highly concentrated market share. As of 2023, the two companies collectively hold approximately 70% of the global DRAM market and over 50% of the NAND market, controlling the supply chain for core components in key application areas such as AI servers, data centres, smartphones, and high-performance computing. Among them, Samsung's DRAM product portfolio covers various forms from DDR5 to LPDDR5X, and it was the first to achieve mass production of 14 nm DRAM and 176-layer V-NAND, ranking among the world's leading companies in terms of technology.

In the logic foundry field, Samsung is also actively expanding its advanced process capabilities. As the only IDM company with full-process capabilities in both memory and logic foundry, Samsung was the first to achieve mass production of 3-nanometre process technology based on GAA (Gate-All-Around) transistor structure in 2022, aiming to challenge TSMC's leading position in logic process technology. Its 'vertical integration + advanced process' strategy enables it to have strong penetration in the AI chip, mobile processor, and custom chip markets.

SK Hynix is focusing on the high-bandwidth memory (HBM) sector, dedicated to meeting the extremely high demands for bandwidth density and energy efficiency in AI inference and training processes. Its HBM3 products are widely used in NVIDIA's H100 AI accelerators, securing a leading position in the HBM market. In addition, SK Hynix is actively pursuing strategic partnerships with global leaders such as AMD and NVIDIA to expand its technological footprint in AI chip modularisation and customisation.

At the policy level, the South Korean government has launched the 'Semiconductor Super Cluster Strategy,' aiming to establish the world's largest wafer manufacturing base by 2030, centred around Seoul and Gyeonggi Province. The strategy comprises four pillars: land policy, tax incentives, R&D investment, and talent recruitment, aiming to establish a closed-loop ecosystem encompassing design, manufacturing, packaging, testing, and materials equipment. According to the Ministry of Industry, Trade, and Energy, South Korea's annual semiconductor export target for 2030 is over $300 billion, with the sector's share of total exports expected to exceed 20%, supporting the country's 'technology-driven, export-led' dual-engine national strategy.

However, despite South Korea's significant achievements in memory and manufacturing, it remains highly dependent on external technology suppliers, primarily from the United States, in foundational areas such as EDA software, IP licensing, and system-on-chip (SoC) design. Particularly in core architecture, system software, and the development of an independent design ecosystem, South Korea still lags behind its US and Japanese counterparts. Additionally, South Korea's semiconductor industry is highly dependent on export markets, with its major customers concentrated in mainland China and the United States, exposing it to heightened external vulnerabilities amid global supply chain disruptions and geopolitical tensions.

In summary, South Korea's semiconductor industry exhibits a multi-layered structure characterised by 'memory dominance, logic foundry catch-up, and design ecosystem development,' occupying a pivotal position in the global semiconductor value chain. Its future competitiveness will hinge on its ability to achieve a structural leap from manufacturing-driven to design-driven growth, as well as its capacity to establish more autonomous strategic footholds within the global technological standards framework.

2.2.5 Chinese Taiwan: Important Position in Contract Manufacturing

Chinese Taiwan has long played a pivotal role as a 'contract manufacturing hub' within the global semiconductor industry. Its industrial structure is centred around wafer foundry services, forming a comprehensive industrial ecosystem that seamlessly integrates IC design, wafer manufacturing, and packaging and testing (P&T) across the entire production chain. The region leverages a three-pronged mechanism of 'manufacturing-driven development, industrial park clusters, and policy support' to form a highly concentrated and specialised technical network, playing a critical role in ensuring the security and efficiency of the global semiconductor supply chain.

TSMC, the world's largest pure-play foundry, held a market share of over 58% in 2023 and possesses absolute technological advantages in advanced process technologies. It has achieved mass production of 5-nanometre and 3-nanometre process nodes and commenced pilot production of 2-nanometre GAA (Gate-All-Around) process technology in 2024, becoming one of the few companies globally capable of stably supplying high-performance logic chip manufacturing capabilities. TSMC's customers include international technology giants such as Apple, Qualcomm, AMD, and NVIDIA, and it has long held a key position in the supply of high-performance chips, serving as the techno-logical foundation for global fabless design companies to achieve cutting-edge innovation.

UMC focuses on mature process nodes of 28 nanometres and above, and has established a stable market share in long-life cycle chip markets such as power management, image processing, automotive electronics, and industrial control, forming a complementary foundry structure with TSMC. In the packaging and testing segment, ASE and SPIL have formed a global-scale packaging and testing service system, providing integrated solutions from packaging design to mass production for small and medium-sized fabless companies. They are important support platforms for the global trend toward 'fabless' semiconductor manufac-turing.

In terms of industrial development policies, Chinese Taiwan has implemented the 'Asia Silicon Valley Plan,' the 'Forward-Looking Infrastructure Development Plan,' and the 'Six Core Strategic Industries' policy framework to continuously promote research and development and ecosystem cultivation in key areas such as 5G, AIoT, semiconductor materials, and advanced packaging. The high-density technology corridor centred on the Hsinchu Science Park, Tainan Science Park (South Science Park) and Central Taiwan Science Park (Central Science Park) has formed one of the world's most important regional innovation clusters in the semiconductor industry, supporting a fully integrated supply chain from design and testing to mass production.

Although the region possesses world-class advantages in manufacturing and packaging and testing, its IC design sector remains relatively dependent on interna-tional licensing for high-end core IP and independent architecture R&D, particularly in areas such as EDA tools, RISC-V ecosystem development, and general-purpose processor architecture design. Additionally, original technological accumulation lags behind that of US and European companies, and industrial innovation remains more collaboration-oriented than source-driven.

Currently, rising geopolitical risks, the strengthening of global 'technological sovereignty' awareness, and the trend toward supply chain resilience restructuring have significantly increased the systemic risks faced by Chinese Taiwan's semi-conductor industry. To address this situation, leading companies such as TSMC are accelerating their global expansion, investing in advanced wafer fabs in Arizona, the United States; Kumamoto, Japan; and Dresden, Germany, to achieve a strategic upgrade path of 'localised production + globalised services.' This approach aims to ensure the stability of customer service while mitigating the potential risks to the supply chain from regional political shocks.

In summary, Chinese Taiwan has established itself as an indispensable foundry hub in the global semiconductor industry, leveraging its manufacturing capabilities, industrial organisation, and park synergy advantages. However, the sustainability of its long-term competitiveness will depend on its ability to transition from a 'manu-facturing-dependent' model to a 'technology-driven' one, and to navigate the dual challenges of geopolitical tensions and technological autonomy in the context of global industrial rebalancing.

2.2.6 Emerging Powers: The Strategic Rise of India and Southeast Asia

Against the backdrop of intensifying regionalisation and multipolarisation in the global semiconductor industry, emerging economies such as India and Southeast Asia are gradually emerging as important players in the global semiconductor supply chain. Through policy guidance, high-intensity investment and foreign capital cooperation, they are accelerating their in areas such as wafer manufacturing, packaging and testing, and material support, with the aim of securing a place in the global industrial rebalancing.

In India, the Tata Group officially announced in 2023 that it will invest up to 90 billion US dollars to build a domestic wafer manufacturing plant, covering the entire industrial chain from chip design, wafer manufacturing to packaging and testing. This strategy not only responds to the 'Make in India' and 'Atmanirbhar Bharat' policy initiatives but also reflects the Indian government's clear intention to designate the semiconductor industry as a national strategic pillar industry.

Although there are still significant gaps in terms of technological accumulation, infrastructure, and talent systems, India is attempting to build a dual-cycle development system of 'technology introduction + local incubation' through cooperation with mature companies such as TSMC and UMC, with the goal of gradually transforming itself from a chip consumer to a producer. In Southeast Asia, Vietnam, Malaysia, and Singapore play different roles in the semiconductor supply chain.

In 2023, Intel announced a $1.5 billion investment in Ho Chi Minh City, Vietnam, to expand its local packaging and testing facilities. This marks a key strategic adjustment in Intel's global packaging and testing footprint and underscores Vietnam's growing appeal in the sector, driven by its low labour costs, favourable business environment, and policy stability.

Malaysia, a traditional hub for packaging and testing, holds approximately 13% of the global semiconductor packaging and testing market share(according to SEMI and Yole Développement statistics for 2023). Domestic and international companies such as Taiwan Semiconductor Manufacturing Company (TSMC) and Tongfu Microelectronics have established large-scale packaging and testing facilities in Penang and Johor, forming a complete ecosystem covering the entire outsourced packaging and testing services (OSAT) supply chain.

Singapore, meanwhile, continues to consolidate its competitive advantage in 12-inch wafer manufacturing through its advanced manufacturing capabilities and policy continuity. GlobalFoundries operates multiple 12-inch wafer production facilities in Singapore, focusing on automotive-grade, low-power, and RF chip process nodes. It is one of the few manufacturers in Southeast Asia with mid-to-high-end wafer foundry capabilities. Additionally, the Singaporean government is actively supporting AI chip and compound semiconductor R&D through the 'Semiconductor Future Ready Initiative,' aiming to move up the value chain.

Overall, while India and Southeast Asian countries still lag behind traditional semiconductor powerhouses such as China, the United States, and South Korea in terms of technological depth and supply chain completeness, they have secured an increasingly important position in the global semiconductor landscape through policy-driven initiatives, capital investment, and international collaboration. The industrial expansion in this region not only provides new pathways for global supply chain diversification but may also form a structural constraint on China's manufacturing dominance in the future, warranting continued attention.

2.3 Future Development Trends of the Global Semiconductor Industry

2.3.1 Technological Innovation-Driven Industrial Upgrading Directions

2.3.1.1 The Continuation and Challenges of Moore's Law: A Paradigm Shift from Size Reduction to System Synergy

In the future evolution of the global semiconductor industry, technological innovation will remain the core driving force. While the traditional path of size miniaturisation represented by Moore's Law still holds guiding significance, its driving force has significantly weakened, exhibiting multiple trends such as diminishing returns, exponential cost increases, and the replacement of synergistic technologies. The original 'Moore's Law' principle, which stated that the density of transistors would double every 18–24 months, is now facing significant challenges in the nanoscale era, including increased current leakage, intensified thermal effects, and lithography precision bottlenecks as physical limits are approached.

TrendForce (2024) reported that the combined revenue of the top 10 foundries increased by 7.9% in Q4, reaching US\$111.54 billion for the year. Currently, leading foundry manufacturers such as TSMC and Samsung Electronics have commercialised 3-nanometre process nodes and are accelerating their advancement towards 2-nanometre and even 1.4-nanometre processes. However, as process nodes shrink, the cost per unit area of transistors increases rather than decreases, and yield control becomes significantly more challenging, rendering the traditional logic that 'advanced processes equal performance leadership' no longer economically viable. According to data from industry research firm International Business Strategies (IBS), the chip manufacturing cost for 3-nanometre processes increases by approximately 25%–30% compared to 5-nanometre processes, but performance gains may not increase linearly.

To break through the structural bottleneck of diminishing returns from size reduction, the semiconductor industry is transitioning from 'planar scaling' to 'system-level collaboration,' achieving equivalent performance leaps through packaging innovation, architectural restructuring, and integration method reforms. Among these, new technological pathways represented by Chiplet architecture, three-dimensional packaging (3D stacking), and heterogeneous integration have gradually become mainstream choices, redefining the boundaries of chip design and manufacturing and driving the industry paradigm shift from 'single-chip integration' to 'multi-chip system coupling.'

Typical technical practices include: Intel's Foveros advanced packaging platform, which optimises power consumption distribution and inter-module communication efficiency by vertically stacking logic and storage modules; AMD's Infinity Fabric interconnect architecture, which integrates multiple chiplets through high-speed interconnects to enable flexible configuration of computing modules and I/O modules; TSMC's System on Integrated Chips (SoIC) technology, which tightly couples logic, power, and storage units on the same packaging platform to enhance thermal management capabilities and signal integrity. Recent developments in high-performance, power-efficient three-dimensional system-in-package designs, particularly those using Universal Chiplet Interconnect Express, have demonstrated substantial gains in performance and energy efficiency (Das Sharma et al. 2024).

These technical solutions not only alleviate the cost pressure brought about by physical size miniaturisation, but also promote the development of 'on-demand integration' product development paradigms, helping the development of heterogeneous chip systems for diverse scenarios such as AI, high-performance computing (HPC) and edge devices. At the same time, this trend also places higher demands on EDA design processes, testing and verification mechanisms, and supply chain management systems, driving the entire semiconductor industry chain into a new phase of deep collaboration between design, manufacturing, packaging and systems.

2.3.1.2   Emerging Technology Frontiers: Transformations in Computing Paradigms and Breakthroughs in Materials Systems

With the trend of the 'post-Moore era' becoming increasingly apparent, global semiconductor technology is shifting from the linear evolution of traditional CMOS architecture to a path of diversified and heterogeneous integration. In particular, at the computing architecture and material platform levels, rapid breakthroughs in emerging technologies are reshaping chip design logic and system integration methods, heralding a multi-round technology-driven cycle of 'architecture reconstruction, material substitution, and system coordination' over the next 10 to 15 years.

Quantum computing, as the core breakthrough direction of the next-generation computing paradigm, has entered a transition phase from experimental verification to practical architecture iteration. This technology uses quantum bits (qubits) as the basic computing unit and realises exponential parallel computing capabilities through superposition and entanglement states, demonstrating the potential to disrupt classical computing architectures in specific problems (such as prime factorisation, quantum simulation, and optimisation algorithms). Currently, IBM, Google, Intel, and institutions such as the University of Science and Technology of China and the Institute of Physics of the Chinese Academy of Sciences are competing globally on three key metrics: 'quantum error correction tolerance,' 'gate operation fidelity,' and 'qubit scalability.' In 2023, IBM unveiled the 127-qubit Eagle processor and outlined a roadmap for a thousand-qubit architecture; Google announced that its quantum advantage experiment had achieved a million-fold simulation acceleration, demonstrating its leading progress in both engineering implementation and algorithmic systems. However, quantum computing still faces numerous challenges, including maintaining extremely low temperatures (approximately 15 mK), noise suppression, and error correction costs, and remains several technological milestones away from general commercialisation.

Photonic computing has demonstrated extremely high system efficiency potential in applications such as AI inference acceleration and high-speed data centre interconnections. Using photons as information carriers, it offers inherent advantages such as interference resistance, low latency, and high bandwidth, making it suitable for large-scale parallel processing and neural network mapping tasks. Current development efforts are focused on silicon photonics integrated solutions, which embed optical channels and modulation modules into traditional CMOS platforms, promising to significantly reduce energy consumption bottlenecks and become a key component in future AI chips and edge computing devices. Intel, NVIDIA, Lightmatter and other companies have made substantial progress in silicon photonics interconnects, on-chip optical matrix multiplication and programmable optical accelerators. Among them, Intel's 'Horse Ridge' project has promoted the high integration of Cryo-CMOS and light-controlled interfaces, heralding the initial formation of a low-power quantum-optical coordination platform in a cooled environment.

At the same time, new material systems are providing technical options for breaking through the physical limits of silicon-based materials. Nanoscale channel materials such as carbon nanotubes (CNTs) and two-dimensional materials (such as graphene and molybdenum disulphide MoS_2) outperform traditional silicon materials in key parameters such as electron mobility, flexible packaging, and thermal conductivity, demonstrating significant potential for material substitution. Currently, multiple experimental platforms have successfully constructed CNT-based field-effect transistor (FET) arrays and validated their switching behaviour stability at the sub-10-nanometre node. Graphene and MoS_2 demonstrate broad adaptability in transparent electronics, wearable sensors, and low-power logic devices due to their tunable bandgap structures and single-atom thickness. However, these material systems remain in the early stages of a three-phase development process—experimental validation, process yield improvement, and large-scale manufacturing—with industrialisation progress dependent on breakthroughs in key bottlenecks such as large-area fabrication, consistent doping, and packaging compatibility.

Overall, the future semiconductor technology system will feature a three-pronged approach of process evolution, structural innovation, and material breakthroughs. Among these, advanced packaging and system-in-package (SiP) will serve as a bridge for technology convergence and heterogeneous integration, driving computing platforms toward vertical coupling, high energy efficiency, and cross-domain integration. This trend will also give rise to interdisciplinary collaboration models such as 'semiconductor + quantum information,' 'chip + optical networking,' and 'material + architecture co-design,' marking the entry of next-generation information infrastructure into a new paradigm centred on platformisation and ecosystem development.

2.3.2   Dynamic Changes in Market Demand and Emerging Application Areas

As information technology accelerates its penetration into all sectors of society, the market demand structure of the global semiconductor industry is undergoing a profound transformation. According to the 2024 SIA Factbook, global semiconductor sales reached record levels, with significant shifts in market share among major producing regions (Semiconductor Industry Association 2024). The industry is transitioning from the traditional paradigm of 'general-purpose computing driven by scale' to a more complex system characterised by 'intelligent ubiquity and scenario-driven applications,' forming a new growth logic centred on intelligence, green technology, and multi-scenario integration. Under this trend, the diversification of end-user applications and the increasing heterogeneity of technical requirements are jointly driving a systematic restructuring of semiconductor product structures and design paradigms.

First, the development of artificial intelligence (AI) technology continues to reshape computing architectures and chip design logic. In particular, breakthroughs in large language models (LLMs), graph neural networks (GNNs), and multi-modal fusion models in fields such as natural language processing, recommendation systems, and image generation have driven sustained expansion in demand for high-performance computing platforms. AI chip manufacturers like NVIDIA, with their A100 and H100 series GPUs, have become critical computing resources for training and inference, driving the industry toward higher energy efficiency and specialised acceleration architectures. At the same time, heterogeneous computing architectures such as application-specific integrated circuits (ASICs), field-programmable gate arrays (FPGAs), and neural network processors (NPUs) are being widely deployed, forming a multi-chip collaboration landscape of 'general-purpose + specialised' parallel evolution.

Second, the rapid penetration of automotive electronics and intelligent driving technologies has become a new growth engine for the semiconductor market. According to McKinsey, by 2030, a smart car with L4-level autonomous driving capabilities will be equipped with more than 5,000 chips, covering multiple dimensions such as automotive-grade control chips, environmental perception processors, power management modules, and V2X communication chips. This trend is significantly boosting demand for automotive-grade MCUs, IGBTs, SiC power devices, and millimetre-wave radar sensor chips. Leading companies such as Infineon, NXP, and Horizon Robotics are accelerating product upgrades through technologies like SoC integration and chip platformisation to meet the high integration and reliability requirements of intelligent cockpits and autonomous driving systems.

Third, green energy and carbon neutrality goals are accelerating the evolution of power semiconductor technology. In fields such as photovoltaic inverters, new energy storage systems, and smart grid dispatching, wide bandgap devices (such as silicon carbide SiC and gallium nitride GaN) with high voltage resistance, high frequency, and low conduction losses are gradually replacing traditional silicon-based IGBTs and becoming the main technology for a new generation of power devices. Research shows that SiC devices exhibit higher power density and thermal stability in high-temperature and high-pressure environments and have been widely deployed in electric vehicle main drive inverters and fast charging station systems. With the diversification of application scenarios, chip packaging forms (such as modular and double-sided cooling packaging) are also evolving in parallel, placing higher demands on packaging materials, thermal management structures, and interface protocols.

Additionally, emerging applications such as the metaverse, augmented reality/ virtual reality (AR/VR), edge computing, and low-earth orbit satellite communication are driving rapid growth in demand for customised, highly integrated chips. These applications typically require extremely low power consumption, high bandwidth, and real-time response capabilities, driving the transition of processors from general-purpose architectures to domain-specific architectures (DSA). DSA chips such as Google TPU, Apple Neural Engine, and Cambricon MLU are emerging as the optimal performance solutions in vertical application fields, establishing a new paradigm of tightly coupled technology stacks from 'chip-system-application.'

Overall, the global semiconductor market is shifting from a single logic of 'unified demand and scale dominance' to a diversified landscape of 'heterogeneous scenarios and customised architectures.' The core competitiveness of the industry is gradually transitioning from 'cost efficiency' to 'application adaptability' and 'system coordination.' This transformative trend significantly raises the systemic requirements for upstream design complexity, differentiated process node selection, and downstream supply chain coordination mechanisms. Meanwhile, for emerging nations and startups, this technology migration window presents a 'catch-up' opportunity, particularly in application scenarios such as edge AI, industrial IoT, and green energy, where they can rapidly enter the global market through architectural innovation and application focus.

The future growth path of the semiconductor industry will no longer rely on a single dominant product but will shift toward a 'multi-layered, multi-node, multi-directional' structural growth model driven by the aggregation of multiple long-tail scenarios, accelerating the transition of industrial innovation from local breakthroughs to full-chain collaboration.

References

Das Sharma, D., Pasdast, G., Tiagaraj, S., & Aygün, K. (2024). High-performance, power-efficient three-dimensional system-in-package designs with universal chiplet interconnect express. *Nature Electronics, 7*(3), 244–254.

Rasmussen, E. G., Wilthan, B., & Simonds, B. (2023, August 22). *Report from the Extreme Ultra-violet (EUV) Lithography Working Group Meeting: Current State, Needs, and Path Forward* (NIST Special Publication 1500–208). National Institute of Standards and Technology. https://doi.org/10.6028/NIST.SP.1500-208

Semiconductor Industry Association. (2024). *2024 SIA factbook*. Semiconductor Industry Association. https://www.semiconductors.org/wp-content/uploads/2024/05/SIA-2024-Factbook.pdf

TrendForce. (2024, March 12). *Global top 10 foundries Q4 revenue up 7.9%, annual total hits US$111.54 billion in 2023*. TrendForce. https://www.trendforce.com/presscenter/news/20240312-12072.html

Chapter 3
Development Environment and Trade Structure of China's Semiconductor Industry During the 15th Five-Year Plan Period

Tao Ma

Abstract Chapter 3 examines the external environment and internal restructuring of China's semiconductor industry during the 15th Five-Year Plan period. It analyses how global policy shifts—marked by export controls, fiscal subsidies, and supply chain realignments—have posed systemic challenges to China. In response, the country has pursued key technological breakthroughs, reinforced vertical coordination, and expanded international partnerships to foster a more autonomous and resilient industrial system. Drawing on customs data from 2015 to 2024, the chapter conducts an empirical analysis of trade structures across the upstream, midstream, and downstream segments. It reveals sustained dependence on imported equipment, mounting pressures in midstream manufacturing, and continued export reliance in downstream applications. Faced with the dual pressures of heightened external constraints and accelerated domestic transformation, the chapter argues for the establishment of a strategically resilient framework underpinned by technological innovation, supply chain integration, and diversified market engagement to ensure both national security and high-quality development.

Keywords Semiconductor Policy Environment • Trade Structure • Supply Chain Integration • Strategic Resilience

© The Author(s) 2026
T. Wang et al., *China's Semiconductor Industry Strategy*,
SpringerBriefs in Economics,
https://doi.org/10.1007/978-981-95-3332-9_3

3.1 Impact of the Global Policy Environment on China's Semiconductor Industry

3.1.1 Analysis of Semiconductor Industry Policies in Major Countries and Regions

The global semiconductor industry is undergoing a profound transformation from a 'market-driven' to a 'state-driven' model, with policy intervention increasingly becoming the core variable shaping the evolution of the industry landscape. Driven by factors such as technological bottlenecks, supply chain security, and geopolitical competition, major economies are increasingly adopting measures such as industrial policies, export controls, fiscal subsidies, and international alliances to strengthen the strategic autonomy of their domestic semiconductor systems. In this context, the global policy landscape is characterised by three prominent features: first, 'security first' has replaced 'efficiency first,' with technology and production capacity within national security frameworks becoming the focal point of industrial development; second, 'coalition-based governance' is replacing 'unilateral competition,' with a technology containment system led by the United States accelerating its formation; third, 'local manufacturing' is returning to the forefront of policy priorities, with multiple countries introducing incentive mechanisms to promote the return of wafer fabs and diversify production capacity.

These international policy developments are exerting systemic pressure on China's semiconductor industry. On the one hand, developed countries led by the United States have intensified export restrictions and investment reviews targeting Chinese companies, particularly in areas such as EDA tools, advanced equipment, and AI chips, creating a 'high wall effect' that poses significant obstacles to China's high-end manufacturing capabilities. On the other hand, multiple countries are implementing localisation strategies to induce global supply chains to restructure toward 'de-Chinaisation,' thereby eroding China's comparative advantages in packaging and testing as well as mature manufacturing processes. Meanwhile, some emerging economies are attempting to leverage geopolitical realignment to compete for manufacturing transfers and policy resources, which objectively also creates competitive pressure on China's semiconductor exports and technological expansion.

Against this backdrop, conducting an in-depth analysis of the semiconductor industry policies of major countries and regions can help clarify the logic of global industrial governance and identify the external institutional challenges and opportunity windows facing China.

3.1.1.1 US Export Control and Industrial Protection Policies

As the global leader in technology policy, the United States has adopted a highly concentrated and systematic industrial intervention strategy in the semiconductor sector in recent years. The CHIPS and Science Act, enacted in 2022, explicitly allocates 52.7 billion US dollars in direct fiscal support, tax breaks, and R&D investments to rebuild domestic manufacturing capabilities and advanced process capacity (United States Congress 2022). Concurrently, the United States has imposed targeted restrictions on Chinese companies through measures such as the 'Entity List,' 'export controls,' and 'technology licensing restrictions,' targeting critical sectors including EDA software, advanced manufacturing equipment (such as EUV lithography machines), high-performance computing chips (GPUs), and manufacturing materials. Building on this, the United States has also formed a 'technology containment alliance' with key technology-supplying countries like Japan and the Netherlands to restrict the export of advanced equipment to China by companies such as ASML and Tokyo Electron.

3.1.1.2   European Technical Cooperation and Industrial Support Policies

Europe has adopted a 'strategic autonomy' approach, allocating 43 billion euros through the European Chip Act to support domestic companies in enhancing their production capacity in manufacturing, packaging, key equipment, and materials (European Union 2023). The European Commission has emphasised the importance of building a 'safer, more resilient semiconductor ecosystem,' with a particular focus on achieving self-reliance in the semiconductor supply chain for new energy vehicles, industrial control, and renewable energy. Although Europe has not yet fully aligned with the United States in terms of technological control, the objective impact of 'technological bottlenecks' in areas such as EUV equipment, high-end photoresist, and photomask materials on China cannot be ignored.

3.1.1.3   Industrial Catch-Up Strategies of Asian Countries and Regions

While strengthening its semiconductor revival strategy, Japan is increasingly aligning its policies with those of the United States in terms of technological restrictions. Through its 'Semiconductor and Digital Industry Strategy,' the Japanese government is funding domestic companies to upgrade their equipment and processes, attracting projects such as TSMC and Rapidus to establish factories in Japan, thereby enhancing local manufacturing capabilities (Ministry of Economy, Trade and Industry [Japan] 2023). In 2023, Japan added 23 types of advanced manufacturing equipment to its export control list on the grounds of 'national security,' covering core areas such as etching, deposition, ion implantation, and testing, with the aim of cutting off China's access to equipment needed for expanding its advanced manufacturing capacity.

South Korea and Chinese Taiwan, despite their strong manufacturing capabilities, have adopted policy orientations that emphasise 'market orientation' and 'security balance.' The South Korean government has implemented the 'Semiconductor Super Cluster' plan to support Samsung and SK Hynix in expanding advanced processes, while also establishing factories in the United States to address political pressures (Ministry of Science and ICT [Republic of Korea] 2023). Chinese Taiwan, meanwhile, is advancing capacity in the United States, Japan, and Europe to reduce geopolitical risks through diversified export channels. However, given their technological pathways and supply chains' high dependence on global markets, some policies may indirectly impact mainland Chinese companies, such as reduced orders from TSMC and UMC, and restrictions on the transfer of advanced equipment and technology.

Among emerging economies, India, Vietnam, and Malaysia are actively attracting industrial transfers amid the 'de-Chinaisation' trend through fiscal incentives, land concessions, and policies facilitating foreign investment. The Indian government has launched a $10 billion incentive programme to attract Foxconn and Micron to build packaging and manufacturing plants, aiming to establish an 'alternative' semiconductor supply chain (Press Information Bureau, Government of India, Ministry of Electronics & Information Technology 2021). Malaysia and Vietnam are strengthening cooperation with the United States and Japan to become emerging hubs for wafer testing and packaging outsourcing. While these countries are unlikely to directly replace China in the short term, their policy orientations will exert a subtle yet significant influence on the global supply chain landscape and the flow of foreign investment.

Overall, the current global policy environment is characterised by 'strong intervention, multi-centred, and coordinated' trends, with countries prioritising domestic security and industrial sovereignty to drive a structural transformation of the semiconductor industry from market-driven to policy-driven. Under this trend, China's semiconductor industry faces dual pressures from external technological constraints and internal innovation upgrades. It must seek breakthroughs within constraints, reconstruct advantages amid risks, and achieve the organic unity of strategic transformation and systemic security during the 15th Five-Year Plan period.

3.1.2 China's Response to International Policy Coordination and the Competitive Landscape

Faced with increasingly complex global policy coordination mechanisms and a highly asymmetrical technological governance system, China has gradually built a strategic autonomous response system under the dual pressures of 'external blockade' and 'internal upgrading.' The core of this system lies in promoting technological self-reliance and control, reshaping the security structure of industrial chains, actively participating in global rule-making, and promoting the 'de-risking' transformation of industrial resilience when necessary.

First, in response to the technology blockade and alliance-based encirclement led by the United States, China has adopted a multi-tiered strategy of 'breakthroughs in key areas, coordination across the supply chain, and security across domains.' In critical technology segments, national-level science and technology R&D platforms have been leveraged to advance the independent development of 'chokepoint' technologies such as EUV replacement equipment, EDA tools, photoresist materials, and high-purity silicon materials. For example, the 'extreme ultraviolet light source' R&D project led by the Chinese Academy of Sciences, the domestic EDA software initiatives by BGI Genomics, and the rapid expansion of domestic silicon wafer suppliers like Shanghai Silicon Industry and Hejian Technology have begun to establish a domestic substitution system targeting core manufacturing processes. At the same time, in terms of supply chain organisation structure, China is accelerating upstream-downstream coordination through the establishment of the second phase of the 'Big Fund' and local industry guidance funds, strengthening vertical integration capabilities between IC design, wafer manufacturing, packaging and testing services, and equipment and materials to avoid systemic risks caused by single-point dependence.

Second, in response to the global trend of 'de-Chinaisation' of industrial chains, China is actively promoting a dual-track strategy of 'local re-embedding' and 'diversified overseas layout' at the institutional level. On the one hand, it has set phased goals for breakthroughs in core technologies through policy documents such as the '14th Five-Year Plan for National Science and Technology Innovation' and the 'Outline of the Strategy for Building a Manufacturing Powerhouse,' and is promoting the concentrated allocation of resources through a 'new national system.' On the other hand, through the 'Digital Silk Road,' the 'Belt and Road' semiconductor cooperation mechanism, and the RCEP agreement, China is expanding technical cooperation and capacity output pathways with countries in the Middle East, Southeast Asia, and Africa, aiming to establish a institutional buffer zone outside the technology rule system dominated by the United States and Europe. For example, the China-Saudi Arabia Jizan Industrial Park, the Tongfu Microelectronics Malaysia factory, and the BYD Thailand packaging and testing base all demonstrate regional manufacturing transfers and standard expansion led by Chinese companies.

Third, at the international governance mechanism level, China is transitioning from a 'rule taker' to a 'rule co-builder,' striving to enhance its global voice in areas such as technical standards, industrial access, and platform agreements. Chinese solutions represented by RISC-V and Chiplet open architecture are gaining increasing importance in international foundations and standard-setting organisations, and Chinese enterprises and research institutions have seen a significant increase in their submission and adoption rates in multiple standard systems, including the ISA instruction set, packaging interconnection protocols, and low-power communication. At the same time, China is actively participating in multilateral governance platforms such as the WTO and WIPO, pushing to incorporate restrictions on chip technology exports and digital product taxation into the international rules system to offset the uncertainty of bilateral sanctions systems.

However, China's current policy responses also face numerous challenges. On the one hand, some core technologies have not yet been fully mastered, and the industrial chain remains highly dependent on external sources. On the other hand, the global trends of 'friend-shoring' and 'technology alliances' have weakened the traditional comparative advantages based on market mechanisms, forcing China to rebalance efficiency and security. Additionally, uncertainties in the international environment, such as the US presidential transition, regional conflicts, and global economic fluctuations, are placing higher demands on China's policy continuity and strategic foresight.

In summary, under the context of international policy coordination and the global competitive landscape, China is gradually establishing a systematic response mechanism centred on technological self-reliance as the foundation, supply chain security as the core, and rule-based negotiations as the lever. This response strategy not only demonstrates China's resilience and adaptability in the face of external constraints but also lays the strategic foundation for the subsequent sections on 'security assessment' and 'strategic repositioning.'

3.2 Global Economic Environment and Its Relationship with China's Semiconductor Industry

3.2.1 The Interrelationship Between Global Economic Growth and Semiconductor Market Demand

The global economy and the semiconductor market are highly interconnected. As a foundational industry with extremely high technology penetration rates, the demand for semiconductor products is significantly influenced by the pace of macroeconomic expansion and the speed of industrial structure upgrades. Generally speaking, a rebound in global GDP growth is accompanied by expansion in fixed asset investment and consumption upgrades, which directly drives demand for semiconductor applications such as consumer electronics, automobiles, industrial automation, and cloud computing, thereby creating growth momentum for upstream chip design, wafer manufacturing, and packaging and testing services. However, in recent years, the global economy has continued to exhibit characteristics of 'weak recovery and rising uncertainty.' According to data from the International Monetary Fund (IMF), global economic growth is expected to remain around 3% in 2023–2024, far below the average growth rate in the early 2010s (International Monetary Fund 2024). In particular, the sustained interest rate hikes implemented by major economies in the US and Europe to curb high inflation have led to a tightening of global credit conditions and a decline in corporate capital expenditure intentions, thereby suppressing the release of demand for semiconductor products.

Against this macroeconomic backdrop, China's semiconductor industry chain has significantly felt the ripple effects of demand fluctuations. On the one hand, overseas customers have reduced wafer orders and lowered inventory levels, causing significant fluctuations in the capacity utilisation rates of major foundries such as SMIC and Huahong Power, with mature process lines facing dual pressures from price declines and order reductions; on the other hand, the extended replacement cycles for end-consumer products such as smartphones, tablets, and laptops have led to changes in the product shipment structure of IC design companies like ZTE and Allwinner, with a significant divergence in demand for high-, mid-, and low-end chips. Additionally, the slowdown in global data centre construction has delayed procurement plans for AI servers and high-performance computing chips, indirectly impacting domestic AI chip innovation companies such as Cambricon and Suyuan Technology.

At the same time, increased uncertainty in the global economic environment has made international order structures more conservative and short-term, with multinational customers tending to adopt a 'multiple orders + small batches' strategy in supply chain management. This has increased the pressure on domestic packaging and testing companies to manage their plans flexibly, affecting capital expenditure and the pace of investment in automated equipment. Overall, the slowdown and volatility in global economic growth are being transmitted through multiple channels to China's entire semiconductor industry chain, exerting profound impacts on its capacity allocation, technological iteration pace, and market expectations.

3.2.2   The Impact of International Trade Frictions on China's Semiconductor Industry Chain

The instability of the international trade environment, especially the intensifying structural friction between China and the United States, has become one of the core challenges constraining the security and outward expansion of China's semiconductor industry chain (United States International Trade Commission 2023). Since 2018, the US government has gradually built a 'systemic decoupling' system centred on tariffs, investment reviews, and technology export restrictions. As a highly technical, complex, and strategically sensitive industry, semiconductors have become the primary target of control measures. The United States has successively placed key companies such as Huawei, SMIC, and Yangtze Memory Technologies on the 'Entity List,' restricting their access to US technology, equipment, and software support, particularly manufacturing equipment and EDA tools related to 14-nanometre and below processes. At the same time, the United States has collaborated with technology node countries such as the Netherlands and Japan to establish a multilateral technology export control framework, restricting the export of high-end equipment such as EUV lithography machines, key photoresists, and precision measurement instruments to China.

These institutional restrictions have had a profound impact on China's semiconductor industry chain, manifesting in three aspects: First, at the equipment level, domestic substitution is still in its early stages, particularly in core areas such as lithography, ion implantation, and chemical vapour deposition, where reliance on imports remains high, constraining the expansion of advanced process production capacity. Second, in terms of software tools, although domestic EDA companies such as Huada Jiutian and Guangliwei are rapidly emerging, there is still a generation gap between them and international mainstream tools in high-end analogue design, system verification, and back-end optimisation, affecting design process efficiency and chip yield control. Third, in terms of international cooperation, some overseas customers are constrained by export control regulations and have proactively reduced technical exchanges and procurement from Chinese companies, raising the barriers to entry for Chinese semiconductor products into international markets.

In addition to Sino-US friction, economies such as the EU, Japan, and South Korea have also strengthened reviews and restrictions on the export of critical technologies and equipment in their industrial security strategies. For example, the EU has introduced the 'Economic Security Toolbox,' which proposes to establish an 'export screening mechanism'; Japan has included semiconductor equipment and materials in the revision list of the Foreign Exchange and Foreign Trade Act, which indirectly affects China. Meanwhile, emerging economies such as India and Vietnam are leveraging the 'friend-shoring' trend to attract the relocation of manufacturing operations by multinational companies, eroding China's comparative advantages in packaging and testing as well as mature manufacturing processes.

Overall, the 'geopolitical boundaries' constructed by international trade frictions are deeply reshaping the external ecosystem of China's semiconductor supply chain. This not only restricts access to advanced technologies and equipment upgrades but also exerts pressure on the cost structure and scale advantages of the mid-to-low-end market. In this environment, China must accelerate the achievement of self-reliance in core technologies, enhance vertical integration capabilities within the supply chain, and explore alternative technical and market pathways within the region to enhance its resilience against trade conflicts and institutional changes.

3.3 Opportunities and Challenges for China's Semiconductor Industry in the Global Technology Environment

3.3.1 Current Status and Trends in International Technical Exchange and Cooperation

Despite the increasingly tense global technological competition landscape, international technical exchanges and cooperation in the semiconductor sector have not completely ceased, particularly in non-sensitive areas such as standardisation, basic research, and exploration of cutting-edge technologies, where cross-border collaboration remains vibrant. The current global semiconductor technology cooperation is evolving towards a 'layered interaction and regional coordination' trend, where cooperation in traditional manufacturing processes and commercial applications is significantly contracting, while some cooperation space is maintained in emerging technologies, basic research, and open architecture.

In terms of standardisation, open-source technology ecosystems such as RISC-V, UCIe (Universal Chiplet Interconnect), and the Open Compute Project (OCP) continue to expand, with Chinese companies increasingly participating in these initiatives. For example, in multiple standardisation working groups under the RISC-V Foundation, Chinese institutions rank among the top in terms of the number of proposals submitted and adoption rates, forming a domestic ecosystem led by companies such as PingTouGe, the Institute of Computing Technology of the Chinese Academy of Sciences, and Xilinx. In the UCIe standard, Chinese packaging and testing companies such as Changjiang Microelectronics and Tongfu Microelectronics have also begun to explore the interface specifications for Chiplet packaging standards at the interconnection protocol layer. Such open systems provide Chinese companies with 'technical entry points' to bypass proprietary standard barriers, while also building a potential platform for 'soft connections' with mainstream international systems.

In the field of basic research, Chinese research institutions maintain a certain level of joint research with their counterparts in Europe, the United States, and Japan in areas such as quantum information, photonic integration, third-generation semiconductor materials, and carbon nanotubes. For example, the University of Science and Technology of China and the University of Innsbruck in Austria have collaborated on multiple high-level papers in the fields of quantum entanglement and quantum measurement; The China Academy of Engineering Physics and the Max Planck Institute in Germany have conducted joint research projects on gallium nitride epitaxial growth. Additionally, some international conferences and journal platforms continue to provide channels for technical personnel to exchange experiences and publish research findings, supporting the development of non-state-driven, academically oriented innovation networks.

However, the sustainability of cooperation trends is constrained by multiple factors, including geopolitical tensions, institutional reviews, and public opinion risks. The CHIPS and Science Act of 2022 and the UNITED STATES GOVERNMENT NATIONAL STANDARDS STRATEGY FOR CRITICAL AND EMERGING TECHNOLOGY in the United States have established stricter project review mechanisms for scientific research cooperation, forcing some Sino-US joint laboratories to suspend or freeze their operations. The EU, Japan, and others have also strengthened political review standards for foreign technology cooperation, raising the barriers for exchanges between technical personnel and academic research institutions. Meanwhile, global core equipment and EDA software suppliers have become increasingly cautious in authorising cooperation, restricting the regions, project scope, and redistribution rights, significantly weakening Chinese companies' ability to access cutting-edge tools and testing platforms.

Overall, while structural opportunities for international technology cooperation remain, cooperation models are shifting from 'full-chain collaboration' to 'limited-scenario integration.' China must maintain an open attitude while flexibly assessing cooperation security boundaries and actively building its capacity to independently participate in global standards and open-source platforms to secure a favourable position in the process of systemic restructuring (Asian Development Bank et al. 2023).

3.3.2 Dual Pressures of Technological Barriers and Independent Innovation

Coexisting with limited room for cooperation is the increasingly stringent technical blockade system that continues to exert pressure on China's semiconductor industry. Currently, export controls and technological decoupling led by the United States have expanded from a single entity list model to a comprehensive blockade system covering multiple dimensions, including EDA software, high-end manufacturing equipment, manufacturing materials, core chips, and cloud service platforms, in an attempt to block China's upgrade path in high-end chip manufacturing and application scenarios from the source. This 'systemic blockade' has transcended the scope of traditional trade barriers and exhibits clear strategic containment intentions and a long-term institutionalisation trend.

In terms of critical manufacturing equipment, China remains heavily reliant on overseas imports (Organisation for Economic Co-operation and Development 2023). Take EUV lithography machines as an example: ASML, the sole supplier, has completely halted exports to China, and domestic efforts have yet to achieve breakthroughs in prototype development. Equipment such as etching, ion implantation, and CVD machines are dominated by US and Japanese companies like Tokyo Electron, Applied Materials, and Lam Research, with restrictions increasingly extending to mid-range equipment. Meanwhile, efforts to replace imports of high-end testing and packaging equipment are still in their infancy, with severe technological gaps severely constraining the upgrading of production lines at domestic wafer fabs.

In terms of EDA tools and core IP, three US companies—Cadence, Synopsys, and Mentor—control over 90% of the global market share. Their software licences are directly constrained by US export laws, causing Chinese IC design companies to heavily rely on imported tools in areas such as simulation verification, back-end optimisation, and power consumption analysis. At the same time, the licensing systems for ARM and x86 architectures are highly closed. Although RISC-V offers some open alternatives, it has yet to pose a comprehensive challenge to mainstream architectures in high-performance, server, and desktop-level chips.

It is against this challenging backdrop that China's semiconductor industry is accelerating its path of independent innovation to break free from the structural dilemma of 'low-end manufacturing and reliance on high-end technology.' At the national level, mechanisms such as 'posting challenges and appointing leaders,' "Core Strengthening Project,' and the 'Second Phase of the National Integrated Circuit Industry Investment Fund" to channel funds, talent, and policy resources toward key technological nodes. Companies such as Huada Jiutian and Guangliwei have made phased progress in EDA domestication, establishing preliminary toolchains covering logic design, functional verification, and post-layout simulation; research institutions including the Chinese Academy of Sciences, Northern HuaChuang, and Shanghai Microelectronics have gradually achieved small-scale domestic substitution in lithography equipment, etching processes, and special gas materials. In terms of chip architecture, Alibaba PingTouGe's Xuan Tie series and the Chinese

Academy of Sciences' Xiangshan processor have been deployed at scale in low-power scenarios.

However, the current path of independent innovation still faces internal bottlenecks such as an insufficient innovation ecosystem, lack of economies of scale, and weak application-driven demand. The domestic toolchain is highly fragmented, lacking unified interfaces and middleware standards, with slow progress in ecosystem construction; some domestic equipment still struggles to support large-scale stable production, and manufacturing yield rates are difficult to control; At the same time, domestic terminal manufacturers still prefer mature foreign solutions during the selection process, leading to frequent situations where local companies 'can produce but cannot use' their products.

In summary, China's semiconductor industry is in a critical transition period from 'technological catch-up' to 'breakthrough within the system.' On one hand, we must be vigilant against the structural technological constraints imposed by evolving blockade systems; on the other hand, we need to adopt a systems engineering approach to transform 'point innovations' into 'chain-based collaboration,' and build an autonomous and controllable technological system across multiple layers, including standards, ecosystems, verification, and applications, to ensure a relatively independent and sustainable leading position in the global technological restructuring.

3.4 Trade Structure of China's Semiconductor Industry Chain

Based on the identification of the six-digit customs codes for products through the supply chain analysis, we obtained import and export values, trade partner data for upstream, midstream, and downstream products in the supply chain, as well as semiconductor products from the customs database for the period 2015–2024. The trade partners were then categorised into three main groups for analysis:The first category consists of G7 countries, which are the world's major developed economies with significant influence in international politics, economics, and technology, and maintain close cooperation with the United States; The second category includes countries that have signed the 'Belt and Road' trade agreements with China. These 'Belt and Road' countries have strong economic and trade ties with China and represent a key direction for China's future foreign trade development; the third category includes East Asian economies, such as South Korea, Japan, and Hong Kong, Macao, and Chinese Taiwan. These countries (regions) are geographically close to China and have close economic and trade ties. Additionally, imports where the origin is marked as China (due to reasons such as free trade zones or products originally produced in China) are also included in this category for analysis. There may be overlapping statistics within these three categories, but this does not affect the overall trend analysis (Italy is both a G7 country and a 'Belt and Road' country; Japan is both a G7 country and an East Asian country; South Korea is both a 'Belt and Road' country and an East Asian country). Additionally, countries such as the Netherlands, which play a key role in the global semiconductor supply chain, should also be considered in the analysis to account for their potential impact.

3.4.1 Trade Structure in the Upstream Industry Chain

3.4.1.1 Total Imports and Exports

In 2014, the State Council issued the 'National Integrated Circuit Industry Development Promotion Outline' and designated semiconductors as a key area in plans such as 'Made in China 2025,' propelling China's semiconductor industry into a period of rapid development. According to the analysis in Fig. 3.1, from 2015 to 2024, the import volume of the upstream segment of the semiconductor industry chain consistently exceeded the export volume, with the gap widening over time. This indicates that this sector represents a weak link in China's industrial chain, as domestic products cannot meet domestic production needs, resulting in high reliance on imports. Furthermore, as shown in Fig. 3.2, when breaking down the data by production equipment and raw materials, it is evident that the growth and fluctuations in total imports from the upstream sector primarily stem from production equipment. As the 'mother machines' of semiconductor manufacturing, production equipment is of critical importance and represents one of the core 'chokepoint' technological challenges China faces in its semiconductor industry. For the upstream segment of the semiconductor supply chain, import supply—especially of high-end semiconductor production equipment—is a critical factor affecting supply chain security. Insufficient import supply will have adverse effects on supply chain security.

During the period from 2015 to 2024, the total import volume of upstream products showed an overall upward trend. However, there was a temporary decline in

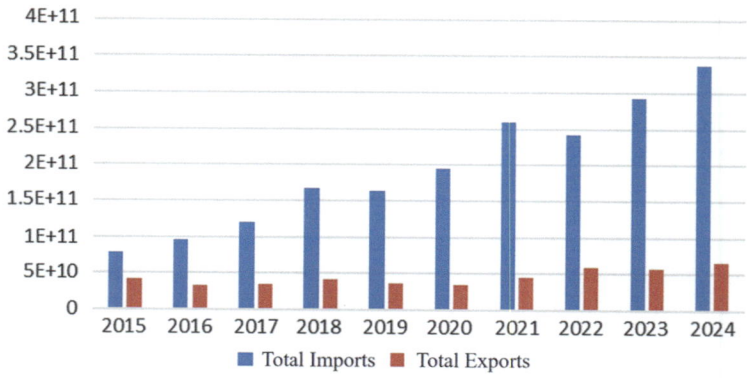

Fig. 3.1 Total imports and exports of China's upstream semiconductor industry chain from 2015 to 2024

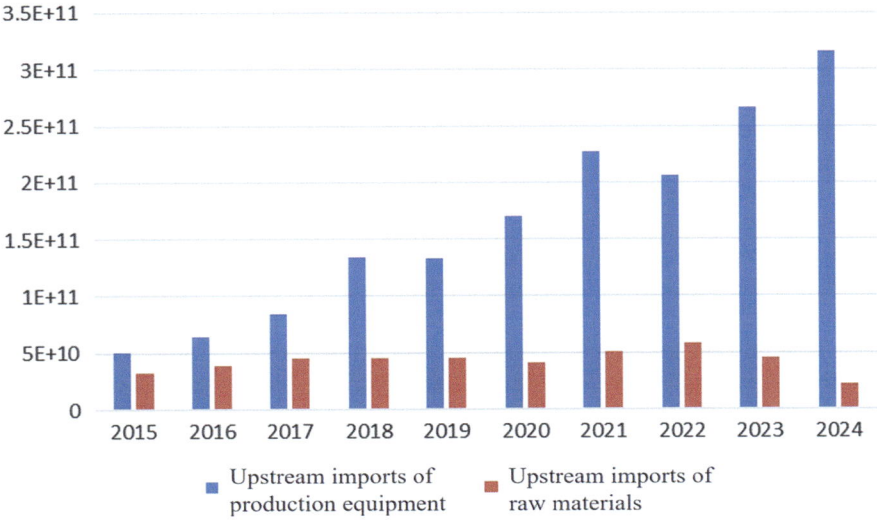

Fig. 3.2   China's semiconductor industry chain upstream imports, 2015–2024

the volume of upstream product imports in 2019 and 2022, which coincided with the US government's inclusion of Huawei and other Chinese semiconductor industry leaders on the Entity List in 2019, as well as the enactment of the CHIPS and Science Act in 2022, which temporarily disrupted China's imports of upstream production equipment.

3.4.1.2   Import Situation from Different Trading Partners

According to the analysis in Fig. 3.3, the main import sources for upstream products in China's semiconductor industry chain are G7 countries and East Asian economies. Excluding the duplicate statistics of Japan, the proportion of upstream imports from these two categories of countries (regions) decreased from 82% in 2015 to 57% in 2024, although there was a significant decline, it still accounted for more than half of the total.

Upstream products have high technological barriers, with import sources being relatively concentrated and single-sourced, posing risks to supply chain security.

Prior to 2019, the import share from East Asian countries was slightly higher than that from G7 countries. However, after 2019, the share from East Asian countries continued to decline and was overtaken by G7 countries, before slightly recovering in 2024. The share from G7 countries increased in 2019 and remained relatively stable until 2022, but saw a significant decline in 2023–2024. The continuous decline in the share of East Asia after 2019 may have been affected by the semiconductor trade friction between Japan and South Korea. As the United

States and its allies strengthened product export restrictions for the purpose of technological blockade and industrial suppression, China was forced to reduce imports from G7 countries, resulting in a significant decline. At the same time, with the agreement reached between Japan and South Korea in 2023, the share of East Asia rebounded.

'Belt and Road' countries account for a low proportion of imports of upstream products in the industrial chain. Except for South Korea, the remaining countries are not major trading partners for China's imports of upstream semiconductor products. Since upstream imports primarily consist of high-end production equipment, and 'Belt and Road' countries are mainly developing countries lacking the production capacity for such products, their imports of upstream products have shown an upward trend, with the import proportion stabilising after 2018. In the future, as more countries join the Belt and Road trade agreements and as countries improve their technology and production capabilities, Belt and Road-related countries may play a greater role in the supply of upstream products in the industrial chain.

Further analysis reveals that G7 countries and the East Asian region overall show a declining trend, while the share of Belt and Road countries remains relatively stable, indicating that other trading partners have experienced significant increases in their import shares. Upon examining the data for other countries individually, it was found that China's imports from the Netherlands accounted for a rapidly growing share of total imports, particularly after 2022, rising from 8% to 21% by 2024. This has diverted import trade shares from G7 countries and East Asian economies,

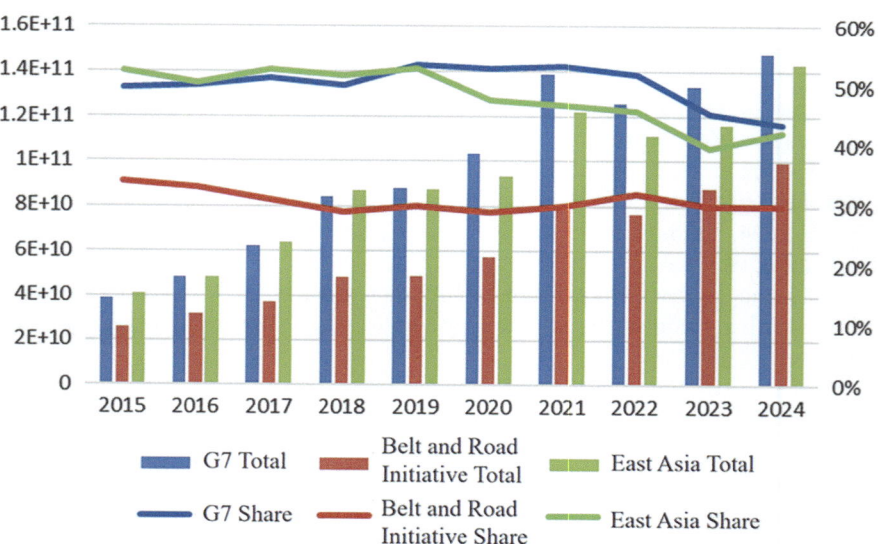

Fig. 3.3   Upstream imports from different trading partners, 2015–2024

with the Netherlands gradually emerging as a country with significant influence on China's upstream semiconductor supply chain.

3.4.1.3   Export Situation to Different Trading Partners

As shown in Fig. 3.4, the export situation of upstream products in China's semiconductor industry chain to different trading partners exhibits different trends. G7 countries account for less than 20% of China's exports of upstream products in the semiconductor industry chain, with a relatively low export share. Although there has been fluctuating growth, the overall trend remains relatively stable. In terms of 'Belt and Road' countries and the East Asia region, the trends show significant differences. During the period from 2015 to 2022, the export share of upstream semiconductor products from China to 'Belt and Road' countries continued to rise, but began to decline in 2023. Meanwhile, the export share to East Asia showed a significant downward trend, with Hong Kong's share dropping from 48% to 6%, primarily due to a decline in exports of raw materials such as silicon. This may be because Hong Kong's semiconductor manufacturing industry is gradually transitioning towards services and finance. Many semiconductor companies have relocated their production facilities to mainland China or other low-cost regions while retaining their headquarters functions and high-value-added operations in Hong Kong, such as research and development, supply chain management, and finance. As a result, the demand for raw materials has decreased.

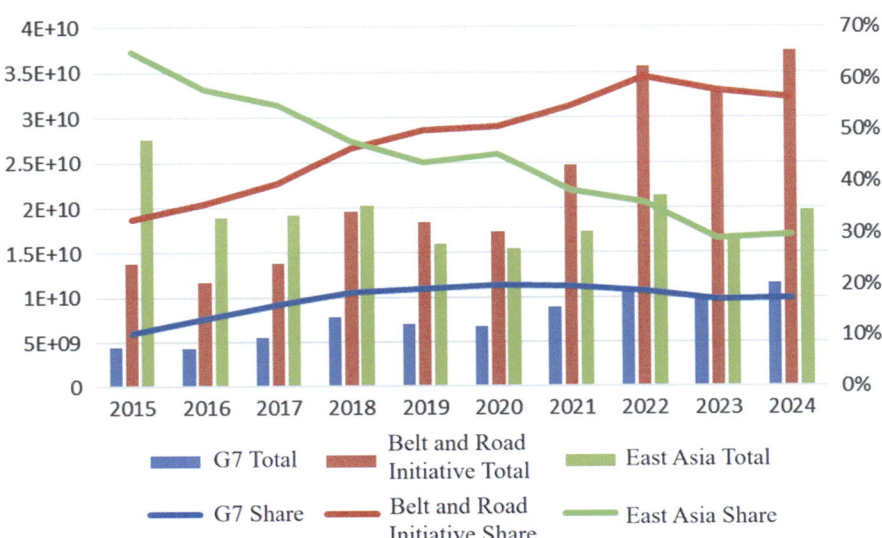

Fig. 3.4   Exports from upstream industries to different trading partners, 2015–2024

3.4.2 Trade Structure in the Midstream of the Industry Chain

3.4.2.1 Total Imports and Exports

According to the analysis in Fig. 3.5, the trends in the total imports and exports of midstream products in China's semiconductor industry chain are converging, with overall import values exceeding export values. The gap between imports and exports in the upstream and downstream segments of the industry chain is relatively small, but it widens after 2022, indicating that midstream products in China's semiconductor industry currently have a high degree of reliance on imports.

From 2017 to 2021, the total volume of imports and exports of midstream products showed an upward trend, but began to decline from 2021 to 2024. Due to factors such as supply-demand mismatches, 'chip shortages' and price hikes, manufacturers hoarding inventory, and consumers' advance spending on consumer electronics during the pandemic, semiconductor prices reached a peak around 2021 and subsequently entered a destocking phase. As a result, 2021 became a turning point for the semiconductor industry in China and globally. The midstream segment of the semiconductor industry chain is the core manufacturing process of semiconductors, closely linked to semiconductor products themselves. Changes in the semiconductor product market directly impact the trend in the total import and export value of midstream products.

3.4.2.2 Import Situation from Different Trading Partners

According to the analysis in Fig. 3.6, imports from East Asia accounted for the highest proportion of China's total imports from 2015 to 2024, exceeding half of

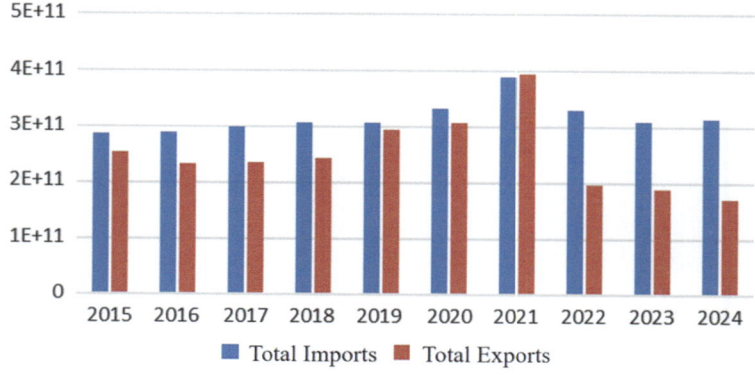

Fig. 3.5 Total imports and exports of China's midstream semiconductor industry chain from 2015 to 2024

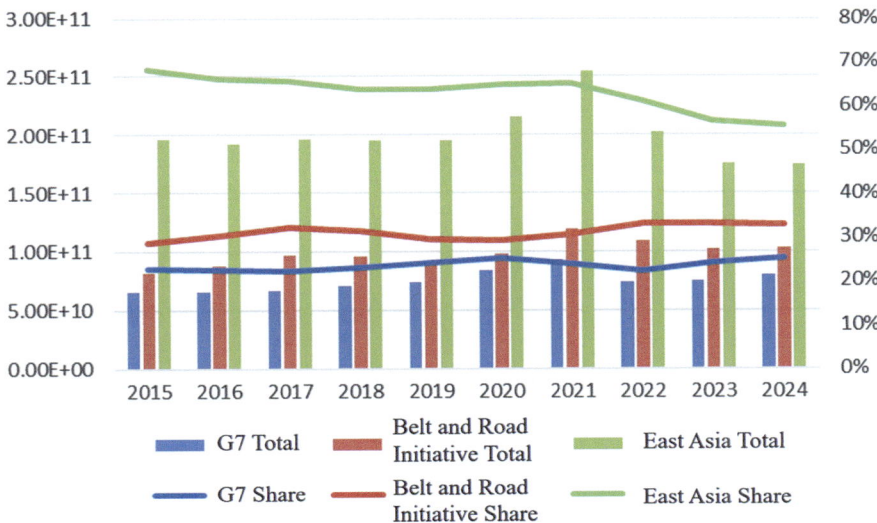

Fig. 3.6   Imports of intermediate goods from different trading partners, 2015–2024

the total, but the overall proportion showed a downward trend. Further analysis of import data revealed that the top countries and regions in terms of import share were China, Japan, Chinese Taiwan, and South Korea, with China having the highest share and a significant gap from Japan, which ranked second, with a share exceeding 20%.

In customs import data, cases where the import country is listed as China are typically due to special circumstances such as bonded zone imports, processing trade, in-kind processing/imported materials processing, or re-exports. This also highlights China's critical role in the midstream of the global semiconductor supply chain.

The import share of 'Belt and Road' countries and G7 countries fluctuates within the range of 35% to 20%, showing a significant gap compared to East Asian countries. The share of 'Belt and Road' countries has consistently been higher than that of G7 countries, but the difference between the two is not significant, and both show a steady upward trend.

3.4.2.3   Export Situation to Different Trading Partners

According to the analysis in Fig. 3.7, the proportion of China's exports of midstream products in the semiconductor industry chain to three categories of countries (regions) varied significantly and followed different trends between 2015 and 2024. China's exports to G7 countries accounted for the lowest proportion and showed an overall downward trend, stabilising at around 13% after 2022.

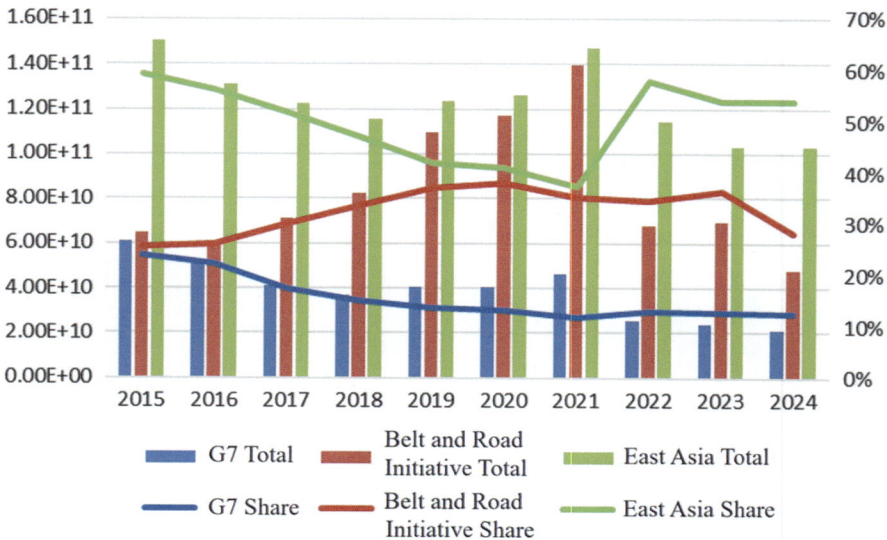

Fig. 3.7 Exports of midstream products to different trading partners, 2015–2024

China's exports to 'Belt and Road' countries showed an overall trend of first increasing and then decreasing, with the largest change in total export volume among the three types of countries (regions). After reaching a peak in 2021, exports dropped sharply in 2022, indicating that midstream products have market potential in 'Belt and Road' countries, but market stability still needs to be improved. The proportion of exports to East Asia decreased from 2015 to 2021, but saw a rapid increase in 2022. However, the total volume change was not significant, and the shift in the proportion was primarily driven by changes in exports to other countries, indicating a relatively stable overall export market.

3.4.3 Trade Structure in the Downstream Industry Chain

3.4.3.1 Total Imports and Exports

The downstream segment of the semiconductor industry chain primarily consists of its application fields. Against the backdrop of rapid development in digital technology and information technology, downstream application fields not only require semiconductors but also demand them in increasing quantities, with quality requirements also rising steadily.

As shown in Fig. 3.8, China's exports of downstream semiconductor products significantly exceed imports, indicating that China holds a competitive advantage in the production of downstream semiconductor products. However, this also implies a high degree of reliance on exports, necessitating efforts to stabilise and continuously expand international markets. The total import volume has remained relatively

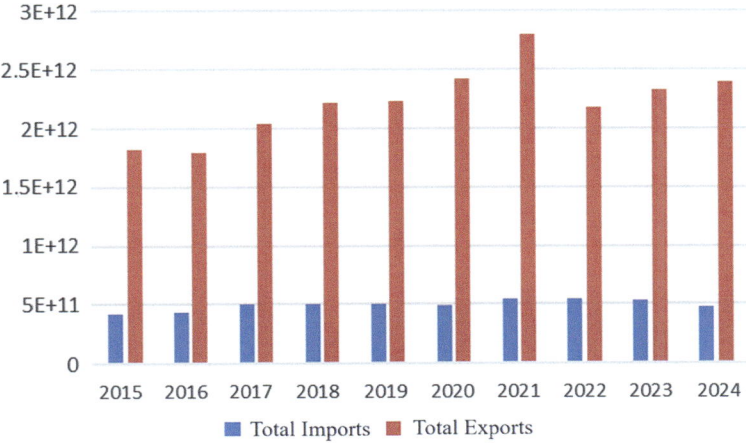

Fig. 3.8   Total imports and exports of China's downstream semiconductor industry chain from 2015 to 2024

stable overall. However, the total export volume experienced a sharp decline in 2022 due to factors such as the global economic downturn, reduced demand, and shifts in the global supply chain. Although it has gradually recovered since then, it has not yet reached the level of 2021.

3.4.3.2   Import Situation from Different Trading Partners

According to the analysis in Fig. 3.9, G7 countries are the primary trading partners for China's imports of downstream products in the semiconductor industry chain, accounting for more than half of the total. However, this proportion has been declining since 2017, dropping from 71% in 2017 to 57% in 2024, with the total import value in 2024 reaching the lowest level since 2015.

Meanwhile, while imports from East Asia have remained relatively stable overall, they have also gradually declined since 2019, with the total import value in 2024 reaching the lowest level since 2015. As China's downstream production capacity and technological capabilities have improved, its reliance on and demand for imports from G7 countries and East Asia have also decreased. Meanwhile, the proportion and total volume of imports from 'Belt and Road' countries have shown an overall upward trend, with import volumes exceeding those from East Asia in 2024.

3.4.3.3   Export Situation to Different Trading Partners

As shown in Fig. 3.10, G7 countries are the main trading partners for exports of downstream products in China's semiconductor industry chain. They have consistently accounted for the highest proportion among the three categories of countries (regions) until 2024, but both their export share and total volume have gradually

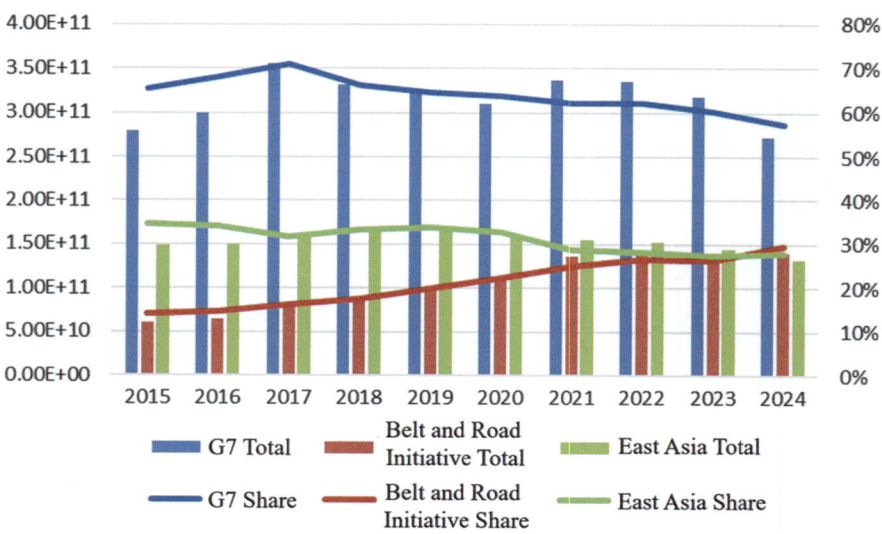

Fig. 3.9 Downstream imports from different trading partners, 2015–2024

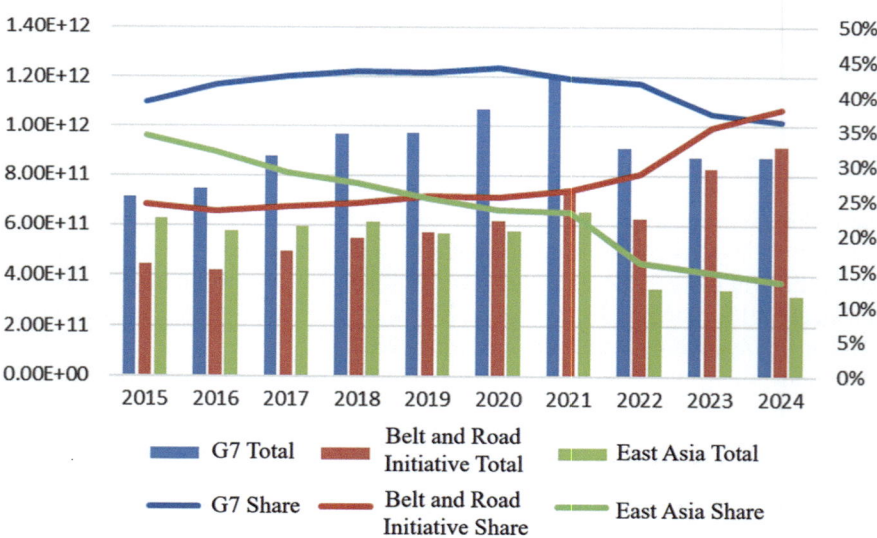

Fig. 3.10 Exports to different trading partners in the downstream sector, 2015–2024

declined since 2021. This situation may stem from three factors: first, insufficient supply of high-end semiconductors has impacted the production and export of downstream high-end products; second, the supply chain has shifted, as countries have strengthened their supply chains and supply chains amid complex international circumstances, leading to a gradual shift in global orders toward Southeast Asian countries such as India; third, the pandemic has exacerbated economic downturn pressures, resulting in shrinking demand.

China's exports to East Asian countries have also shown a significant downward trend. A detailed analysis of individual countries and regions reveals that this is primarily due to the decline in exports from Hong Kong, which dropped from 23% in 2015 to 6% in 2024. The reduction in Hong Kong's exports may be attributed to the rise of e-commerce and the rapid development of mainland ports, leading to a gradual weakening of Hong Kong's role as a trade hub.

China's exports to 'Belt and Road' countries have shown an upward trend, surpassing East Asian countries in 2019 and G7 countries in 2024, accounting for the highest proportion among the three categories of countries (regions). Although the total volume decreased in 2022 due to the overall export environment, it quickly rebounded thereafter. This has to some extent alleviated the impact of reduced exports to G7 countries and East Asian regions on the production and exports of downstream products in China's semiconductor industry chain, while continuously expanding new international markets.

3.5 Summary

As the global semiconductor industry enters a critical phase of strategic restructuring and systemic transformation, China's semiconductor industry is facing unprecedented external complexity and internal development urgency. This chapter systematically analyses the impact of the current global environment on China's semiconductor industry from three dimensions—policy, economy, and technology—and the room for response, presenting a multidimensional picture of 'strengthened external constraints and unleashed internal potential.'

In terms of the global policy environment, major economies have generally intensified state intervention in the semiconductor industry, manifested in a combination of large-scale fiscal subsidies, the repatriation of domestic manufacturing, and restrictions on technology exports. The United States has passed the CHIPS and Science Act to drive domestic manufacturing and technology lockdown mechanisms, while the European Union and Japan have established industrial security frameworks. South Korea and Chinese Taiwan are accelerating their global capacity layout, and emerging countries are taking over some of the transfer paths. This trend is not only reshaping the global industrial division of labour, but also forcing China to accelerate the construction of a semiconductor ecosystem with autonomy and resilience.

In terms of the global economic environment, overall recovery is weak, trade frictions are intensifying, and capital flows are unstable, all of which are exerting multiple impacts on China's semiconductor market demand, export structure, and investment and financing environment. On the demand side, global consumer electronics and industrial investment are slowing down, exacerbating cyclical fluctuations. On the supply side, against the backdrop of 'de-Chinaisation,' order transfers and foreign capital outflows are occurring, and the manufacturing and packaging and testing segments are facing structural adjustment pressures. Against this backdrop, enhancing domestic demand-driven growth and strengthening regional cooperation and layout have become key pillars for China to mitigate external risks.

In terms of the global technological environment, China faces ongoing challenges from technological blockades and the upgrading of standard exclusivity, particularly in high-tech categories such as EDA, advanced process equipment, and core IP, where access rights are restricted, forming multi-layered 'technological bottlenecks.' At the same time, the expansion of emerging areas such as chiplets, RISC-V, quantum computing, and third-generation semiconductors has provided China with limited but real strategic breakthrough opportunities. By strengthening national major projects, focusing on open architectures, and promoting standardisation, China is building an independent innovation path from 'product substitutability' to 'system self-sufficiency.'

Between 2015 and 2024, the import and export structure of China's semiconductor industry chain exhibited phased and regional characteristics. The upstream segment remains highly dependent on imports, particularly in high-end production equipment, where long-standing technical bottlenecks have constrained development. While G7 countries and East Asian economies remain the primary suppliers, their share has declined annually. The Netherlands has rapidly emerged as a key trading partner due to its advanced equipment technology. The midstream segment, as the manufacturing core, has seen its total imports and exports remain largely balanced. However, since 2022, the import advantage has expanded significantly, with East Asian countries remaining the primary import source, though their share has been declining, while 'Belt and Road' countries have gradually begun to demonstrate their potential as alternative suppliers. The downstream segment highlights China's competitive advantage in the manufacturing and export of application-oriented products, with export volumes far exceeding imports. However, in recent years, traditional markets such as the G7 and East Asian countries have seen a decline in export shares due to factors including the global economic downturn, the pandemic, and the relocation of supply chains. BRI countries have grown against the trend, emerging as new growth poles. Overall, China's integration and dominance in the global semiconductor industry chain are steadily increasing. However, it still faces multiple challenges, including reliance on advanced equipment, geopolitical interference, and the restructuring of the trade landscape. It urgently needs to accelerate core technology breakthroughs and expand into diversified markets.

In summary, the global external environment presents both systemic challenges and real opportunities for reshaping the path of China's semiconductor industry. How to achieve a structural balance of 'manageable risks, sustainable growth, and reversible competition' amid geopolitical rivalry, technological restrictions, and economic fluctuations has become the core issue for the development of China's semiconductor industry during the 15th Five-Year Plan period.

References

Asian Development Bank, WTO, IDE–JETRO, OECD, UIBE, & World Bank. (2023). *Global value chain development report 2023: Resilient and sustainable GVCs in turbulent times.* Asian Development Bank. https://www.adb.org/publications/global-value-chain-development-report-2023

European Union. (2023). *Regulation (EU) 2023/1781 of the European Parliament and of the Council of 13 September 2023 establishing a framework of measures for strengthening Europe's semiconductor ecosystem (Chips Act). Official Journal of the European Union, L* 229, 1–53. https://eur-lex.europa.eu/eli/reg/2023/1781/oj/eng

International Monetary Fund. (2024, April). *World economic outlook: Steady but slow—Resilience amid divergence and fragmentation.* International Monetary Fund. https://www.imf.org/en/Publications/WEO/Issues/2024/04.

Ministry of Economy, Trade and Industry (Japan). (2023, March 31). *Press conference by Minister Nishimura (excerpt)* [Press release]. https://www.meti.go.jp/english/speeches/press_conferences/2023/0331001.html

Ministry of Science and ICT (Republic of Korea). (2023, May 16). *Government to establish the world's largest and most advanced mega semiconductor cluster.* https://www.msit.go.kr/eng/bbs/view.do?bbsSeqNo=42&mId=4&nttSeqNo=952&sCode=eng

Organisation for Economic Co-operation and Development. (2023). *Vulnerabilities and resilience in the semiconductor supply chain.* OECD Publishing. https://www.oecd.org/en/publications/vulnerabilities-in-the-semiconductor-supplychain_6bed616f-en.html

Press Information Bureau, Government of India, Ministry of Electronics & Information Technology. (2021, December 16). *Cabinet approves programme for development of semiconductors and display manufacturing ecosystem in India.* https://www.pib.gov.in/PressReleasePage.aspx?PRID=1781723

United States Congress. (2022). *CHIPS and Science Act of 2022, Pub. L. No. 117–167, 136 Stat. 1392.* https://www.congress.gov/117/plaws/publ167/PLAW-117publ167.pdf

United States International Trade Commission. (2023, November). *Recent developments in the global semiconductor industry (Executive Briefings on Trade).* https://www.usitc.gov/publications/332/recent_developments_global_semiconductor_industry.htm

Chapter 4
Current Distribution of China's Semiconductor Industry

Tao Ma

Abstract Chapter 4 provides a comprehensive overview of the current spatial distribution of China's semiconductor industry and evaluates its alignment with global industrial development trends. It first analyses the regional characteristics and development potential of the eastern coastal and central–western regions, highlighting their respective roles in innovation, manufacturing, and packaging/testing. The chapter then compares China's semiconductor clusters with global counterparts—such as Silicon Valley, Chinese Taiwan, and South Korea—identifying key gaps in technological capability, manufacturing strength, and industrial chain integration. It also explores structural challenges confronting China's industrial geography, including weak inter-regional coordination, inefficient resource allocation, and limited responsiveness to global shifts. Finally, the chapter assesses historical patterns and emerging dynamics of global semiconductor relocation, underscoring the urgency for China to optimise its regional layout, enhance industrial synergy, and reinforce resilience amid intensifying international competition.

Keywords Regional Industrial Distribution • Semiconductor Clusters in China • Eastern Coastal Innovation Hub • Emerging Inland Manufacturing Centres • Global Cluster Comparison

© The Author(s) 2026
T. Wang et al., *China's Semiconductor Industry Strategy,*
SpringerBriefs in Economics,
https://doi.org/10.1007/978-981-95-3332-9_4

4.1 Regional Distribution of China's Semiconductor Industry and Comparison with the Global Landscape

4.1.1 Characteristics and Development Potential of Industrial Distribution in the Eastern Coastal, Central and Western Regions

China's semiconductor industry chain layout exhibits significant regional differences, which are closely related to factors such as local resource endowments, policy support, and infrastructure, as well as the unique characteristics of the semiconductor industry, such as its high technology and capital intensity. Different regions play distinct roles and have unique characteristics within China's semiconductor industry chain. The eastern coastal regions are generally regarded as the core and vanguard of the semiconductor industry, while central and western regions are increasingly demonstrating unique advantages in manufacturing and packaging segments. The following sections will discuss the industrial distribution characteristics and development potential of the eastern coastal and central-western regions, respectively.

4.1.1.1 Characteristics of Industrial Layout and Development Potential in the Eastern Coastal Regions

The eastern coastal regions, particularly the Yangtze River Delta (Shanghai, Jiangsu, Zhejiang) and the Pearl River Delta (Guangdong, Shenzhen, Xiamen), are key hubs for China's semiconductor industry. This region holds a significant position in the global semiconductor supply chain, serving not only as a centre for technological innovation in China's semiconductor industry but also as a major hub for production and manufacturing capabilities.

Technology Innovation and R&D Hubs: The Yangtze River Delta region, particularly Shanghai, is one of China's key technology innovation centres for the semiconductor industry. Shanghai serves as a major base for semiconductor design and R&D, hosting numerous domestic and international semiconductor design companies and research institutions, including leading firms such as SMIC and Hua Hong Semiconductor. The region's strengths lie in its accumulation of advanced technologies, particularly in integrated circuit design and high-end manufacturing processes, which have attracted a large number of high-tech enterprises and top-tier talent.

Manufacturing and Packaging/Testing Capabilities: The Pearl River Delta region, especially Shenzhen, primarily handles semiconductor manufacturing and packaging/testing functions. Shenzhen is not only an important component of the global semiconductor manufacturing industry but also one of the world's major production bases for semiconductor packaging and testing.

With investments from global semiconductor giants such as TSMC and Samsung in the region, Shenzhen's semiconductor manufacturing industry is gradually transitioning to advanced processes, while the region's packaging and testing companies are driving the coordinated development of the entire electronics industry. Policy Support and Market Demand: The eastern coastal region has benefited from government policy support and mature market demand. In recent years, local governments have introduced a series of supportive policies to further promote the rapid development of the semiconductor industry.

For example, the Shanghai municipal government has increased financial subsidies and R&D funding for the semiconductor industry to further enhance the region's industrial technology level and innovation capabilities. In addition, market demand in the Yangtze River Delta and Pearl River Delta regions has provided a broad market space for the development of the semiconductor industry, especially in the rapid growth of smart hardware, consumer electronics, and automotive electronics.

Development Potential: In the future, the semiconductor industry in eastern coastal regions is expected to maintain its strong growth momentum. As the global semiconductor industry shifts toward high-end manufacturing and intelligentisation, the Yangtze River Delta and Pearl River Delta regions will leverage their robust innovation capabilities and manufacturing strengths to drive technological breakthroughs and industrial upgrading. The rapid emergence of emerging fields such as advanced process technologies (e.g., 7 nm and 5 nm processes), AI chips, and 5G communication chips will also unlock greater development potential for these regions.

4.1.1.2 Industrial Layout Characteristics and Development Potential of Central and Western Regions

Compared to the eastern coastal regions, the semiconductor industry in central and western regions started later, but in recent years, with the continuous advancement of policy support and infrastructure construction, it has gradually demonstrated unique industrial advantages, particularly in manufacturing, packaging and testing, as well as certain specialised equipment sectors, where it holds significant development potential.

Manufacturing bases and production capacity advantages: Central and western regions (such as Chongqing, Chengdu, Xi'an, and Wuhan) have recently emerged as manufacturing bases for the semiconductor industry.

The advantages of central and western regions lie in their abundant land resources, low labour costs, and policy support. In particular, some local governments have introduced tax incentives and land subsidies to attract high-end manufacturing industries. Xi'an, as one of China's integrated circuit industry bases, has attracted investments from multiple domestic and international semiconductor manufacturing companies, with capabilities in packaging and testing, material manufacturing, and other fields steadily improving.

Supply Chain Integration: In central and western regions, many semiconductor companies and related supply chain firms (such as packaging and testing, and materials production) have gradually formed industrial clusters, further enhancing the regional semiconductor supply chain. For example, Chengdu has emerged as a key semiconductor packaging and testing hub in China, housing multiple packaging and testing companies and supply chain support firms, providing abundant resources for downstream product production.

Innovation and Talent Resources: Although the central and western regions started their technological innovation efforts later, they have made significant progress with the active promotion of local governments. For example, Xi'an and Wuhan have become important centres for semiconductor design and material research and development in China. With the increasing number of higher education institutions and research institutes, these cities are also enhancing their potential in semiconductor technology research and development. The gradual accumulation of talent resources and the construction of industrial innovation platforms will drive the central and western regions to gradually elevate their status in the semiconductor industry.

Development Potential: The semiconductor industry in central and western China has significant growth potential, particularly in manufacturing and supply chain support. As the global trend toward outsourcing in the semiconductor industry intensifies, central and western China will have the opportunity to attract more investment in manufacturing and become an important base for domestic and international semiconductor manufacturing. At the same time, strong government support and ongoing improvements in infrastructure provide a solid foundation for the development of the semiconductor industry in central and western China.

4.1.1.3   Summary

Overall, the eastern coastal regions remain the core area of China's semiconductor industry, leveraging their technological innovation capabilities, robust manufacturing bases, and well-developed market demand. They will continue to drive the high-end and intelligent development of the semiconductor industry in the future. Meanwhile, central and western regions are gradually forming industrial agglomeration effects, particularly in areas such as packaging and testing, and material production, thanks to their manufacturing advantages, low-cost advantages, and policy support.

With ongoing technological advancements and policy support, central and western regions will play an increasingly important role in the semiconductor supply chain, providing strong support for the overall development of China's semiconductor industry. The differences and development potential of these regions also offer valuable insights for optimising industrial layout. In the future, efforts should be made to enhance regional coordination and optimise resource allocation to improve the overall competitiveness of the supply chain.

4.1.2 Spatial Differences Analysis with Major Global Semiconductor Industry Clusters

The global semiconductor industry has formed multiple industrial clusters with unique advantages, distributed across different countries and regions (Organisation for Economic Co-operation and Development 2023, 2025). These clusters each possess distinctive strengths in terms of technological innovation, manufacturing capabilities, and market competitiveness. China's semiconductor industry holds an important position in the global industrial chain, but compared to global major semiconductor industry clusters such as Silicon Valley, TSMC's headquarters in Chinese Taiwan, South Korea, and Singapore, there are still certain gaps. This article will analyse the differences between China's semiconductor industry and other major global industry clusters in terms of technological innovation, manufacturing capabilities, industrial chain integration, and global market competitiveness.

First, in terms of technological innovation, Silicon Valley is undoubtedly the global hub for semiconductor technological innovation. Silicon Valley is not only the primary base for global high-end integrated circuit design and chip architecture but also the gathering place for the world's leading semiconductor companies, such as Intel, NVIDIA, and AMD, whose research and development headquarters are all located there. Silicon Valley's advantage lies in its continuous technological innovation capabilities, particularly in cutting-edge technologies such as AI chips, quantum computing, and system-level chip design, where it leads the rest of the world. In comparison, although China has a certain foundation in integrated circuit design and has seen the emergence of a number of outstanding design companies such as Huawei HiSilicon and Tsinghua Unigroup, it still faces pressure to catch up in terms of high-end chip design and system-level integrated circuits.

Second, in terms of manufacturing capabilities, Chinese Taiwan is an important manufacturing base for the global semiconductor industry, with TSMC as its representative. TSMC maintains a leading position globally in semiconductor foundry and advanced process technologies (such as 7 nm and 5 nm technologies). TSMC has unrivalled competitive advantages in terms of technological maturity, manufacturing scale and market share in the foundry market. Although China's semiconductor manufacturing industry is gradually gaining market share in areas such as packaging and testing and mid-to-low-end manufacturing, it still lags behind TSMC in high-end process technologies. China still has a significant gap compared to Chinese Taiwan and South Korea in terms of mass production capabilities for 7 nm and below processes.

Furthermore, in terms of industrial chain synergy, regions such as Silicon Valley, Chinese Taiwan, and South Korea have formed highly integrated industrial chains, especially in R&D, manufacturing, packaging, and testing. Synergy between these links promotes rapid technological innovation and industrial development. For example, Silicon Valley's semiconductor industry has strong technical synergies in design, testing, and production, while TSMC has formed complementary advantages in the industrial chain through its close cooperation with design companies and its world-leading foundry technology. In comparison, although China's semiconductor industrial chain has gradually formed clusters in manufacturing and packaging and testing, there are still certain shortcomings in the depth of synergy between the design and manufacturing links. Some high-end design and manufacturing segments rely on imported or foreign-owned technologies, resulting in weak self-reliance and control over the industrial chain.

In terms of global market competitiveness, TSMC and Samsung of South Korea have secured dominant positions in the global semiconductor market, particularly in the memory (DRAM, NAND flash) and high-end process foundry segments, where their market shares are unmatched. Semiconductor companies in Silicon Valley dominate the global consumer electronics, AI, and high-performance computing markets. Although China is gradually emerging in markets such as consumer electronics, 5G communications, and smart hardware, its overall share of the global semiconductor market, especially in the high-end chip market, is still unable to compete with global leaders. Chinese semiconductor companies need to continuously strive to improve their global competitiveness in terms of technological breakthroughs, brand influence, and global market penetration.

In summary, although China's semiconductor industry has demonstrated strong competitiveness in certain areas, such as packaging and testing and low-end manufacturing, it still lags behind major global semiconductor industry clusters in terms of technology, manufacturing capabilities, industrial chain coordination, and market competitiveness. In the future, China must strengthen R&D in core technologies, enhance supply chain synergy, and leverage policy support and industry consolidation to drive the industry's transformation from traditional manufacturing to high-end manufacturing and innovation hubs, thereby further narrowing the gap with global leading clusters.

4.2 Issues Facing the Current Industrial Layout and Challenges in International Competition

4.2.1 Insufficient Industrial Synergy and Competitive Disadvantages

In the development of China's semiconductor industry, insufficient industrial synergy has been a key issue constraining the overall competitiveness of the industry. The semiconductor industry is inherently a highly complex and highly concentrated industrial chain system, involving every link from design, manufacturing, packaging to testing. Against the backdrop of increasingly fierce global competition, close synergy among all links within the industrial chain is the foundation for enhancing the overall competitiveness of the industry. The lack of industrial synergy in China's semiconductor industry has directly led to competitive disadvantages in areas such as technological innovation, production efficiency, cost control, and market responsiveness.

4.2.1.1 Poor Technical Coordination Leads to Lagging Innovation

Although China's semiconductor industry has made some progress in technological innovation, its overall innovation speed still lags behind the global advanced level. A key factor is the lack of technical coordination between different links in the industrial chain, especially in the areas of design, manufacturing, packaging, and testing. Leading global semiconductor industry clusters such as Silicon Valley and Chinese Taiwan have formed powerful technological innovation ecosystems through close cooperation within the industrial chain.

Information flows rapidly and efficiently between design companies, manufacturers, and packaging and testing companies, enabling them to iterate technologies in a short period of time and promote the application and commercialisation of new technologies. However, the level of technical coordination between the various links in China's semiconductor industry chain is relatively low, and there are often disconnects in technical alignment between design companies and manufacturing companies.

Design companies often rely on external contract manufacturers for production, which results in insufficient technical feedback between design and manufacturing, often constraining manufacturing process innovation and new product development. The lack of efficient coordination between design, manufacturing, and packaging and testing has prevented China's semiconductor industry from responding quickly to market demand for high-end technologies, further affecting the overall innovation capacity of the industry.

4.2.1.2 Inadequate Resource Integration Affects Production Efficiency and Cost Control

The semiconductor industry involves deep integration across multiple stages, including raw material supply, equipment procurement, and manufacturing process improvements. Leading global semiconductor clusters achieve efficient integration in resource allocation, production processes, and supply chain management through close collaboration within the industrial chain, thereby reducing production costs and improving efficiency. For example, TSMC's close collaboration with its clients enables it to precisely control manufacturing processes during production, shorten production cycles, and increase output.

In contrast, China's semiconductor industry has obvious shortcomings in resource integration. Some enterprises lack sufficient cooperation and information sharing in areas such as raw material procurement, production equipment, and technological innovation, resulting in low production efficiency and imprecise cost control. In particular, Chinese semiconductor companies are still highly dependent on imports for the procurement of high-end equipment and raw materials, which is even more prominent in the context of insufficient industrial chain integration. The lack of effective cooperation and resource sharing between various links in the industrial chain has led to relatively high production costs for China's semiconductor industry, further affecting its global market competitiveness.

4.2.1.3 Insufficient Industrial Chain Coordination Leads to Slow Market Response

In the context of globalisation, market demand is changing at an increasingly rapid pace, especially in emerging fields such as 5G communications, artificial intelligence, and the Internet of Things, where the market demand for semiconductor products is becoming increasingly diversified and high-end.

Leading global semiconductor industry clusters can form a virtuous cycle between technological innovation and market application by responding quickly to market demand. However, China's semiconductor industry lags behind in this regard due to insufficient coordination within the industrial chain, resulting in slow market response. For example, in the research, development, and commercialisation of 5G chips, companies in major global semiconductor clusters were able to quickly collaborate with operators and terminal manufacturers to transform 5G technology into marketable products.

In contrast, some Chinese semiconductor companies, especially in the design and manufacturing segments, lag behind. This not only leads to the loss of market share in emerging markets but also affects the competitive position of China's semiconductor industry in the global market.

4.2.1.4 Limitations of Talent Mobility and Industrial Synergy

The high technical barriers of the semiconductor industry determine the core role of talent in the industrial chain. However, the Chinese semiconductor industry lacks synergy, and talent mobility and technical exchanges are infrequent, limiting innovation within the industry. Leading global clusters, such as Silicon Valley and Chinese Taiwan, often use efficient talent mobility mechanisms to quickly introduce key personnel, such as R&D personnel, engineers, and technical experts, into various links of the industrial chain, promoting technological innovation and industrial synergy.

In China, despite the support of research institutions and universities such as the Chinese Academy of Sciences and Tsinghua University, the concentration of high-end talent in the industrial chain is relatively low, and cross-industry and cross-domain talent mobility has not yet achieved sufficient coordination. Restricted talent mobility has led to delays in technological innovation across different links in the industrial chain, further exacerbating the problem of insufficient industrial synergy.

4.2.1.5   Summary

In summary, the lack of industrial synergy in China's semiconductor industry directly results in a competitive disadvantage in the global market. The lag in technological innovation, inadequate resource integration, slow market response, and limitations on talent mobility are all factors constraining the global competitiveness of China's semiconductor industry. Therefore, enhancing industrial chain synergy is one of the core issues facing China's semiconductor industry. Only by strengthening deep cooperation across design, manufacturing, packaging and testing, and materials can we effectively promote technological breakthroughs, reduce production costs, improve market response speed, and ultimately enhance the industry's overall competitiveness.

4.2.2   Risk of Industrial Layout Not Matching Global Industrial Development Trends

As the global semiconductor industry enters a new phase characterised by advanced manufacturing, intelligentisation, 5G, and artificial intelligence (AI), the global industrial chain is evolving towards higher technological content, shorter product life cycles, more intelligent production processes, and more flexible supply chain layouts. If China's semiconductor industry fails to adapt to these global trends in a timely manner, it may face the risk of being unable to effectively compete in the international market.

4.2.2.1   Lagging Technological Innovation and Disconnect from Global Industrial Upgrading

With the rapid development of technologies such as 5G communications, artificial intelligence, quantum computing, and big data, global demand for high-performance computing chips, AI chips, 5G chips, and other products is continuously increasing. In contrast, China's semiconductor industry has yet to fully adapt its layout in key technological areas such as advanced chip design and advanced manufacturing processes to meet the latest global industrial development needs.

Global trend: As technology continues to advance, the mass production and application of advanced manufacturing processes (such as 7 nm, 5 nm, and even lower processes) have become key competitive points in the global semiconductor industry. Major companies such as TSMC, Samsung, and Intel are increasing their investments in these areas. However, China's progress in R&D and capacity building for these high-end technologies remains relatively slow. Although China has achieved breakthroughs in certain technical fields, the gap between its technical capabilities and the world's most advanced levels still exists.

Risks: If China's semiconductor industry fails to adjust its layout in a timely manner and continues to rely on traditional technologies and the production of low-end products, it may be at a disadvantage in global market competition, especially in future markets with rapid growth such as 5G and AI chips. Global demand for high-performance chips has entered a stage of high-end customisation. If China's industrial layout fails to adapt to this change in a timely manner, it will face the risk of its market share being gradually eroded by international competitors.

4.2.2.2 Over-Reliance on Low-End Segments of the Semiconductor Industry Chain

The current layout of China's semiconductor industry, especially in low-end manufacturing and packaging and testing, is overly reliant on traditional segments with relatively low technical barriers. Although these segments occupy an important position in the global semiconductor industry chain, with the development of the global industry, especially the rise of high-end technologies, market competition in low-end manufacturing is becoming increasingly fierce and cost advantages are gradually being eroded.

Global trend: The global semiconductor industry has entered a new era of high-end manufacturing and intelligent manufacturing. In the international market, the focus of manufacturing has gradually shifted to high value-added and high-tech areas, such as advanced processes and high-end AI chips. These areas have increasingly stringent technical requirements, and production processes are gradually moving towards intelligent, automated, and customised development.

Risks: China's industrial layout in low-end manufacturing and packaging and testing, although cost-competitive, will face increasingly fierce market competition as global competition intensifies and technological progress accelerates. Meanwhile, if China's semiconductor industry fails to timely upgrade its technology and expand into high-end manufacturing, it will be at a disadvantage in global industrial competition and struggle to secure a share of the high-end market.

4.2.2.3 Mismatch Between Regional Development and Global Industrial Transfer Trends

There are significant regional disparities in the layout of China's semiconductor industry. The eastern coastal regions, especially the Yangtze River Delta and Pearl River Delta, have long been the core areas of China's semiconductor industry, attracting a large influx of high-tech enterprises and capital (Economics Observatory 2025). However, with the global industrial transfer, the demand for low-cost, high-efficiency manufacturing is beginning to shift towards the central and western regions. If China's semiconductor industry fails to effectively align with this global industrial shift trend, it may lose its cost competitiveness, leading to lagging production capacity and technology in certain segments (Financial Times 2025).

Global Trend: As global industrial shifts and manufacturing outsourcing intensify, many developed countries are gradually relocating low-end manufacturing and some foundational segments of their semiconductor industries to emerging markets, particularly Southeast Asia and the Middle East. These regions not only offer low-cost labour but also accelerate industrial relocation through policy support and market access.

Risks: If China's semiconductor industry continues to maintain its current industrial layout, it may be unable to effectively adapt to the global industrial relocation trend, leading to the gradual loss of production capacity and technological advantages in certain production segments to other countries and regions, resulting in the waste of industrial resources.

4.2.2.4   Internationalisation of the Industrial Chain and Insufficient Global Cooperation

Global competition in the semiconductor industry increasingly relies on international cooperation and cross-border resource integration, but China's semiconductor industrial chain still has certain shortcomings in international cooperation. The Chinese semiconductor industry has limited access to advanced international technologies and markets, especially in terms of technical cooperation and innovation in core equipment and materials, and has not yet fully integrated into the coordinated development of the global industrial chain.

Global trend: The internationalisation of the global semiconductor industry is becoming increasingly evident, with international cooperation and resource integration among global multinational semiconductor companies in design, manufacturing, packaging, and testing gradually becoming the mainstream. This trend of cross-border cooperation not only helps reduce costs but also promotes technological innovation and market expansion.

Risks: If China's semiconductor industry fails to strengthen its in-depth cooperation with the global semiconductor industry chain, especially in international cooperation in core equipment, key materials, and technology research and development, it will face challenges such as resource shortages and technological bottlenecks, which will in turn affect the competitiveness of the entire industry chain.

4.2.2.5   Summary

There is a certain disconnect between the layout of China's semiconductor industry and global industry development trends, especially in terms of high-end technology, intelligent manufacturing, and industry chain coordination.

If the industry fails to adjust its layout in a timely manner, especially in response to key trends such as technological innovation, changes in market demand, and global industrial shifts, China's semiconductor industry will face significant competitive risks. To effectively address these risks, China must accelerate industrial restructuring by increasing R&D investment, promoting advanced manufacturing, and strengthening international cooperation to enhance the overall competitiveness of the industry and ensure a favourable position in the global semiconductor supply chain.

4.2.3 Regional Development Imbalances and Resource Allocation Issues

The layout of China's semiconductor industry across different regions exhibits significant regional imbalances. This issue primarily manifests in the development gaps between eastern and central-western regions, uneven resource allocation, and disparities in infrastructure. This regional imbalance not only affects the overall synergy of China's semiconductor industry but also hinders the efficient integration of the industrial chain, limiting the improvement of overall competitiveness. Especially in the context of rapid changes in the global semiconductor industrial chain and increasingly fierce international competition, regional development imbalances and resource allocation issues have become increasingly urgent and need to be optimised and adjusted through effective policies and industrial planning.

4.2.3.1 Development Gap Between Eastern Coastal and Central-Western Regions

China's semiconductor industry, particularly in terms of technological innovation and manufacturing capabilities, is primarily concentrated in eastern coastal regions such as the Yangtze River Delta (Shanghai, Jiangsu, Zhejiang) and the Pearl River Delta (Guangdong, Shenzhen, Xiamen).

The eastern coastal regions not only possess strong technological foundations and abundant industrial resources but also hold advantages in infrastructure development, talent recruitment, and capital aggregation (Wikipedia contributors 2025). In contrast, central and western regions, such as Xi'an, Wuhan, and Chengdu, although they have made significant progress in recent years and attracted some semiconductor manufacturing and design companies, still lag behind the eastern coastal regions in terms of overall technological level, R&D investment, and production capacity.

Differences in gaps: Disparities in technological accumulation and innovation capabilities: Eastern regions have accumulated strong technical capabilities in high-end chip design and integrated circuit manufacturing, with leading companies such as SMIC and Hua Hong Semiconductor. Central and western regions have begun to emerge in packaging and testing, as well as manufacturing processes, but their overall technical capabilities and innovation outcomes remain relatively lagging.

Differences in industrial infrastructure: The eastern coastal regions possess advanced production facilities, efficient supply chain networks, and extensive market demand, making them important bases for the global semiconductor industry. In contrast, the central and western regions lag behind in infrastructure development, particularly in terms of high-end equipment and technological R&D platforms, which constrains the rapid development of their local semiconductor industries.

4.2.3.2   Regional Imbalances in Resource Allocation

China's semiconductor industry also faces issues of uneven resource allocation. Eastern regions have a high concentration of resources, particularly in terms of capital, talent, technology, and market advantages. However, as global competition in the semiconductor industry intensifies, especially in high-end manufacturing and advanced technology R&D, the advantages of resource concentration are beginning to show limitations. Even technologically advanced eastern regions are facing challenges such as talent shortages and land resource constraints.

On the other hand, central and western regions, although benefiting from lower land and labour costs, have relatively low resource utilisation efficiency due to insufficient technological innovation and capital investment. For example, while semiconductor industries in cities like Xi'an and Chongqing have achieved initial development and attracted some enterprises to settle, funding and resource allocation in areas such as high-end manufacturing equipment, material production, and technological R&D remain inadequate, leading to insufficient completeness of the industrial chain and synergistic effects.

Impact of Uneven Resource Allocation:

Disparities in Capital Investment: Eastern regions, particularly the Yangtze River Delta and Pearl River Delta, receive relatively more government policy support and capital investment, enabling enterprises to access greater fiscal support such as R&D subsidies and tax incentives. While central and western regions also benefit from certain policy support, their overall capital investment and corporate financing capabilities remain weak, constraining local enterprises' technological R&D and industrial expansion.

Talent Mobility and Technical Support: Eastern regions, with their well-developed research institutions, universities, and technical platforms, attract a large number of high-end talents, forming a strong talent aggregation effect. In contrast, central and western regions, with relatively scarce educational resources and a weaker innovation environment, face certain constraints in attracting and retaining high-end technical talents, further leading to lagging technological innovation.

4.2.3.3   Challenges in Policy Support and Regional Resource Integration

Policy support has played a crucial role in promoting the development of the semiconductor industry, particularly in terms of regional industrial layout. Eastern regions have more mature industrial policies and significant government investment, with local governments introducing a series of preferential policies to promote industrial development. In contrast, policy support in central and western regions remains inadequate. Although the central government has proposed relevant regional development strategies, such as supporting western development, the implementation of local policies, policy precision, and the intensity of financial investment are relatively weak.

Impact of policy differences:

Insufficient policy implementation capacity: Although central and western regions enjoy certain policy advantages, there are disparities in policy implementation capacity and the level of support provided by local governments across different regions. Some local governments have failed to provide sufficient funding, tax incentives, and technical support to enterprises, resulting in the policy effects not being fully realised.

Regional disparities in policy support: Local governments in eastern regions typically provide more support for industrial development, particularly in terms of R&D funding and the construction of innovation platforms, creating a more favourable environment for industrial development.

In contrast, local policies in central and western regions often focus more on infrastructure construction than on supporting technological innovation, which has slowed down technological progress in the semiconductor industry in these regions.

4.2.3.4   Summary

The imbalance in regional development and resource allocation in China's semiconductor industry is one of the core factors constraining the overall competitiveness of its industrial chain. Eastern coastal regions concentrate technological, market, and capital resources, driving technological innovation and market development in the semiconductor industry; however, inadequate resource allocation and insufficient policy support in central and western regions have resulted in their relatively low position in the global supply chain. To enhance the overall competitiveness of the supply chain, it is essential to strengthen regional resource integration, promote the development of central and western regions, and facilitate collaborative innovation and efficient operation across the national supply chain.

4.3   Trends in the Transfer of the Semiconductor Industry and the Urgency of Adjusting China's Semiconductor Industry Layout

4.3.1   Historical Characteristics and Lessons Learned from the Transfer of the Semiconductor Industry

The development of the semiconductor industry has undergone typical phased transitions, with its focus evolving continuously in response to factors such as technology diffusion, cost changes, and policy drivers. Starting in the United States, the industry rose to prominence in Japan and Chinese Taiwan before gradually expanding to mainland China and Southeast Asian countries, forming a historical evolution path characterised by 'core technology control—manufacturing capability transfer—global rebalancing.' Understanding this transition trajectory is of great reference value for China's current efforts to optimise its semiconductor industry layout.

From the 1950s to the 1970s, the United States was the absolute centre of the semiconductor industry. Benefiting from Silicon Valley's research and development clusters, military demand, and venture capital ecosystem, the United States was the first to establish an integrated industrial system centred on design, manufacturing, and equipment, giving rise to global leaders such as Intel and Texas Instruments. The industrial model during this period was characterised by high concentration and vertical integration, with the state playing a key role in research funding and military demand orientation. The experience of this stage indicates that strong original innovation capabilities and government strategic guidance are the foundation for a semiconductor industry to achieve international dominance.

In the 1980s and 1990s, semiconductor manufacturing capabilities gradually shifted from the United States to Japan and Chinese Taiwan. Japan relied on its conglomerate system, long-term R&D investments, and advantages in materials and equipment to achieve major breakthroughs in memory and other fields, securing a dominant position in the global market. Chinese Taiwan, on the other hand, established science and technology parks, attracted foreign investment, and promoted local talent development, successfully fostering a foundry industry model represented by TSMC. The industrial layout adjustments during this phase reflected the trend of high-cost countries shifting to regions with lower manufacturing costs and more favourable policies. It also demonstrated the importance of 'focusing on core links in the industrial chain' and 'building policy-driven aggregation platforms' for latecomers to overtake their competitors.

In the twenty-first century, with the deepening of globalisation and the extension of supply chains, the semiconductor industry has further shifted to mainland China and some Southeast Asian countries. Mainland China, relying on its huge market demand, complete manufacturing base and policy support, has gradually established an industrial system covering major links such as design, manufacturing and packaging and testing, becoming the world's largest semiconductor market. At the national level, in 2014, the State Council issued the 'National Integrated Circuit Industry Development Promotion Outline,' clearly stating the goal of achieving international advanced levels in the main links of China's semiconductor industry chain by 2020 and 2030, and established the 'National Integrated Circuit Industry Investment Fund' (the 'Big Fund') to form a support system combining policy guidance and capital-driven development. The development experience of this stage highlights the strategic role of industrial policies and the significant driving effect of capital aggregation on technological breakthroughs.

In summary, the transfer of the semiconductor industry reflects a continuous logic of 'technology-driven—manufacturing transfer—system restructuring.' The experience of each stage shows that, on the one hand, relying solely on low-cost manufacturing cannot solidify the industrial foundation; it is necessary to focus on forming sustainable capabilities in key technologies, core design, and basic research. On the other hand, institutional design and policy direction play an irreplaceable role in the rise of industries in late-developing countries. For China, while embracing global industrial transfer, it is even more important to focus on transforming from a manufacturing powerhouse to a technological powerhouse, accelerating self-reliance in key areas, and building an innovative system with international competitiveness to provide a more solid foundation for future industrial restructuring.

4.3.2 New Trends and Underlying Logic in the Current Transfer of the Semiconductor Industry

Against the backdrop of global geopolitical turmoil, supply chain security restructuring, and intensifying technological competition, the global division of labour in the semiconductor industry is undergoing profound changes, exhibiting new trends of relocation and adjustment logic. This round of industrial relocation is no longer driven solely by traditional cost considerations but by 'multiple driving factors,' including national security, technological self-reliance, market layout optimisation, and green and low-carbon requirements, demonstrating more complex systemic evolutionary characteristics. Gaining a deep understanding of the new trends and underlying logic of the current industrial shift is of great significance for China to timely adjust its industrial layout and enhance its global competitiveness.

First, the semiconductor industry has exhibited clear trends toward 're-localisation' and 'de-Chinaisation,' with some countries promoting the repatriation of key industries to their home countries or their relocation to 'friendly nations.' Led by the United States, countries have recently enacted legislation such as the CHIPS Act to strengthen policy support for domestic chip manufacturing, encouraging companies like TSMC and Samsung to establish factories in the United States, thereby concentrating manufacturing capabilities. This 'security-driven' transfer logic has become a key feature of the current global industrial restructuring, reflecting a systemic reassessment of supply chain resilience, strategic autonomy, and national security. Meanwhile, economies such as the European Union and Japan are also leveraging fiscal subsidies, industrial incentives, and regional collaboration to strengthen manufacturing and design capabilities within their own borders or among 'allied nations,' driving partial retrenchment and redistribution of the supply chain.

Second, green manufacturing and low-carbon transformation are gradually emerging as new drivers of industrial transfer. Against the backdrop of global 'dual carbon' strategic goals and the deepening of ESG (environmental, social, and governance) principles, semiconductor manufacturing companies are increasingly demanding improvements in energy structure, carbon emission targets, and environmental standards. Traditional production bases with high energy consumption and pollution are being replaced by regions with advantages in clean energy. Southeast Asia, India, and Mexico are gradually becoming new destinations for the global semiconductor industry thanks to their low-carbon resources, policy support, and labour cost advantages. Such transfers are not only the result of cost spillovers but also reflect the trend of reshaping the 'green resilience' of supply chains.

Third, the trend toward regionalisation, modularisation, and localisation of supply chains is becoming increasingly evident, with the global integrated supply chain system evolving toward a 'multi-centre collaboration' model. Global companies are increasingly prioritising the risk-resilience and emergency response capabilities of their supply chains, leading to the adoption of 'decentralisation' principles in supply chain planning. For example, an increasing number of multinational companies are adopting a strategy of 'design at headquarters, manufacturing locally, and distributed packaging and testing' to shorten supply chain paths and enhance operational flexibility. This logic was particularly evident during the COVID-19 pandemic, when governments and companies in many countries recognised the risks of relying on a single country or region and began to adjust their industrial layouts to build multi-layered, distributed, and complementary industrial networks.

In addition, rapid technological evolution and the emergence of new market demands are reshaping the global industrial landscape. Emerging technologies such as artificial intelligence, the Internet of Things, intelligent driving, and edge computing are driving the diversification and customisation of chip design, prompting the semiconductor industry to transition from general-purpose chips to specialised high-end chips. This trend imposes higher demands on supply chain responsiveness, design service capabilities, and collaborative development models, prompting some companies to deploy local design and packaging/testing capabilities in regions closer to market endpoints to enhance innovation efficiency and market adaptability. In particular, the strategy of 'high-end manufacturing coupled with local market integration' is emerging as a new investment direction for multinational corporations, accelerating the expansion of emerging regions such as India, Vietnam, and Malaysia in the mid-to-low-end segments of the semiconductor industry.

In summary, the current semiconductor industry transfer is characterised by a new logic driven by geopolitical factors, security-oriented demands, green manufacturing support, and market diversification. These trends are not only profoundly reshaping the global semiconductor industry's spatial structure but also imposing higher requirements on China to establish an efficient, secure, and self-reliant industrial layout.

4.3.3 Opportunities and Challenges for China in the Global Semiconductor Industry Shift

The global semiconductor industry chain is currently undergoing a major restructuring. As the world's largest semiconductor consumer market and manufacturing hub, China faces unprecedented external pressures in this round of transformation, but also harbours significant strategic opportunities. Against the backdrop of complex international circumstances, intensified technological barriers, and the diversification and restructuring of the global supply chain, China must seek a new balance between leveraging the benefits of industrial transfer and mitigating structural risks. This can be achieved through optimising strategic, enhancing self-reliance, and strengthening strategic cooperation to redefine its core position within the global supply chain.

First, from the perspective of opportunities, China still possesses strong appeal in terms of manufacturing capabilities, supply chain completeness, and domestic market potential. China boasts the world's most comprehensive mid-to-low-end manufacturing and packaging/testing capabilities, having established a relatively complete supply chain system spanning design, manufacturing, and packaging/testing. Additionally, the 'supply chain strengthening and gap-filling' policies implemented by the state over the past decade, such as the National Integrated Circuit Industry Investment Fund (the 'Big Fund'), have effectively enhanced the layout capabilities of domestic enterprises in critical segments. Furthermore, China's massive downstream market demand, particularly the strong growth in sectors such as smartphones, home appliances, and automotive electronics, makes it an indispensable market for global semiconductor companies. This dual advantage of 'domestic demand-driven growth and manufacturing support' provides China with the practical foundation to continue to take on part of the global manufacturing and service segments.

Second, China's 'strategic window of opportunity' driven by emerging technologies is gradually opening up. With the rapid development of artificial intelligence, the Internet of Things, automotive-grade chips, and edge computing, global semiconductor technology is evolving toward diversification, customisation, and small-batch, high-value production. This trend provides Chinese start-ups and emerging forces with opportunities to 'overtake on a curve.' Particularly in niche areas such as AI chips, power semiconductors, and advanced packaging, some Chinese companies have accumulated certain technological capabilities and are poised to achieve breakthroughs in specific fields. At the same time, central and western regions such as Xi'an, Wuhan, and Chengdu are accelerating the development of semiconductor manufacturing and design capabilities under policy guidance, promoting a more balanced regional layout.

However, China must also face the structural challenges it faces in the global industrial transfer. First, the most serious challenge is the unresolved issue of core technology 'chokepoints.' China remains highly dependent on foreign countries in key areas such as EDA software, lithography machines, high-end materials, and manufacturing equipment. Especially against the backdrop of ongoing technology export controls and sanctions by the United States and Western countries, Chinese domestic enterprises face long-term risks of technological blockade in advanced processes, EDA tool chains, and IP cores, which severely restricts the overall improvement of technological capabilities.

Second, globalisation is facing headwinds, and the environment for cross-border cooperation is becoming more complex. As the United States and European countries strengthen their 'technology alliances' and 'industrial circles' strategies, some key links in the supply chain have begun to intentionally decouple or shift to 'friendly outsourcing' (Springer 2024). This trend is putting pressure on China's position in the global industrial chain, not only restricting the introduction of and cooperation with high-end segments, but also reducing the voice of Chinese companies in the formulation of international rules and supply chain governance. In addition, some foreign companies are increasingly concerned about the policy environment and intellectual property protection, which may affect their long-term investment plans in China.

Furthermore, China's semiconductor industry has weaknesses in talent, original R&D capabilities, and industrial coordination. The reserve and mobility mechanisms for high-end talent are still immature, R&D investment is still mainly enterprise-led, basic research lacks continuity and breakthroughs, and the efficiency of resource allocation between regions needs to be improved (Information Technology and Innovation Foundation 2024). Although some central and western regions have the potential to take over industrial transfers, they still need to address shortcomings in infrastructure, technology platforms, and high-end manufacturing capabilities.

In summary, while China possesses the practical advantages of absorbing production capacity and expanding markets in the global semiconductor industry transfer, it also faces severe challenges posed by technological barriers, deteriorating international conditions, and structural weaknesses. Future strategic adjustments should prioritise enhancing core technological self-reliance, strengthening regional coordination, while balancing internal structural optimisation and external resource integration, to drive China's transition from a global manufacturing hub to an innovation-driven industrial powerhouse.

References

Economics Observatory. (2025, May 28). *What's happening in China's semiconductor industry?* Retrieved from https://www.economicsobservatory.com/whats-happening-in-chinas-semiconductor-industry

Financial Times. (2025, August 6). *China hits roadblock in drive for 'national champions' in chip industry.* Retrieved from https://www.ft.com/content/579fbffe-9add-466a-8d72-31d12151c040

Hamdani, M., Belfencha, I. (2024). Strategic implications of the US-China semiconductor rivalry. *Discover global society, 2*(67). https://doi.org/10.1007/s44282-024-00081-5

Information Technology and Innovation Foundation. (2024, August 19). *How innovative is China in semiconductors?* Retrieved from https://itif.org/publications/2024/08/19/how-innovative-is-china-in-semiconductors/

Organisation for Economic Co-operation and Development. (2023, June). *Vulnerabilities in the semiconductor supply chain (OECD Working Papers)*. OECD Publishing. Retrieved from https://www.oecd.org/en/publications/vulnerabilities-in-the-semiconductor-supply-chain_6bed616fen.html

Organisation for Economic Co-operation and Development. (2025, June). *Mapping the semiconductor value chain (OECD Reports)*. OECD Publishing. https://doi.org/10.1787/4154cdbf-en

Wikipedia contributors. (2025, June). *Guangdong–Hong Kong–Macao Greater Bay Area*. In *Wikipedia*. https://en.wikipedia.org/wiki/Guangdong%E2%80%93Hong_Kong%E2%80%93Macao_Greater_Bay_Area

Chapter 5
Comprehensive Quantitative Assessment of the Security Level of China's Semiconductor Industry Chain

Tiantian Wang

Abstract Chapter 5 presents a comprehensive quantitative assessment of the security level of China's semiconductor industry chain. It introduces an evaluation model integrating principal component analysis (PCA), entropy weighting, and the TOPSIS method, and details key methodological steps, including indicator standardisation, principal component extraction, weight determination, and final ranking based on relative closeness to ideal solutions. A longitudinal analysis covering the years 2015 to 2023 reveals an initial decline in supply chain security, followed by a steady recovery, culminating in the highest level recorded in 2023. A cross-sectional analysis of 29 provinces and municipalities in 2024 indicates that Guangdong ranks highest in security, while Shanxi ranks lowest, with the Eastern region leading overall. Segment-level trade analysis identifies downstream sectors as the most secure and upstream sectors as the most vulnerable. The chapter concludes with an in-depth assessment of import concentration risks, based on trade data from 2019 to 2024, highlighting structural vulnerabilities across countries and product categories that warrant strategic policy attention.

Keywords PCA–Entropy–TOPSIS Model • Security Assessment • Regional Security Comparison • Trade Segment Security • Import Concentration Risk

5.1 Safety Level Measurement Based on Indicator System

5.1.1 Construction of the PCA-Entropy Weight-TOPSIS Model

The Entropy Weight-TOPSIS model does not strictly require independence among indicators, but high correlation among indicators can affect the model's validity and

---

T. Wang et al., *China's Semiconductor Industry Strategy,*
SpringerBriefs in Economics,
https://doi.org/10.1007/978-981-95-3332-9_5

the accuracy of the results (Zhang & Xu, 2015; Li & Zou 2014). The semiconductor industry chain is highly interconnected, and some indicators may exhibit strong correlations. Therefore, we first conduct a correlation analysis of all indicators. If strong correlations exist, we perform principal component analysis (PCA) to transform multiple correlated indicators into a few uncorrelated principal components, thereby eliminating correlations among indicators. The weights in PCA are based on the variance contribution rate of principal components, but this metric only reflects data variability and does not necessarily reflect the importance of indicators (Jolliffe & Cadima 2016; Jolliffe 2002). The entropy weight method, however, determines weights based on the information content (dispersion degree) of the principal components, enabling a more objective reflection of the importance of principal components in cases with multiple indicators and avoiding the limitations of relying solely on variance contribution rates (Zou et al. 2006; Li & Wang 2014). Therefore, PCA is first used for dimension reduction and to eliminate correlations among indicators. The resulting principal components are then further analysed using the entropy weight method to determine the weights of each principal component. Finally, the weighted principal components are used for TOPSIS evaluation to obtain the final ranking results.

5.1.1.1 Establish the Evaluation Matrix

Assume there are n evaluation objects and m evaluation indicators. Construct the original evaluation matrix X_x. Among them, the value corresponding to the j_{th} evaluation object under the i_{th} evaluation indicator is denoted as X_{ij}:

$$X = \begin{bmatrix} X_{11} & \cdots & X_{n1} \\ \vdots & \ddots & \vdots \\ X_{1m} & \cdots & X_{nm} \end{bmatrix}$$

5.1.1.2 Standardisation of Original Indicators

Standardisation is used to eliminate the impact of differences in magnitude, ensuring that evaluation indicators are consistent in terms of dimensions and units.

Evaluation indicators are positive indicators:

$$x'_{ij} = \frac{X_{max}-X_{ij}}{X_{max}-X_{min}} \tag{5.1}$$

Evaluation indicators are negative indicators:

$$x'_{ij} = \frac{X_{ij}-X_{min}}{X_{max}-X_{min}} \tag{5.2}$$

Obtain the standardised matrix:

$$X' = \begin{bmatrix} X'_{11} & \cdots & X'_{n1} \\ \vdots & \ddots & \vdots \\ X'_{1m} & \cdots & X'_{nm} \end{bmatrix}$$

5.1.1.3   Calculate the Covariance Matrix, Eigenvalues, and Eigenvectors

Calculate the covariance matrix C of the standardised data:

$$C = \tfrac{1}{n-1} X'TX', \text{where XT is the transpose matrix of X.} \tag{5.3}$$

Perform an eigenvalue decomposition on the covariance matrix C to obtain the eigenvalues $\lambda_1, \lambda_2, \ldots, \lambda_m$ and the corresponding eigenvectors $v_1, v_2, \ldots, v_m$. Sort the eigenvalues in descending order and adjust the order of the corresponding eigenvectors accordingly.

5.1.1.4   Select Principal Components and Calculate Principal Component Scores

Calculate the variance contribution ratio and cumulative variance contribution ratio for each principal component:

$$\text{variance contribution ratio} = \frac{\lambda_j}{\sum_{k=1}^{m} \lambda_k} \tag{5.4}$$

$$\text{Cumulative variance contribution ratio} = \sum_{k=1}^{j} \frac{\lambda_k}{\sum_{k=1}^{m} \lambda_k} \tag{5.5}$$

Determine the number of principal components p (p<m) to be retained based on the cumulative variance contribution ratio (usually select principal components with a cumulative contribution ratio ≥ 85%) or the size of the eigenvalues (e.g., select principal components with eigenvalues ≥ 1).
Construct projection matrix V using the first m feature vectors = $[v_1, v_2, \ldots, v_m]$
Calculate principal component scores:

$$Y = VX' \tag{5.6}$$

5.1.1.5   Standardise and Non-Normalise the Principal Components

Standardise the principal components obtained using formulas (5.1) and (5.2). Standardisation based on the maximum and minimum values may result in values of

0. Since the entropy weight method requires the calculation of logarithms, a standardised value of 0 would be meaningless. Therefore, add 0.001 to the matrix to form a new matrix.

$$y'_{ij} = y_{ij} + 0.001 \tag{5.7}$$

$$Y' = \begin{bmatrix} X'_{11} & \cdots & X'_{n1} \\ \vdots & \ddots & \vdots \\ X'_{1P} & \cdots & X'_{nP} \end{bmatrix}$$

5.1.1.6 Normalisation Processing

$$P_{ij} = y'_{ij} / \sum_{i=1}^{n} y'_{ij} \tag{5.8}$$

5.1.1.7 Calculate the Entropy Value e_j, Differentiation Coefficient g_j, and Entropy Weight w_j

$$e_j = -k \sum_{i=1}^{n} P_{ij} \ln\left(P_{ij}\right), \ 其中 k = 1/\ln(n) \tag{5.9}$$

$$g_j = 1 - e_j \tag{5.10}$$

$$w_j = g_j / \sum_{i=1}^{n} g_j \tag{5.11}$$

5.1.1.8 Construct a Weighted Normalised Decision Matrix

Use the TOPSIS method to objectively rank the evaluation objects and reduce the influence of subjective factors. Multiply the entropy weight w_j of each evaluation indicator by the observation value X'_{ij} of all evaluation objects under each evaluation indicator.

$$Y''_{ij} = w_j * Y'_{ij} \tag{5.12}$$

Obtain the weighted normalised decision matrix Y:

$$Y'' = \begin{bmatrix} Y''_{11} & \cdots & Y''_{n1} \\ \vdots & \ddots & \vdots \\ Y''_{1P} & \cdots & Y''_{nP} \end{bmatrix}$$

5.1.1.9   Determine Positive and Negative Ideal Solutions

Positive and negative ideal solutions are the basis for subsequent evaluation calculations, aiming to distinguish between different indicators. The closer the indicator vector is to the positive ideal solution (Y_+), the better its performance; conversely, the closer it is to the negative ideal solution (Y_-), the worse its performance.

$$Y''_+ = \max \quad (Y''_1, Y''_2 \ldots Y''_P) \tag{5.13}$$

$$Y''_- = \min \quad (Y''_1, Y''_2 \ldots Y''_P) \tag{5.14}$$

5.1.1.10   Calculate the Euclidean Distance

After determining the positive and negative ideal sets, calculate the Euclidean distance between them and each evaluation object. D_{i+} represents the magnitude of the distance to the positive ideal value, and D_{i-} represents the magnitude of the distance to the negative ideal value.

$$D_{i+} = \sqrt{\sum_{j=1}^{P} \left(Y''_{ij} - Y''_j{}^+\right)^2} \tag{5.15}$$

$$D_{i-} \sqrt{\sum_{j=1}^{P} (Y''_{ij} - Y''_j{}^-)^2} \tag{5.16}$$

5.1.1.11   Calculate Relative Progress

Calculate relative progress, rank n evaluation objects based on this, and thereby measure the level of semiconductor industry chain security. The higher the relative progress, the higher the level of industry chain security, and vice versa.

$$Z_i = \frac{D_i^-}{D_i^- + D_i^+} \tag{5.17}$$

5.1.2 Vertical Analysis of the Security Level of China's Semiconductor Industry Chain

Based on the original data, the evaluation indicators were first standardised according to formulas (5.1) and (5.2). A correlation analysis was conducted on the standardised indicators, revealing strong correlations between some indicators. However, due to the limited number of samples (only nine from 2015 to 2023) for the 17 secondary indicators, it was not possible to form a positive matrix for principal component analysis. The purpose of principal component analysis is to eliminate potential correlations between upstream, midstream, and downstream data, which primarily exist within each primary indicator. Therefore, we selected the two primary indicators of 'external dependence' and 'self-reliance' for principal component analysis.

First, a KMO test was conducted, with a KMO value greater than 0.6 and a Bartlett test <0.01, indicating significant results and suitability for principal component analysis. Then, the principal components were selected according to formulas (5.3), (5.4), and (5.5), with the results shown in Tables 5.1, 5.2, and 5.3. Under the external dependence primary indicator, the three retained principal components explain 92% of the original data; under the self-reliance primary indicator, the two retained principal components explain 90% of the original data; and under the policy environment primary indicator, the two retained principal components explain 98% of the original data. The principal components have a strong explanatory power for the original data, so a total of six principal components were selected for analysis.

The principal components were calculated according to formula (5.6) and are shown in Table 5.4.

Standardise the obtained principal components using formula (5.1), non-normalise the results using formula (5.7), and then normalise the processed data using formula (5.8). The normalised results are shown in Table 5.5.

Substitute the normalised data into formulas (5.9), (5.10), and (5.11) in order to calculate the entropy values e, differentiation coefficients g, and entropy weights w for each evaluation indicator. The specific results are shown in Table 5.6.

According to formula (5.12), the standardised data was weighted using the entropy weight method, and the specific results are shown in Table 5.7.

Based on formulas (5.13) and (5.14), calculate the positive and negative ideal solutions for each evaluation indicator. Using formulas (5.15), (5.16), and (5.17), calculate the European distance and relative progress of China's semiconductor industry chain security from 2015 to 2024. The specific results are shown in Table 5.8.

Relative proximity is a vertical evaluation result   analysis of the security of China's semiconductor industry chain. The higher the relative proximity calculation result, the higher the security level of the semiconductor industry chain; conversely, it indicates a low security level. As shown in Fig. 5.1, the security level of China's semiconductor industry chain declined from 2015 to 2017, with 2017 being the

Table 5.1   Principal component analysis of external dependence

	Total	% of Variance	Cumulative %	Total	% of Variance	Cumulative %	Total	% of Variance	Cumulative %
1	4.756	59.447	59.447	4.756	59.447	59.447	3.250	40.625	40.625
2	1.950	24.370	83.816	1.950	24.370	83.816	2.547	31.832	72.457
3	.622	7.774	91.591	.622	7.774	91.591	1.531	19.134	91.591
4	.393	4.915	96.506						
5	.203	2.537	99.043						
6	.044	.555	99.598						
7	.027	.334	99.932						
8	.005	.068	100.000						

Table 5.2   Principal component analysis of autonomous ability

	Total	% of Variance	Cumulative %	Total	% of Variance	Cumulative %	Total	% of Variance	Cumulative %
1	3.785	63.078	63.078	3.785	63.078	63.078	3.723	62.043	62.043
2	1.639	27.312	90.390	1.639	27.312	90.390	1.701	28.347	90.390
3	.452	7.536	97.926						
4	.092	1.528	99.453						
5	.022	.369	99.822						
6	.011	.178	100.000						

Table 5.3   Principal component analysis of the policy environment

	Total	% of Variance	Cumulative %	Total	% of Variance	Cumulative %	Total	% of Variance	Cumulative %
1	2.468	82.252	82.252	2.468	82.252	82.252	1.794	59.809	59.809
2	.462	15.388	97.640	.462	15.388	97.640	1.135	37.831	97.640
3	.071	2.360	100.000						

lowest point. From 2017 to 2023, the overall security level of the supply chain showed an upward trend, but there was a brief decline in 2022, which may be due to the short-term impact of external shocks.

5.1.3   Horizontal Analysis of China's Semiconductor Industry Chain Security Level

A further horizontal analysis of the semiconductor industry chain security level in various provinces and municipalities of mainland China in 2024 is conducted. Excluding regions with missing data (Tibet Autonomous Region and Xinjiang Uyghur Autonomous Region), a total of 29 provinces and municipalities are

Table 5.4 Matrix after dimension reduction

	External dependency			Self-reliance		Policy environment	
	1	2	3	4	5	6	7
2015	0.12	−2.13	0.22	−1.39	0.11	1.60	−0.52
2016	−0.49	−1.06	−1.08	−1.10	−0.31	0.89	−0.71
2017	−0.83	0.18	−0.98	−0.90	−0.31	0.36	−0.85
2018	−0.77	0.76	−0.44	−0.48	0.09	−0.02	−0.47
2019	−0.96	0.77	0.98	0.07	0.60	−1.21	−0.75
2020	−0.54	0.48	0.85	0.71	1.10	−1.72	−0.49
2021	0.46	−0.20	1.57	1.00	1.49	0.14	0.57
2022	1.01	0.87	−1.21	0.81	−1.69	−0.21	1.64
2023	2.00	0.33	0.10	1.29	−1.07	0.17	1.57

Table 5.5 Normalised matrix

	2015	2016	2017	2018	2019	2020	2021	2022	2023
1	0.12	0.05	0.02	0.02	0.00	0.05	0.16	0.23	0.34
2	0.00	0.06	0.12	0.15	0.15	0.14	0.10	0.16	0.13
3	0.13	0.01	0.02	0.07	0.20	0.19	0.26	0.00	0.12
4	0.00	0.02	0.04	0.07	0.12	0.17	0.19	0.18	0.21
5	0.12	0.09	0.09	0.12	0.15	0.18	0.21	0.00	0.04
6	0.21	0.17	0.13	0.11	0.03	0.00	0.12	0.10	0.12
7	0.04	0.02	0.00	0.05	0.01	0.05	0.19	0.32	0.32

Table 5.6 Entropy values, differentiation coefficients, and entropy weights

	Entropy value (e)	Differential coefficient (g)	Entropy weights (w)
1	0.78	0.22	0.21
2	0.93	0.07	0.07
3	0.83	0.17	0.16
4	0.87	0.13	0.13
5	0.91	0.09	0.09
6	0.91	0.09	0.09
7	0.73	0.27	0.26

involved. In the horizontal regional analysis, the policy environment and independent innovation data (secondary indicators x14-x17) are difficult to further subdivide horizontally. Therefore, based on the two primary indicators of external dependence and independent capability (secondary indicators x1-x13), a horizontal analysis of the semiconductor industry chain security levels of all provinces and municipalities in 2024 is conducted.

Table 5.7 TOPSIS Weighted Matrix

	2015	2016	2017	2018	2019	2020	2021	2022	2023
1	0.08	0.03	0.01	0.01	0.00	0.03	0.10	0.14	0.21
2	0.00	0.02	0.05	0.06	0.06	0.06	0.04	0.07	0.05
3	0.08	0.01	0.01	0.04	0.13	0.12	0.16	0.00	0.08
4	0.00	0.01	0.02	0.04	0.07	0.10	0.11	0.10	0.13
5	0.05	0.04	0.04	0.05	0.06	0.08	0.09	0.00	0.02
6	0.09	0.07	0.06	0.05	0.01	0.00	0.05	0.04	0.05
7	0.03	0.02	0.00	0.04	0.01	0.04	0.15	0.26	0.25

Table 5.8 Euclidean distance and relative proximity of evaluation indicators

	Ideal value(D+)	Negative ideal value(D-)	Relative proximity(Z)
2015	0.31	0.16	0.33
2016	0.36	0.09	0.20
2017	0.38	0.09	0.19
2018	0.33	0.12	0.26
2019	0.34	0.17	0.33
2020	0.30	0.19	0.38
2021	0.16	0.29	0.64
2022	0.20	0.32	0.61
2023	0.12	0.37	0.76

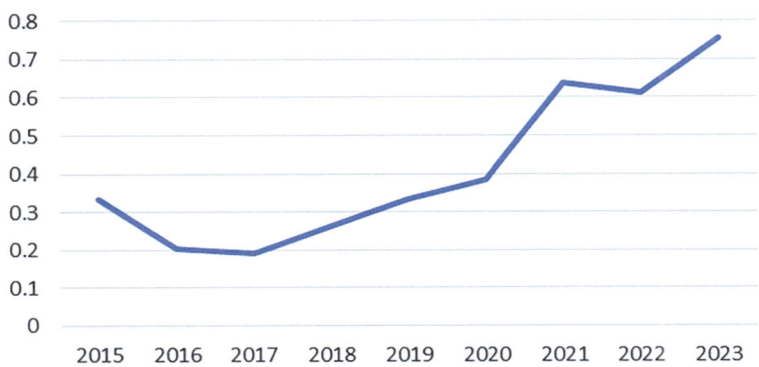

Fig. 5.1   China's semiconductor industry chain security level from 2015 to 2023

First, the correlation between indicators is analysed, and it is found that some indicators have strong correlations. Since the number of samples exceeds the number of indicators, principal component analysis can be directly applied to all indicators. The subsequent calculation and analysis steps are identical to those in the vertical annual analysis. The KMO value exceeds 0.6, and the Bartlett test yields a p-value <0.01, indicating statistical significance and suitability for principal component analysis. Through principal component analysis, seven principal components were retained, explaining 89% of the original data, demonstrating strong explanatory power of the principal components (Table 5.9). Further calculations yielded the principal component scores (Table 5.10). The principal components were standardised, non-normalised, and normalised to obtain the normalised matrix. The information entropy values, information utility, and weight coefficients were calculated using the formula, and the weighted matrix was further obtained. Finally, the positive and negative ideal solutions and relative progress were calculated using the formula (Table 5.11).

The semiconductor industry chain security levels of provinces and municipalities across China in 2024, ranked from highest to lowest, with Guangdong Province having the highest security level and Shanxi Province the lowest. Further classification is based on China's economic regions: Northeast Region (Liaoning Province, Jilin Province, Heilongjiang Province); Eastern Region (Beijing Municipality, Tianjin Municipality, Hebei Province, Shanghai Municipality, Jiangsu Province, Zhejiang Province, Fujian Province, Shandong Province, Guangdong Province, Hainan Province); Central Region (Shanxi Province, Anhui Province, Jiangxi Province, Henan Province, Hubei Province, Hunan Province); Western Region: (Inner Mongolia Autonomous Region, Guangxi Zhuang Autonomous Region, Chongqing Municipality, Sichuan Province, Guizhou Province, Yunnan Province, Shaanxi Province, Gansu Province, Qinghai Province, Ningxia Hui Autonomous Region), the weighted average of the relative proximity (Z) for each region was calculated. The security levels of China's semiconductor supply chain in 2024, ranked from highest to lowest by region, are as follows: Eastern Region, Western Region, Central Region, and Northeast Region (Fig. 5.2).

Table 5.9 Principal component analysis

	Total	% of Variance	Cumulative %	Total	% of Variance	Cumulative %	Total	% of Variance	Cumulative %
1	4.999	38.455	38.455	4.999	38.455	38.455	3.039	23.374	23.374
2	1.829	14.069	52.523	1.829	14.069	52.523	2.272	17.475	40.849
3	1.547	11.901	64.424	1.547	11.901	64.424	1.496	11.507	52.356
4	1.126	8.665	73.089	1.126	8.665	73.089	1.250	9.619	61.975
5	.834	6.417	79.506	.834	6.417	79.506	1.215	9.343	71.319
6	.691	5.315	84.822	.691	5.315	84.822	1.190	9.157	80.476
7	.512	3.939	88.761	.512	3.939	88.761	1.077	8.285	88.761
8	.455	3.499	92.260						
9	.324	2.492	94.751						
10	.294	2.259	97.010						
11	.176	1.355	98.366						
12	.148	1.137	99.503						
13	.065	.497	100.000						

The eastern region has the highest level of semiconductor industry chain security and is the main area for the development of China's semiconductor industry chain. It is centred on the Yangtze River Delta, Pearl River Delta, and Hainan Free Trade Zone. In comparison, the Beijing-Tianjin-Hebei region still has room for improvement in terms of security. The western region has advantages in terms of resources and production costs, with Inner Mongolia Autonomous Region and Guangxi Zhuang Autonomous Region having relatively high levels of industry chain security. The central and northeastern regions still have room for improvement in terms of semiconductor industry chain security, with Jiangxi Province and Liaoning Province having relatively high levels of security.

Table 5.10 Principal component scores

	1	2	3	4	5	6	7
Anhui	0.50	0.91	0.55	−0.90	−0.59	0.42	−0.20
Beijing	0.71	0.18	−0.02	0.49	0.11	−2.51	0.20
Fujian	0.88	0.08	−0.22	−0.03	0.59	0.60	0.28
Gansu	0.04	−0.76	0.56	−0.55	0.13	0.37	−0.57
Guangdong	0.11	0.01	−0.68	0.06	−0.17	0.04	4.44
Guangxi	−0.87	−0.68	1.63	1.07	−1.12	0.25	−0.17
Guizhou	−1.34	0.15	−1.49	0.26	−2.67	0.12	−0.72
Hainan	−1.38	−0.46	2.43	2.02	0.88	0.26	0.04
Hebei	0.05	−0.25	−0.22	1.41	1.79	0.90	−0.43
Henan	−1.97	1.48	−0.82	−1.14	0.74	0.85	−0.15
Heilongjiang	−0.59	−0.19	0.32	−0.69	−0.55	0.87	−0.49
Hubei	0.70	0.97	−0.14	−0.58	0.31	0.51	−0.49
Hunan	0.60	0.92	−1.27	0.42	0.29	0.42	−0.61
Jilin	1.13	−0.83	−0.56	−0.81	1.25	−2.02	−0.58
Jiangsu	0.31	0.15	0.58	−0.26	1.14	0.43	1.81
Jiangxi	0.14	0.07	−1.12	0.82	0.20	0.35	−0.28
Liaoning	0.30	0.07	2.21	0.08	−0.40	−0.09	−0.45
Inner Mongolia	−0.57	−1.29	−2.01	2.72	0.00	0.31	−0.02
Ningxia	−2.94	0.10	0.14	−0.99	0.23	−2.38	0.23
Qinghai	0.76	−4.00	−0.27	−1.42	−0.83	0.75	−0.05
Shandong	0.68	0.77	0.14	0.17	−1.19	0.07	−0.13
Shanxi	−0.53	−0.71	−0.08	−1.40	0.40	−1.14	−0.12
Shannxi	0.41	0.11	1.13	−0.12	0.81	0.43	−0.28
Shanghai	1.00	0.88	0.57	0.29	−2.70	−0.57	0.59
Sichuan	1.06	0.44	0.01	−1.03	0.32	0.59	−0.34
Tianjin	1.03	0.35	−0.58	1.13	0.35	−1.89	−0.91
Yunnan	−1.17	−0.01	−0.85	−0.93	0.58	1.14	−0.31
Zhejiang	0.39	0.75	0.14	0.01	0.09	0.49	0.46
Chongqing	0.56	0.79	−0.08	−0.09	0.00	0.44	−0.73

Table 5.11 Euclidean Distance and Relative Closeness of Evaluation Indicators

	Ideal value(D+)	Negative ideal value(D-)	Relative proximity(Z)
Anhui	0.37	0.15	0.29
Beijing	0.32	0.17	0.34
Fujian	0.32	0.18	0.36
Gansu	0.37	0.14	0.28
Guangdong	0.18	0.37	0.67
Guangxi	0.32	0.20	0.39
Guizhou	0.39	0.13	0.25
Hainan	0.29	0.26	0.47
Hebei	0.33	0.22	0.40
Henan	0.38	0.14	0.27
Heilongjiang	0.38	0.14	0.27
Hubei	0.37	0.15	0.28
Hunan	0.36	0.16	0.31
Jilin	0.40	0.12	0.24
Jiangsu	0.24	0.24	0.49
Jiangxi	0.34	0.18	0.35
Liaoning	0.35	0.18	0.34
Inner Mongolia	0.31	0.26	0.45
Ningxia	0.37	0.12	0.24
Qinghai	0.38	0.14	0.27
Shandong	0.34	0.16	0.32
Shanxi	0.39	0.11	0.23
Shannxi	0.34	0.17	0.34
Shanghai	0.30	0.18	0.37
Sichuan	0.38	0.15	0.28
Tianjin	0.37	0.18	0.32
Yunnan	0.38	0.14	0.27
Zhejiang	0.30	0.18	0.37
Chongqing	0.37	0.15	0.29

5.1.4 Security of China's Semiconductor Industry Chain from Upstream to Downstream from a Trade Perspective

Further analysis of the security status of China's semiconductor industry chain from a trade perspective (import concentration, export concentration, and trade competitive advantage) is conducted separately for the upstream, midstream, and downstream segments. The corresponding indicators for the upstream segment are $x1$, $x5$, and $x9$; for the midstream segment, $x2$, $x6$, and $x10$; and for the downstream segment, $x3$, $x7$, and $x11$. The Entropy Weighted TOPSIS model was applied to calculate the relative proximity of the upstream, midstream, and downstream segments of the supply chain. The specific results are presented in Table 5.12.

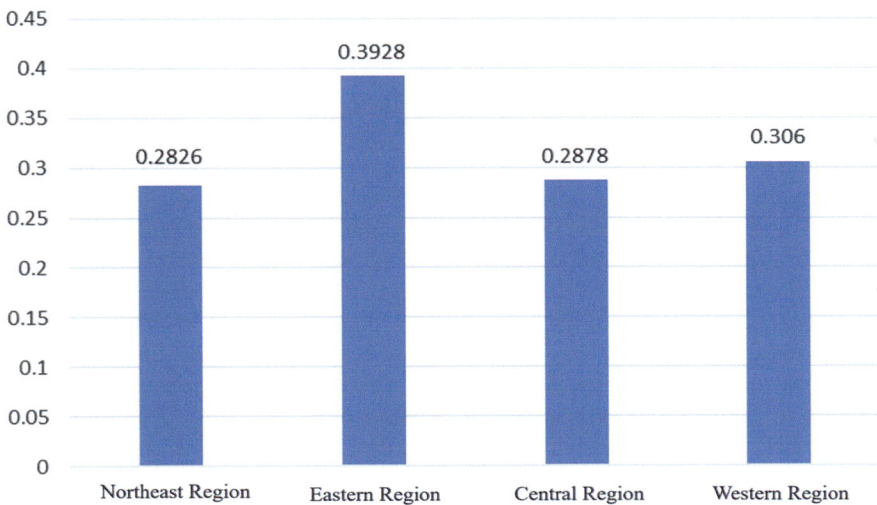

Fig. 5.2 2024 semiconductor industry chain security levels in various regions of China

Table 5.12 Relative Proximity of Evaluation Indicators for the Upstream, Midstream, and Downstream Sectors of the Industrial Chain

	Upstream proximity	Midstream proximity	Downstream proximity
2015	0.78	0.42	0.11
2016	0.55	0.45	0.02
2017	0.44	0.50	0.06
2018	0.37	0.57	0.19
2019	0.27	0.65	0.23
2020	0.22	0.58	0.38
2021	0.22	0.58	0.52
2022	0.38	0.40	0.46
2023	0.26	0.54	0.66
2024	0.22	0.48	0.96

During the period from 2015 to 2024, the overall security level of the upstream segment of China's semiconductor industry chain showed a downward trend. Although there was a brief rebound from 2021 to 2022, the trend continued to decline thereafter. The security level reached its peak in 2015 and hit its lowest point in 2020. Further analysis of the original data reveals that the import concentration of upstream products is higher than that of midstream and downstream products, while the trade competitive advantage is significantly lower than that of midstream and downstream products. As a result, the upstream segment of the semiconductor industry chain faces more severe security risks. In 2015, the security level of China's semiconductor industry chain was at its highest, primarily because the semiconductor industry was still in its growth stage at the time, resulting in relatively low demand pressure for upstream products. Additionally, the relatively stable international environment ensured the smooth supply of critical equipment and raw materials. However, as China's semiconductor industry continued to develop, demand pressure for upstream products also increased. Since China is unable to independently manufacture high-end production equipment, its reliance on imports has risen, leading to a continuous decline in the security level of the upstream segment of the industry chain. Additionally, the escalation of Sino-US trade friction has restricted imports of high-end equipment, causing the security level of the upstream segment to drop to its lowest point in 2020. In 2021–2022, the security level saw a brief rebound, partly due to the government's intensified policy efforts to promote domestic substitution and supply chain adjustments by enterprises, which led to breakthroughs in some areas. However, this was offset by the impact of reduced imports of high-end equipment due to import restrictions. After 2022, the security level of the upstream segment of China's semiconductor supply chain declined again. The core reason lies in the significant gap between domestic technological capabilities and international advanced levels, making it difficult to achieve complete import substitution. Although countries led by the United States have imposed technological blockades and export restrictions on China, leading to a temporary reduction in imports, domestic companies will still seek new trade partners or find other ways to circumvent export restrictions to meet demand in the face of a significant supply gap.

During the 2015–2024 period, the security level of China's midstream semiconductor industry chain fluctuated. From 2015 to 2019, the security level continued to rise, reaching its peak in 2019; however, from 2020 to 2024, despite fluctuations, the overall trend was downward, with the lowest point occurring in 2022. From 2015 to 2019, the security level of China's midstream semiconductor industry chain continued to rise, primarily due to the rapid expansion of domestic wafer manufacturing and semiconductor electronic component production capacity, improvements in technological capabilities, policy support, and market demand. Additionally, the strengthening of local supply chain played a significant role, enabling the security level to reach its peak in 2019. From 2020 to 2024, the overall security level showed a downward trend, particularly reaching its lowest point in 2022. The main reasons include the intensification of Sino-US trade friction leading to technological blockades and export restrictions, constraints imposed by the technological gap in domestic high-end wafer manufacturing and testing equipment, supply-demand imbalances, and the impact of the global supply chain crisis.

As shown in Figure 5.3, during the period from 2015 to 2024, the security level of the downstream segment of China's semiconductor industry chain showed a short-term decline in 2016 and 2022 but overall presented an upward trend, with the lowest security level in 2016 and the highest in 2024. The overall upward trend was driven by rapid growth in market demand, policy support and industrial upgrading, the rise of domestic enterprises, and the rapid development of emerging fields such as new energy and intelligent vehicles. Additionally, the in-depth implementation of the Belt and Road Initiative has provided important support for the improvement

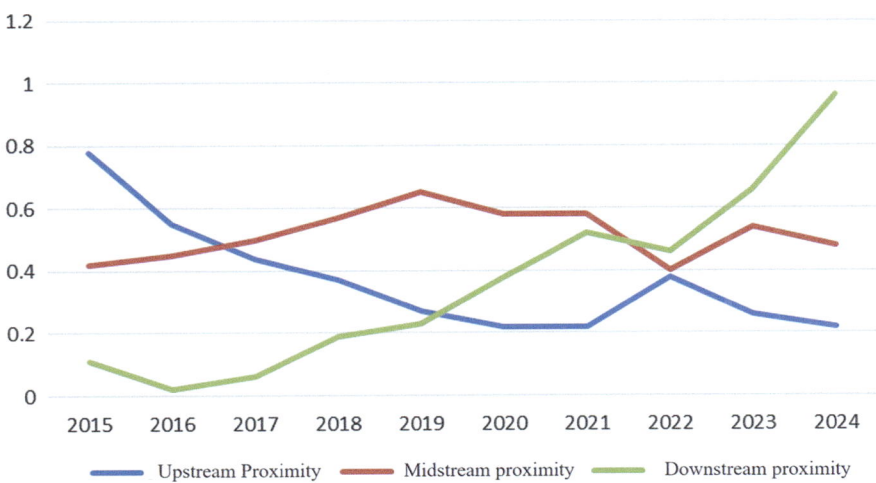

Fig. 5.3 Security Levels of Each Link in China's Semiconductor Industry Chain from 2015 to 2024

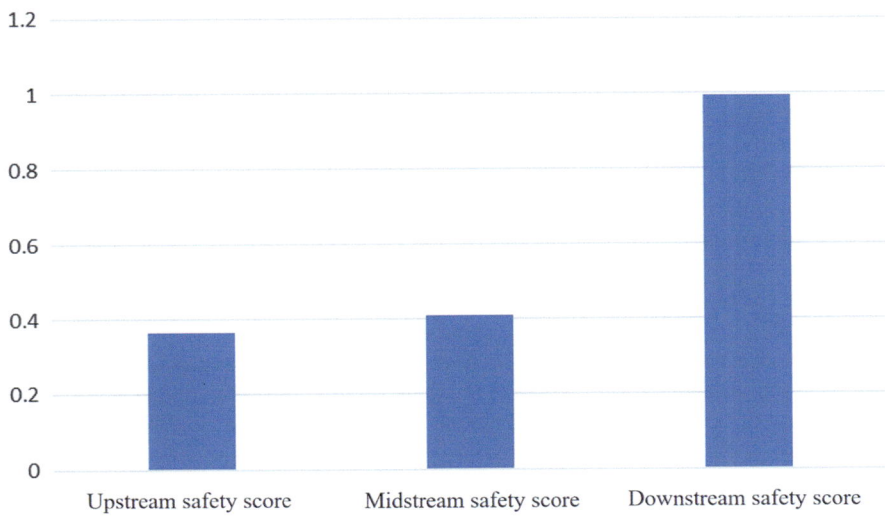

Fig. 5.4 Security Levels of China's Semiconductor Industry Chain in 2024

of the security level of China's downstream semiconductor industry chain. First, by expanding cooperation with countries along the Belt and Road, export markets have been diversified, reducing reliance on traditional developed markets. Second, the establishment of close economic and trade relations with countries along the Belt and Road has enhanced supply chain stability, while the establishment of production bases and sales networks in these regions has improved risk-resistance capabilities. Additionally, the rapid growth in demand for consumer electronics, communication equipment, new energy, and intelligent vehicles in emerging markets along the Belt and Road has provided new growth opportunities for domestic enterprises.

At the same time, a horizontal analysis of the security levels of the upstream, midstream, and downstream segments of China's semiconductor industry chain in 2024 was conducted from a trade perspective. According to the entropy-weighted TOPSIS ranking results (Fig. 5.4), the downstream segment of China's semiconductor industry chain has the highest security level, while the upstream segment has the lowest security level.

5.2 Assessing Semiconductor Industry Chain Security Risks from the Perspective of Import Concentration

5.2.1 Construction of Import Concentration Indicators

Based on the global value chain theory, the concentration of intermediate goods imports can directly reflect the specific embedding pattern of an industry in the global division of labour system (Gereffi & Fernandez-Stark 2016). When import concentration is high, the industry exhibits a single-dimensional characteristic in its global value chain layout. This leaves industries with insufficient buffer space and flexible response mechanisms when facing external shocks such as fluctuations in the trade policies of importing countries or supply shortages, making them highly susceptible to severe impacts. Additionally, this highly concentrated import pattern may suppress the intrinsic motivation for technological innovation and supply chain optimisation within industries, rendering them unable to flexibly adjust their development paths in the face of intensifying global competition and rapid technological iteration, thereby further exposing the inherent fragility of industrial chains. From a systems theory perspective, the industrial chain can be viewed as a complex and organic system, with intermediate product imports serving as a critical subsystem; In complex systems, diversity is a key guarantee of stability (Simon 1962; Levin 1998). When intermediate product imports are concentrated in a few sources, the stability of the entire industrial chain system is threatened. Based on risk management theory and supply chain resilience theory, adopting a strategy of diversifying import sources can effectively reduce the risk of supply disruptions caused by sudden issues with a single supply source, thereby enhancing the overall safety of the supply chain system. From the perspective of trade network relationships, intermediate products with more concentrated supply sources tend to occupy more critical positions in the industrial chain (Caldarelli et al. 2012). The greater the number of critical intermediate products in an industrial chain, the more complex its structure becomes, and the greater its vulnerability to external shocks. Therefore, when facing external supply shocks, intermediate inputs highly dependent on a few supply sources are highly prone to supply disruptions, which in turn affect the normal operation of the entire industry. In summary, the intermediate product import concentration index, with its inherent logical correlation and quantitative representation capabilities, can effectively and scientifically characterise the safety level of industrial chains, providing a theoretical basis for subsequent research and policy recommendations.

The import concentration index (Herfindahl-Hirschman Index, HHI) is used to measure the diversity of intermediate goods imports. It is calculated as the square of the ratio of the scale of intermediate goods imports from various countries to the total scale of intermediate goods imports in the semiconductor industry chain. A higher HHI value indicates higher import concentration of intermediate goods in the semiconductor industry chain, which implies higher industry chain risks; conversely, a lower HHI value indicates better industry chain security.

$$HHI = \sum_{i=1}^{n} S_i^2 \tag{5.18}$$

Where n is the number of import source countries, and HHI is the market share of the i-th source country. The value of HHI typically ranges between 0 and 1.

Using HS 6-digit customs trade data for China's semiconductor intermediate imports from January 2019 to October 2024, the data was organised into a dataset with dimensions of Chinese provinces—source countries (regions)—products—months. The data was sourced from the General Administration of Customs.

5.2.2   Overall Assessment of the Security Level of the Semiconductor Industry Chain

Fig. 5.5 illustrates the changes in the concentration of intermediate product imports in China's semiconductor industry chain from 2019 to 2024. Risks in the semiconductor industry chain remained relatively stable in the first half of 2019, with minimal fluctuations, but began to rise in the second half of 2019, peaking around the fourth quarter of 2019. This growth reflects the intensifying impact of the US-China trade war and the interaction between the dynamic uncertainty of global trade policies and the complex and volatile factors affecting the semiconductor supply chain. In 2020, due to the outbreak of COVID-19, risks in the semiconductor industry chain surged sharply in the first and second quarters. The spread of factory shutdowns and production halts, supply chain disruptions and interruptions, and profound adjustments and changes in global demand structures, among other adverse factors, combined to push semiconductor industry chain risks to new highs. The semiconductor industry was severely affected by disruptions in manufacturing and distribution channels, further exacerbating uncertainty within the industry. Since 2021, due to the sustained expansion of demand in the electronics and automotive industries and the prolonged and intractable supply chain bottlenecks, global semiconductor shortages have become more pronounced, and risks in the semi-conductor industry chain have continued to fluctuate, with noticeable peaks and troughs. Despite the proactive efforts of all relevant parties to resume operations, supply chain issues persisted into the middle of 2021, resulting in persistently high risk levels that continued to exert pressure and constraints on industry development. In early 2022, the risk level of the semiconductor supply chain remained relatively stable. However, in April 2022, geopolitical tensions (including the Russia-Ukraine war) and ongoing supply chain issues caused the risk landscape to fluctuate again. In the second half of 2022, stabilisation began to emerge, potentially due to policies introduced by various countries aimed at alleviating risk pressures in the semicon-ductor industry and promoting industrial stability, leading to a slight decline in sup-ply chain risks. In 2023, risks showed a relatively slow downward trend. However, the semiconductor industry chain still experienced some peaks, possibly reflecting the combined impact of multiple factors such as supply chain resilience and tech-nological iteration and transformation. Additionally, macroeconomic disturbances such as global inflationary pressures and energy crises further complicated and intensified the dynamics of risk changes in the industry chain. By 2024, the overall stability of risks in the semiconductor industry chain had significantly improved.

Overall, from 2019 to 2024, driven by geopolitical events, the COVID-19 pan-demic, and supply chain issues, risks in the semiconductor industry chain have shown a fluctuating upward trend. Although the semiconductor industry has under-gone years of development and has to some extent adapted to and adjusted for the challenges it faces, risk factors associated with the ongoing instability of the geo-political landscape, intensifying international competition, and rapid technological advancements continue to influence market dynamics. These factors remain critical

Fig. 5.5 Semiconductor Industry Chain Security Assessment

considerations that must be closely monitored and addressed with caution as the industry seeks to achieve sustained and steady growth.

5.2.3   Country (Region) Heterogeneity in the Security Level of the Semiconductor Industry Chain

This section selects the top 30 source countries (regions) in terms of import scale for China's semiconductor industry chain and assesses the import concentration of the semiconductor industry chain in these countries (regions). The analysis results are shown in Fig. 5.6. Overall, the risk is highest in the Netherlands, Saudi Arabia, and other countries, followed by the Philippines, Australia, Chinese Taiwan, and other countries, while the risk is lowest in Germany, Switzerland, Italy, France, the United Kingdom, and other countries.

China's imports of intermediate products from the Netherlands primarily consist of machinery and equipment used in the manufacture of semiconductor devices or integrated circuits, as well as digital integrated circuits. Among these, machinery and equipment used in the manufacture of semiconductor devices or integrated circuits account for 89.50% of China's total imports of semiconductor-related intermediate products from the Netherlands, highlighting the Netherlands' dominant position in China's semiconductor manufacturing equipment sector. China should consider diversifying its import sources, reduce reliance on a single country, and promote domestic research, development, and production of semiconductor equipment to reduce dependence on external suppliers. The main intermediate products

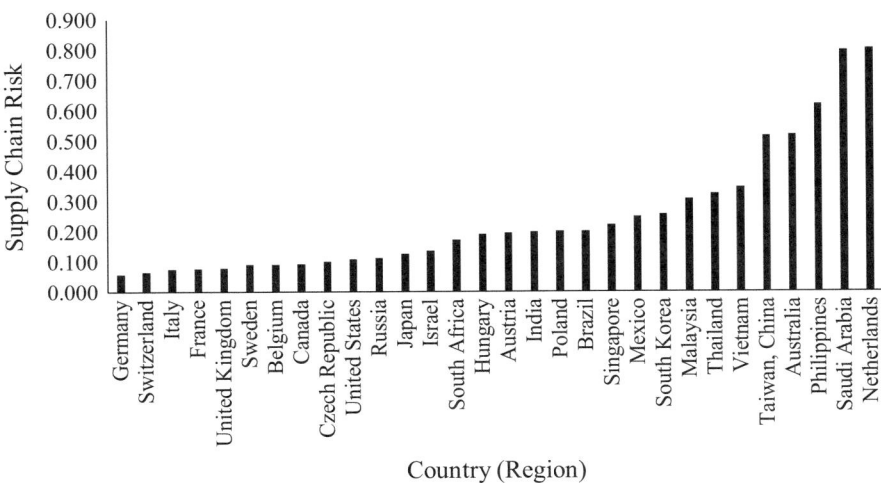

Fig. 5.6   Security Assessment of the Semiconductor Industry Chain in Key Countries (Regions) in 2023

imported from Saudi Arabia are high-purity solvents and high-purity metals. China's imports of acetone from Saudi Arabia account for 33.69% of its total acetone imports, indicating that Saudi Arabia may influence the stability of China's semiconductor manufacturing material supply chain in terms of high-purity chemicals and metals. Imports of high-purity metals (primarily aluminium oxide) from Australia account for 70.90% of China's total imports of semiconductor-related intermediate products from Australia and 52.70% of China's total imports of aluminium oxide, making Australia the primary source of aluminium oxide for China. Integrated circuits imported from South Korea for use as memory account for 39.04% of the total value of semiconductor-related intermediate products imported from South Korea and 53.23% of China's total imports of integrated circuits for memory; digital integrated circuits imported from South Korea account for 13.46% of China's total imports of digital integrated circuits and 30.54% of the total value of semiconductor-related intermediate products imported from South Korea. Chinese Taiwan is also a key supplier of digital integrated circuits, with imports accounting for 53.91% of total digital integrated circuit imports and 70.47% of total imports of semiconductor-related intermediate products from Chinese Taiwan. In the digital integrated circuit sector, China should strengthen cooperation with South Korea and Chinese Taiwan to promote technology sharing and industrial collaboration, which may help maintain import stability and drive technological progress. Imports of other organic light-emitting diode flat-panel display modules from Vietnam accounted for 53.88% of total imports of semiconductor-related intermediate products from Vietnam and 98.63% of total imports of other organic light-emitting diode flat-panel display modules. This indicates that China is almost entirely dependent on Vietnam in this sector, posing certain supply risks. Relevant policies could promote the enhancement of domestic production capacity, explore cooperation with other countries or regions, and gradually reduce reliance on a single country. China's imports of digital integrated circuits from Thailand account for 51.07% of its total imports of other integrated circuits from Thailand, while imports from Malaysia account for 53.88% of its total imports of other integrated circuits from Malaysia. Both countries rank among the top ten in terms of China's imports of digital integrated circuits. The semiconductor intermediates imported most from Germany, Switzerland, and Italy are all measurement or testing instruments, apparatus, and machinery, which are critical equipment in semiconductor production. Relevant policies can promote technology introduction and domestic R&D to enhance China's semiconductor industry's technological level and quality control capabilities.

This section further categorises countries (regions) into four major categories using a quadrant classification method based on the import concentration of the semiconductor industry chain in each country (region) and the scale of semiconductor industry chain imports. It identifies that the five major economies face the risk of both high import concentration and high import scale, which requires high attention. Fig. 5.7 shows that in the first quadrant, imports from Chinese Taiwan, South Korea, Vietnam, Malaysia, and Thailand are large in scale and have high import concentration, indicating relatively higher supply chain risks. In the second quadrant, while the import scale from Saudi Arabia, the Philippines, and Australia is

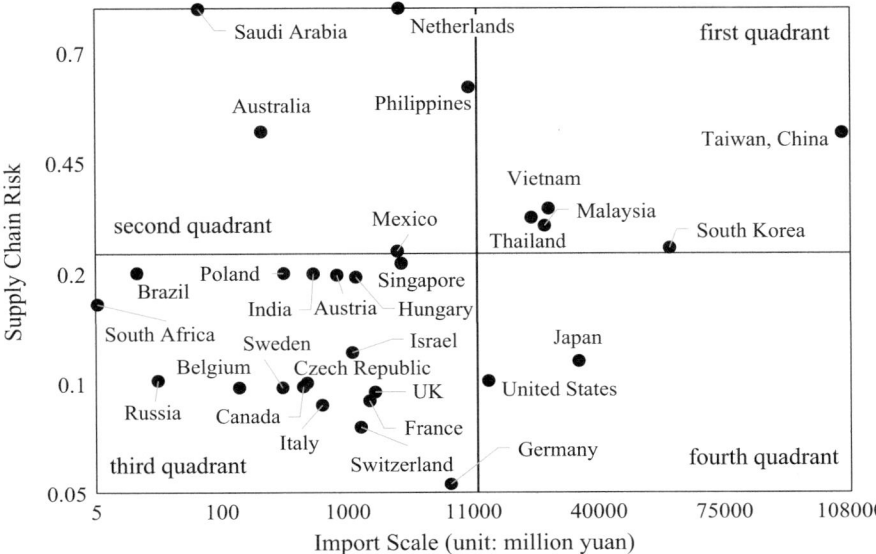

Fig. 5.7   Quadrant diagram of semiconductor industry chain risks and import scale in key countries (regions) in 2023

relatively small, the import concentration is high, necessitating measures to mitigate the risk of an overly concentrated import structure in the semiconductor industry chain. In the third quadrant, both the import concentration and import scale from France, Canada, and the United Kingdom are low, indicating relatively lower risks in the industry chain. In the fourth quadrant, while China's import concentration from Japan and the United States is low, the import scale is large.

5.2.4   Heterogeneity of the Semiconductor Industry Chain Security Level

Figures 5.8, 5.9, and 5.10 illustrate the import concentration of various segments in the upstream, midstream, and downstream segments of the semiconductor industry chain. Overall, the downstream segments of data transmission modules, wind turbine generators, accelerator cards, industrial robots, and upstream segments such as electronic-grade special gases pose relatively higher risks. When broken down by major segments, the upstream segments of electronic-grade special gases, chemical mechanical polishing liquids, photoresists, and photoresist substrates pose relatively higher risks, with electronic-grade special gases having the highest import concentration. The midstream segments of the supply chain generally pose lower risks, but the segments related to cutting equipment, digital integrated circuits, and solder balls exhibit relatively prominent risks and should be closely monitored. The import concentration levels vary significantly across different segments of the downstream supply chain. Segments such as data transmission modules, wind turbine generators, accelerator cards, industrial robots, touchscreens, RF front-end modules, and AI chips have higher import concentration levels and face higher supply chain risks.

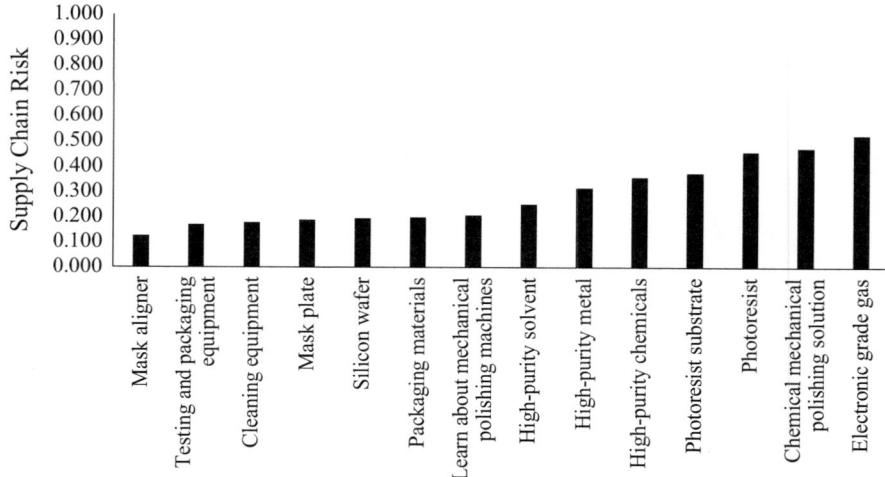

Fig. 5.8   2023 Upstream Semiconductor Industry Chain Security Assessment

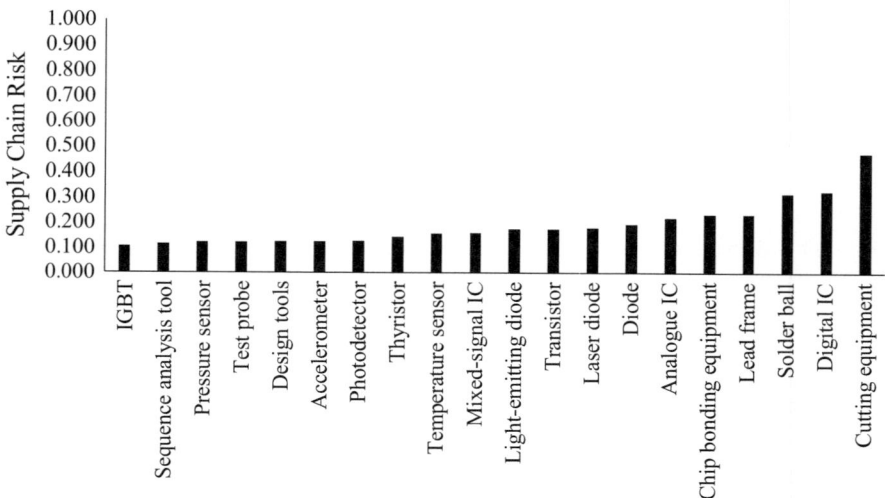

Fig. 5.9   2023 Midstream Semiconductor Industry Chain Security Assessment

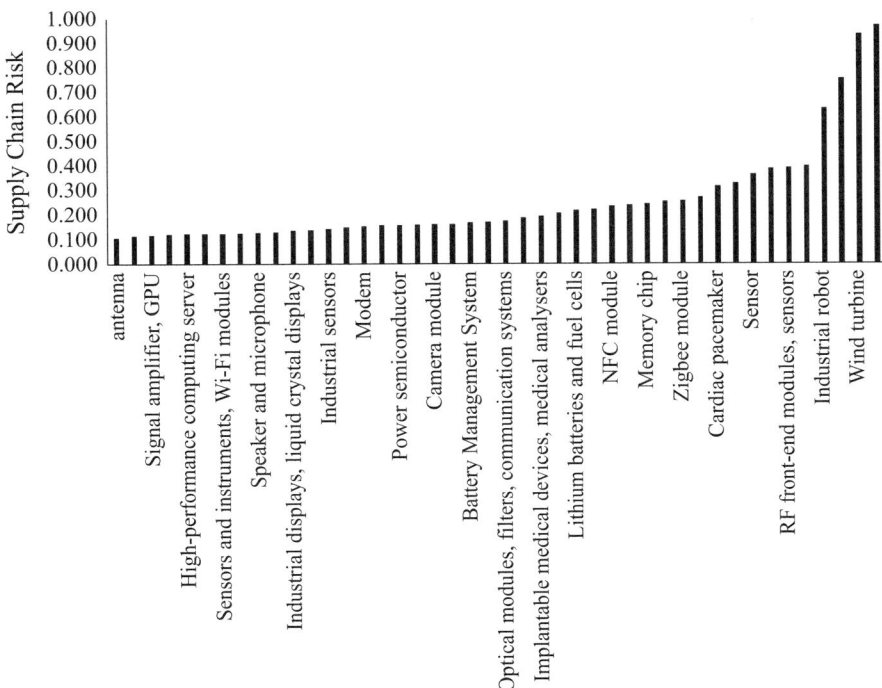

Fig. 5.10   2023 Downstream Semiconductor Industry Chain Security Assessment

References

Caldarelli, G., Chessa, A., Gabrielli, A., Pammolli, F., & Scala, A. (2012). A network analysis of countries' export flows: Firm grounds for the building blocks of the economy. *PLoS ONE*, *7*(10), e47278.

Gereffi, G., & Fernandez-Stark, K. (2016). *Global value chain analysis: A primer* (2nd ed.). Center on Globalization, Governance & Competitiveness (CGGC), Duke University.

Jolliffe, I. T. (2002). *Principal component analysis* (2nd ed.). Springer.

Jolliffe, I. T., & Cadima, J. (2016). Principal component analysis: A review and recent developments. *Philosophical Transactions of the Royal Society A: Mathematical, Physical and Engineering Sciences*, *374*(2065), 20150202.

Levin, S. A. (1998). Ecosystems and the biosphere as complex adaptive systems. *Ecosystems*, *1*(5), 431–436.

Li, M., & Wang, X. (2014). An improved entropy weight method and its application in water quality assessment. *Procedia Environmental Sciences*, *10*, 2849–2854.

Li, P., & Zou, J. (2014). An improved TOPSIS method for multi-attribute decision making problems. *Mathematical Problems in Engineering*, *2014*, 1–10.

Simon, H. A. (1962). The architecture of complexity. *Proceedings of the American Philosophical Society*, *106*(6), 467–482.

Zhang, X., & Xu, Z. (2015). A method based on TOPSIS and entropy weight for supplier selection. *Journal of Systems Science and Systems Engineering*, *24*(2), 204–217.

Zou, Z. H., Yun, Y., & Sun, J. N. (2006). Entropy method for determination of weight of evaluating indicators in fuzzy synthetic evaluation for water quality assessment. *Journal of Environmental Sciences, 18*(5), 1020–1023.

Chapter 6
The Reshaping of the US Supply Chain and the Security Level of China's Semiconductor Industry Chain

Tiantian Wang

Abstract Chapter 6 investigates the impact of US supply chain review policies on the security of China's semiconductor industry chain. Taking Executive Order No. 14017 as a policy intervention point, the chapter constructs a continuous difference-in-differences (DID) model using monthly trade data from 2019 to 2024. The empirical analysis indicates that US policy measures have significantly increased the import concentration of China's semiconductor intermediate goods, thereby undermining the resilience of its supply chain. Further results suggest that rationalising industrial structure, enhancing innovation capacity, and increasing fiscal support can partially offset these negative effects. The chapter concludes with policy recommendations centred on diversifying import sources, strengthening regional coordination, reinforcing key segments of the supply chain, advancing indigenous innovation, and optimising industrial structure to enhance national supply chain security and systemic resilience.

Keywords US Supply Chain Policy • Semiconductor Import Concentration • Supply Chain Security • Difference-in-Differences (DID) • Industrial Resilience

In recent years, the global industrial chain has accelerated its shift from efficiency-driven to security-driven, with geopolitical rivalry fuelling a wave of technological nationalism (Baldwin & Freeman 2022). Since 2021, the United States has shifted its supply chain review policy from strategic defence to proactive reshaping, centred on technology export controls and alliances with allies, systematically restructuring the global division of labour in key industries such as semiconductors. As the cornerstone of the digital economy, the security of the semiconductor supply chain directly impacts a nation's technological sovereignty and industrial competitiveness. However, China's semiconductor supply chain faces severe external dependency risks: the self-sufficiency rate for high-end chips is less than 10% (Shen & Wang 2024), and the reliance on imports for critical equipment and materials

© The Author(s) 2026
T. Wang et al., *China's Semiconductor Industry Strategy,*
SpringerBriefs in Economics,
https://doi.org/10.1007/978-981-95-3332-9_6

exceeds 80%. Additionally, US policies have further exacerbated the risk of import source concentration (Fajgelbaum et al. 2021). Against this backdrop, clarifying the mechanisms through which US supply chain review policies impact the security level of China's semiconductor industry chain has become a core issue in breaking the 'chokepoint' dilemma.

6.1   Theoretical Mechanisms and Research Hypotheses

6.1.1   The Direct Impact of US Supply Chain Review Policies on the Security Level of Industrial Chains

The Global Value Chain (GVC) theory (Gereffi et al. 2005) emphasises that dominant countries establish structural power over dependent countries by controlling 'strategic links.' According to the technology-economic paradigm theory (Perez 2002), the semiconductor industry, as the core carrier of general-purpose technology (GPT), exhibits path dependence and systemic synergy in its technological progress. The United States has upgraded its technology export controls through the Wassenaar Arrangement, restricting the supply of critical equipment such as extreme ultraviolet lithography (EUV) and atomic layer deposition (ALD) to China. This has left China's semiconductor industry isolated in advanced process technologies, with its ability to iterate processes systematically constrained. Based on network power theory (Castells 2011), the United States has restructured the global semiconductor supply chain network through domestic manufacturing and alliances with allies (White House 2021), excluding China from high-end foundry and memory chip segments. This exercise of network power has exacerbated the 'peripheral node' status of China's industrial chain, reducing its bargaining power and risk buffer space in the global value chain.

Hypothesis H1: US supply chain review policies have a significant negative impact on the security level of China's semiconductor industrial chain.

6.1.2   Moderating Effect Mechanism

6.1.1.1   Positive Moderating Effect of Industrial Structure Rationalisation

Based on transaction cost theory (Stone 1986), rationalisation of industrial structure reduces vertical coordination costs within the industrial chain, thereby mitigating external shocks. For example, higher concentration in the manufacturing segment can accelerate the verification and adoption of domestically produced photoresist and special gases, thereby shortening the repair cycle for supply chain disruptions. Industrial cluster theory (Porter 1998) suggests that regional industrial clusters build localised capacity redundancy through knowledge spillovers and factor sharing. In semiconductor industry clusters such as the Yangtze River Delta and Pearl River Delta, joint laboratories between universities and enterprises can cultivate process technology talent in a targeted manner, accelerate the verification of domestically produced materials, and shorten the repair cycle of supply chain disruptions.

Hypothesis H2a: The degree of industrial structure rationalisation can positively regulate the negative relationship between US supply chain review policies and the security level of China's semiconductor industry chain.

6.1.1.2 Positive Moderating Effect of Innovation Capabilities

Based on the technology catch-up theory (Lee & Lim 2001) technological break-throughs in the semiconductor industry require following a progressive path of 'reverse engineering → process improvement → architectural innovation.' High R&D intensity firms can break through US patent barriers in areas such as FinFET transistor structures and multiple exposure technology by increasing the number of trial wafer runs and accumulating defect databases, thereby reducing the negative impact of technology supply disruptions.

According to the dynamic capability theory (Teece et al. 1997), independent innovation not only depends on R&D investment but also requires the construction of a full-cycle capability of 'technology monitoring-absorption-reconstruction.' For example, establishing a global patent early warning system can identify the risk of US technology blockade in advance, and acquiring overseas R&D teams can achieve reverse technology transfer, both of which can enhance the adaptive adjustment ability of the industrial chain.

Hypothesis H2b: The level of independent innovation can positively moderate the negative relationship between US supply chain review policies and the security level of China's semiconductor industry chain.

6.1.1.3 Positive Moderating Effect of Fiscal Policy Support

Based on the market failure correction mechanism (Arrow 1962), semiconductor equipment R&D has strong positive externalities and high risk. Fiscal subsidies reduce firms' marginal costs, redirect social capital toward high-uncertainty sectors, and address innovation market failures caused by insufficient private investment. Based on the demand-side policy complementarity (Rodrik 2004), government procurement and tax incentives can expand domestic firms' market share, forming a positive feedback loop of 'demand scale ↑ → R&D investment ↑ → technological iteration ↑' (Aghion et al. 2015). For example, the mass application of domestically produced etching machines in the production lines of Yangtze Memory Technologies Co., Ltd. has accelerated process optimisation through a 'learning by doing' effect, enhancing the substitution elasticity of American equipment.

Hypothesis H2c: Fiscal policy support can positively moderate the negative relationship between US supply chain review policies and the security level of China's semiconductor industry chain.

6.2 Empirical Design

Executive Order No. 14017 of the United States targets six industries and four categories of critical products for supply chain vulnerability reviews. Since the order was signed on 24 February 2021, February 2021 is set as the starting point for the impact of the US supply chain review policy. This section constructs a continuous double difference measurement model to explore the impact of the US supply chain review policy on the security of China's semiconductor industry chain. The model is set as follows:

$$\ln HHI_{prct} = \alpha + \beta \, \text{Treat}_c \times \text{post}_t + X_{prct} \gamma + \omega_p + \mu_t + \varepsilon_{prct} \tag{6.1}$$

In this context, p represents imported intermediate products in the semiconductor industry chain, r denotes a province (autonomous region, municipality), c denotes a key country (region), and t denotes the month. The dependent variable $\ln HHI_{prct}$ is the import concentration of China's semiconductor industry chain. The explanatory variables include treatment variables Treat_c and experimental period variables post_t. It indicates the scale of China's imports of semiconductor intermediate products from various countries (regions). It is a dummy variable, taking 1 for February 2021 and thereafter, and 0 otherwise. X_{prct} is a control variable vector, with control variables including: (1) Economic freedom ($\ln ECO_{ct}$), which represents the economic freedom of the key country (region) c in period t; economic freedom reflects the degree of relaxation of a country's (region's) economic policy environment and the degree of free market competition. Countries (regions) with higher economic freedom may have advantages in semiconductor production and trade, thereby influencing the scale and stability of China's semiconductor intermediate product trade with them, and ultimately affecting the import concentration of China's semiconductor supply chain. (2) The logarithm of the weighted geographical distance between China and the target country (region) c (in thousands of kilometres)($\ln DIS_c$); geographical distance affects trade costs, including transportation costs and communication costs. The greater the distance, the higher the trade costs, which may reduce China's imports of semiconductor intermediate products from the corresponding countries (regions), thereby affecting import concentration. (3) The logarithm of the per capita GDP of key countries (regions) (in US dollars); per capita GDP reflects a country's (region's) level of economic development and residents' purchasing power, and to some extent represents the market size and development potential of its semiconductor industry. Countries (regions) with higher levels of economic development may have more advanced semiconductor industries and technologies, which can influence China's trade relations with them in the semiconductor sector and impact the import concentration of China's semiconductor supply chain.(4) Whether China shares a common border (BORD$_c$) or a common language (LANG$_c$) with key countries (regions). If so, the value is 1; otherwise, it is 0. Countries (regions) with common borders or languages may have more convenient trade, smoother cultural exchanges, and better information communication, which helps reduce trade costs, promote trade in semiconductor intermediates, and thereby influence import concentration. Additionally, the model includes product fixed effects and month fixed effects to control for the impact of product characteristics and time trends on import concentration. ε_{prct} represents the random error term, whose standard error is adjusted through cluster analysis at the country (region) level to ensure the accuracy and reliability of the estimation results. The economic freedom data in the control variables are sourced from the Heritage Foundation database, while the remaining control variable data are obtained from the CEPII-Gravity database.

6.3   Benchmark Regression Analysis

Based on Formula (2), this study analyses the impact of the United States' supply chain review policy on the security level of China's semiconductor industry chain. As shown in Table 6.1, Column (1) includes only product and

Table 6.1   Impact of US Supply Chain Reviews on the Security of China's Semiconductor Industry Chain

	(1)	(2)	(3)
Treat × post	1.812***	1.562***	1.562***
	(310.00)	(209.61)	(18.01)
BORD		−1.346***	−1.346
		(−19.13)	(−1.28)
LANG		0.339***	0.339
		(6.33)	(0.55)
lnDIS		−2.489***	−2.489***
		(−85.84)	(−4.55)
lnGDPPC		0.700***	0.700
		(31.83)	(1.53)
lnECO		−0.285**	−0.285
		(−2.28)	(−0.26)
Constant	−28.112***	−8.459***	−8.459
	(−531.94)	(−13.10)	(−1.06)
Product Fixed Effects	Yes	Yes	Yes
Monthly Fixed Effects	Yes	Yes	Yes
Clustering Hierarchy	No	No	Country (Region)
Observations	88427	72040	72040
R^2	0.580	0.564	0.564

month fixed effects, Column (2) further includes control variables, and Column (3) performs standard error clustering based on Column (2). The results indicate that the coefficients of the explanatory variables are significantly positive, suggesting that the US supply chain review policy has increased the import concentration of semiconductor intermediate products, thereby reducing the security level of China's semiconductor industry chain, and Hypothesis 1 is supported.

Note: The statistics in brackets are t statistics; *, *, and **** indicate significance at the 10%, 5%, and 1% levels, respectively. If the regression results of the main variables are decimals, they are retained to three decimal places; otherwise, they are rounded to three decimal places. The same applies below.

6.4 Parallel Trend Test

One of the key assumptions of the double difference model is the parallel trend assumption (PTA). This assumption requires that, prior to the policy shock, the import concentration of the experimental group and the control group should have the same characteristics or trends. After the implementation of the US supply chain review policy, the import concentration of the two groups should exhibit significant differences. If the sample data does not meet the parallel trend assumption, it may lead to an overestimation or underestimation of the effectiveness of the US supply chain review policy. To address this, a parallel trend test is conducted, with the model as follows:

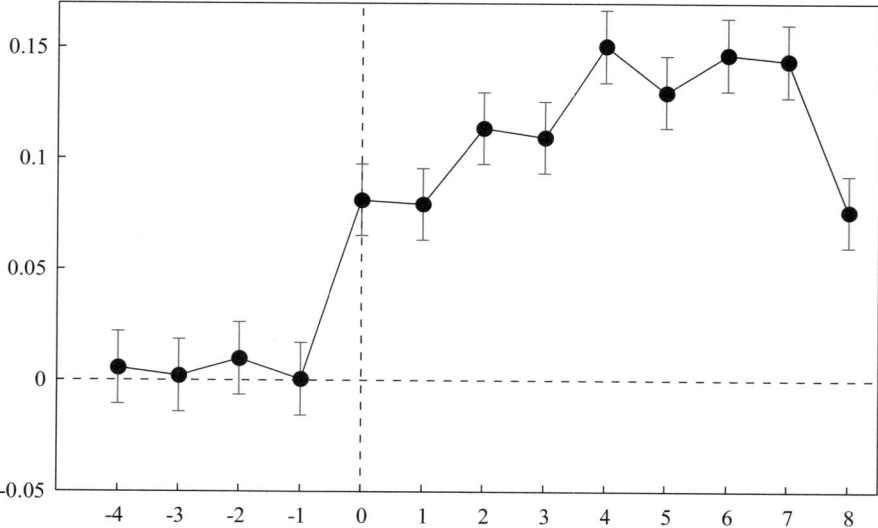

Fig. 6.1 Parallel trend test chart

$$\ln\mathrm{HHI}_{\mathrm{prct}} = \varphi + \sum_{m=-4}^{8} \theta^m \mathrm{Treat}_c \times \mathrm{post}_t^m + X_{\mathrm{prct}}\gamma + \omega_p + \mu_t + \varepsilon_{\mathrm{prct}} \qquad (6.2)$$

Among these, post_t^m represents the month in the virtual variable. The value rule is as follows: if the month t is the same as February 2021, the value is 1; otherwise, it is 0. Other variables are the same as those in the baseline model formula (6.1).

As shown in Fig. 6.1, prior to the impact of the US supply chain review policy (i.e., before February 2021), the import concentration of the treatment group and the control group remained parallel. However, after the impact of the US supply chain review policy, the import concentration of semiconductor intermediate products in the treatment group began to significantly exceed that of the control group. This indicates that the US supply chain review has a significant impact on the security level of China's semiconductor industry chain, consistent with the conclusions drawn from the basic regression analysis.

6.5   Endogeneity and Robustness Tests

6.5.1   Endogeneity Test

To reduce endogeneity and estimation biases caused by systematic differences between samples, the propensity score matching method (PSM-DID) was used to test endogeneity. Following the 1:1 nearest neighbour matching method using PSM (Zhao & Li 2021), we selected economic freedom, the logarithm of the geographical distance between China and trading partner country c, the logarithm of per capita GDP of trading partner country j, whether China and trading partner country j share a common border, and whether they share a common language as feature variables to select and match the control group, thereby enhancing the comparability of the two sample groups. Table 6.2, columns (1) and (2), respectively represent the results with and without the inclusion of control variables. The results indicate that the regression coefficients of the core explanatory variables are significant at the 1% level, suggesting that the impact of US supply chain review policies on the security level of China's semiconductor industry chain is significant and robust.

6.5.2   Robustness Tests

Exogenous Shock Tests. The global COVID-19 pandemic that began at the end of 2019 led to sustained economic downturns across countries, resulting in a significant decline in global trade volumes. The various policies and economic stimulus measures implemented by governments during the pandemic further disrupted the

Table 6.2   Regression results of endogeneity test

	(1)	(2)
Treat × post	1.996***	1.994***
	(2687.22)	(2279.50)
BORD		−0.005
		(−0.52)
LANG		0.004
		(0.53)
lnDIS		−0.015***
		(−3.26)
lnGDPPC		0.004
		(1.33)
lnECO		−0.015
		(−0.89)
Constant	−41.894***	−41.722***
	(−3712.49)	(−454.27)
Product Fixed Effects	Yes	Yes
Monthly Fixed Effects	Yes	Yes
Observations	35398	35398
R^2	0.996	0.996

existing structure of the semiconductor supply chain and international division of labour. The sample period for this section is January 2019 to October 2024, meaning that the pandemic may have had a significant impact on the security level of China's semiconductor supply chain during this period. Although time-fixed effects were controlled for, the pandemic's impact on the security level of China's semiconductor supply chain could not be fully absorbed. Therefore, the samples from 2020, 2021, and 2022, which were affected by the pandemic, were removed, and the regression analysis was conducted again. According to Column (1) of Table 6.3, the relevant conclusions remain valid, indicating that the baseline conclusions drawn in this section possess a certain degree of robustness.

Add control variables. To test the robustness of the research results, this section conducts robustness tests by adding control variables. If the research results remain significant after adding control variables, it indicates that the regression results have strong robustness. Specifically, three control variables are added one by one. The regression results are presented in Table 6.3. Column (2) represents the logarithm of the transportation capacity of trading countries (regions) (lnTransport), aiming to control for the moderating effect of infrastructure endowments on supply chain efficiency. The inclusion of this variable helps to eliminate estimation biases caused by differences in transportation efficiency. The data are sourced from the United Nations Conference on Trade and Development (UNCTAD) database. Column (3) represents the logarithm of the total population of trading countries (regions) (lnPOP), capturing the market size effect. The inclusion of this variable tests whether the research conclusions are influenced by differences in economic size, with data sourced from the World Bank database. Column (4) indicates whether the trading country (region) has signed a free trade agreement (FTA) with China, identifying the impact of institutional arrangements. The inclusion of this variable tests whether the impact of the US supply chain review policy is independent of existing institutional cooperation frameworks. Data are sourced from the CEPII-Gravity database. After adding control variables, the regression coefficients and significance levels of the core explanatory variables did not change significantly. The directions of the regression coefficients for other control variables remained consistent with the results of the baseline regression model, indicating that the results of the baseline model are robust.

Counterfactual test. The starting point for the impact of the US supply chain review policy is February 2021. In the period prior to February 2021, a random year was selected and set as the starting point for the US supply chain review policy. Using this new sample, the estimated coefficients of the core explanatory variables were re-estimated. Fig. 6.2 depicts the kernel density curves of the estimated coefficients obtained from 1,000 counterfactual tests. As shown in Fig. 6.2, randomly advancing the timing of the US supply chain review policy leads to a significant decline in the impact on the security level of China's semiconductor supply chain.

Table 6.3 Regression results of robustness test

	(1)	(2)	(3)	(4)
Treat × post	1.562***	1.564***	1.458***	1.562***
	(209.61)	(209.51)	(198.46)	(210.03)
BORD	−1.346***	−1.487***	−2.465***	−1.190***
	(−19.13)	(−18.87)	(−35.34)	(−16.83)
LANG	0.339***	0.344***	1.415***	0.437***
	(6.33)	(6.43)	(26.30)	(8.15)
lnDIS	−2.489***	−2.494***	−2.594***	−2.704***
	(−85.84)	(−85.94)	(−92.51)	(−86.95)
lnGDPPC	0.700***	0.613***	1.221***	0.653***
	(31.83)	(19.72)	(54.44)	(29.60)
lnECO	−0.285**	−0.389***	−0.043	−0.235*
	(−2.28)	(−3.05)	(−0.36)	(−1.88)
lnTransport		0.396***		
		(3.96)		
lnPOP			1.060***	
			(71.98)	
RTA				−0.739***
				(−18.84)
Constant	−8.459***	−8.555***	−32.004***	−6.087***
	(−13.10)	(−13.24)	(−45.46)	(−9.28)
Product Fixed Effects	Yes	Yes	Yes	Yes
Monthly Fixed Effects	Yes	Yes	Yes	Yes
Observations	72040	72040	72040	72040
R^2	0.564	0.564	0.593	0.566

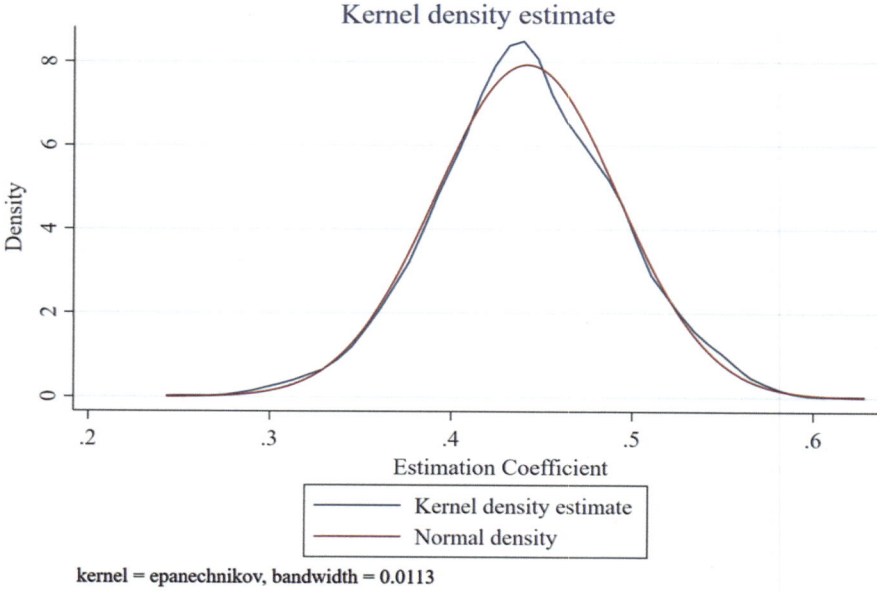

kernel = epanechnikov, bandwidth = 0.0113

Fig. 6.2   Counterfactual test

This also confirms from a counterfactual perspective that the US supply chain review policy has indeed reduced the security level of China's semiconductor supply chain.

6.6   Analysis of Influencing Mechanisms

The main empirical regression results confirm that the restructuring of the US supply chain has a negative impact on the security level of China's semiconductor industry chain. Based on theoretical analysis, this section examines how the security level of China's semiconductor industry chain is influenced by US supply chain reviews through three channels: enhancing the rationalisation of industrial structure, improving independent innovation capabilities, and increasing fiscal support. (1) A higher degree of industrial structure rationalisation implies greater coordination among industries and more efficient resource allocation (Gan et al. 2011). From the perspective of industrial chain security, a more rational industrial structure implies stronger and more stable interconnections between industries, thereby avoiding the vulnerability caused by over-reliance on a single industry or a few key links. Following the methodology (Gan et al. 2011), the Tyer Index is used to measure the rationality of industrial structure (structure$_{rt}$), with data sourced from the China Statistical Yearbook; (2) Enhancing independent innovation capabilities is the key to improving China's supply chain self-reliance and control (Zhang & Chen 2022).

The logarithm of the number of invention patent applications in China is used to represent the level of independent innovation (tech$_{rt}$), with data sourced from the National Intellectual Property Administration. (3) Fiscal policy support can effectively bridge the gap between the efficiency of resource allocation in emerging industries and the optimal allocation efficiency (Wang & Ma 2024). Reasonable and sustained increases in fiscal investment can inject vitality into all links of the industrial chain, help enterprises cope with risks such as market fluctuations and external shocks, and consolidate the coordination and stability of the industrial chain. The fiscal support intensity is measured by the ratio of general budget expenditure to regional GDP (finance$_{rt}$), with data sourced from the National Bureau of Statistics. The following model is established to analyse the channels of the aforementioned three levels:

$$\ln HHI_{prct} = \alpha + \beta Treat_c \times post_t + \delta Treat_c \times post_t \times factor_{rt} + X_{prct}\gamma + \omega_p + \mu_t + \varepsilon_{prct} \quad (6.3)$$

Among these, factor$_{rt}$ represent the degree of rationalisation of the industrial structure (structure$_{rt}$), the level of independent innovation (tech$_{rt}$), and the intensity of fiscal support (finance$_{rt}$).

Table 6.4   Impact of US Supply Chain Reviews on the Security of the Semiconductor Industry Chain

	(1)	(2)	(3)
Treat × post	0.359***	13.759***	5.522***
	(11.15)	(9.17)	(16.01)
Treat × post × structure	−1.803***		
	(−6.64)		
Treat × post × tech		−0.966***	
		(−9.13)	
Treat × post × finance			−18.588***
			(−16.23)
BORD	−2.168	−1.998	−1.874
	(−1.23)	(−1.19)	(−1.25)
LANG	0.595	0.531	0.497
	(0.59)	(0.55)	(0.59)
lnDIS	−3.898***	−3.721***	−3.359***
	(−5.09)	(−4.94)	(−4.96)
lnGDPPC	1.068	1.052	0.919
	(1.50)	(1.55)	(1.50)
lnECO	−0.521	−0.204	−0.436
	(−0.26)	(−0.09)	(−0.28)
Constant	10.275	−219.016***	−66.767***
	(0.75)	(−7.21)	(−4.89)
Product Fixed Effects	Yes	Yes	Yes
Observations	72040	72040	72040
R^2	0.321	0.348	0.420

The empirical results are presented in Table 6.4. Columns (1) to (3) represent the interaction terms between the core explanatory variables and the rationalisation of industrial structure, independent innovation capacity, and fiscal support intensity, respectively. The results indicate that the coefficients of the interaction terms are significantly negative, suggesting that under the impact of US supply chain review policies, improving industrial structure rationalisation, enhancing independent innovation capabilities, and increasing fiscal support can mitigate some of the negative effects of US supply chain review policies on the security of China's semiconductor supply chain, thereby alleviating the unfavourable situation faced by China's semiconductor supply chain.

6.7 Policy Implications

Based on the above conclusions, the following policy implications are drawn:

First, optimise the import structure and diversify supply source risks across multiple dimensions. Currently, the risk volatility of China's semiconductor industry chain is on the rise, and different countries (regions) exhibit differentiated risk characteristics. From a macro level, a systematic import strategy planning mechanism should be established to guide enterprises in expanding diversified import channels based on the risk ratings of each country (region). For high-risk regions such as the Netherlands and Saudi Arabia, trade policy guidance and industrial cooperation adjustments should be used to gradually reduce import dependency. For economies like South Korea, which face both high import volumes and high supply chain risks, dynamic monitoring and quota management mechanisms should be established to reasonably control import scale and timing, thereby mitigating potential risks stemming from supply concentration and enhancing the resilience of the entire supply chain against external shocks.

Second, implement regional coordination policies tailored to local conditions to strengthen overall coordinated development. There are significant imbalances among China's regions in terms of import concentration and risks faced by their semiconductor supply chains. Based on this, regional industrial coordination policies tailored to local conditions should be formulated. Special industrial support funds should be increased for high-risk regions to help them improve industrial infrastructure and reduce import concentration. At the same time, low-risk regions should be encouraged to fully leverage their own advantages through cross-regional industrial alliances, joint industrial park development, and other forms to deepen regional collaboration in areas such as technology, talent, and markets. This will foster a national semiconductor supply chain collaboration framework characterised by complementary strengths and shared risks, thereby comprehensively enhancing the overall security and resilience of the supply chain.

Third, target critical links and comprehensively enhance risk-resilience across all links. In the semiconductor industry chain, downstream data transmission modules, wind turbines, accelerator cards, industrial robots, and upstream electronic-grade special gases have already shown relatively high risk levels. In response, the government should integrate multiple resources to build industrial technology innovation consortiums centred on key links, bringing together the scientific research strengths of universities, research institutes, and enterprises to conduct joint research on key technical challenges. It should also establish ongoing scientific research project funding programmes to ensure the stability of R&D investment.

At the same time, it is necessary to improve the material reserve system for key links, formulate graded and classified emergency response plans, strengthen information sharing and coordination between upstream and downstream enterprises, and ensure that production can be quickly restored and supply guaranteed in the event of various emergencies. Fourth, adhere to independent innovation and build a solid foundation of independence and control. The US supply chain review has had a significant negative impact on the security of China's semiconductor industry chain, highlighting the key role of strengthening independence and control in ensuring the security of the semiconductor industry chain.

Improve mechanisms for cultivating and attracting innovative talent, establish semiconductor talent training bases in collaboration with universities, and introduce preferential policies for attracting high-end overseas talent to build a high-quality, professional domestic innovative talent pool. Additionally, actively foster a favourable industrial innovation ecosystem, strengthen intellectual property protection, encourage enterprises to pursue technological iteration and domestic substitution, and solidify the foundation of self-reliance and control in the semiconductor industry chain from multiple dimensions including technology, talent, and institutional frameworks.

Fifth, systematically promote industrial upgrading and deeply optimise industrial structure and layout. Given that improving the rationality of industrial structure and increasing fiscal support can reduce supply chain risks, a systemic approach should be adopted to promote semiconductor industry upgrading and structural optimisation through comprehensive policy tools. On the one hand, it is necessary to increase financial support for core technology research and development in the semiconductor industry, establish special industrial development funds, and focus on basic research and application development projects in key areas such as chip design and manufacturing processes. Through policy measures such as tax incentives and financial subsidies, guide social capital to flow into weak links and key technology areas of the semiconductor industry chain, and encourage enterprises to carry out technological innovation and product upgrades. On the other hand, industrial planning and guidance should be strengthened. Based on the resource endowments and industrial foundations of various regions, the upstream, midstream, and downstream segments of the industrial chain should be reasonably laid out to promote the cluster-based development of industries, forming an industrial ecosystem with clear divisions of labour and efficient coordination. This will enhance the overall resilience and security of the industrial chain through the deep optimisation of the industrial structure.

References

Aghion, P., Cai, J., Dewatripont, M., Du, L., Harrison, A., & Legros, P. (2015). Industrial policy and competition. *American Economic Journal: Macroeconomics, 7*(4), 1–32. https://www.aea-web.org/articles?id=10.1257/mac.20120103

Arrow, K. J. (1962). Economic welfare and the allocation of resources for invention. In *The rate and direction of inventive activity: Economic and social factors* (pp. 609–626). Princeton University Press. https://doi.org/10.1515/9781400879762-024

Baldwin, R., & Freeman, R. (2022). Risks and global supply chains: What we know and what we need to know. *Annual Review of Economics, 14*, 153–180.

Castells, M. (2011). *The rise of the network society* (2nd ed.). Wiley-Blackwell.

Fajgelbaum, P., Goldberg, P. K., Kennedy, P. J., & Khandelwal, A. K. (2021). The return to protectionism. *Quarterly Journal of Economics, 136*(2), 1–58.

Gan, C., Zheng, R., & Yu, D. (2011). The impact of China's industrial structure transformation on economic growth and fluctuations. *Economic Research, 46*(5), 4–16, 31.

Gereffi, G., Humphrey, J., & Sturgeon, T. (2005). The governance of global value chains. *Review of International Political Economy, 12*(1), 78–104.

Lee, K., & Lim, C. (2001). Technological regimes, catching-up and leapfrogging: Findings from the Korean industries. *Research Policy, 30*(3), 459–483.

Perez, C. (2002). *Technological revolutions and financial capital: The dynamics of bubbles and golden ages*. Edward Elgar.

Porter, M. E. (1998). Clusters and the new economics of competition. *Harvard Business Review, 76*(6), 77–90.

Rodrik, D. (2004). Industrial policy for the twenty-first century. *CEPR Discussion Paper* No. 4767.

Shen, G., & Wang, Y. (2024). The reshaping of the US supply chain and the resilience of China's foreign trade industry chain and supply chain. *Journal of East China Normal University (Philosophy and Social Sciences Edition), 56*(4), 155–177, 182. https://doi.org/10.16382/j.cnki.1000-5579.2024.04.014

Stone, A. (1986). The economic institutions of capitalism: Firms, markets, relational contracting, by Oliver E. Williamson. *American Political Science Review, 80*(4), 1424–1425.

Teece, D. J., Pisano, G., & Shuen, A. (1997). Dynamic capabilities and strategic management. *Strategic Management Journal, 18*(7), 509–533.

Wang, Y., & Ma, Q. (2024). The resource allocation effects of fiscal subsidies on strategic emerging industries: The case of the photovoltaic industry. *Economic Management, 46*(3), 64–85.

White House. (2021). *Building resilient supply chains, revitalizing American manufacturing, and fostering broad-based growth.*

Zhang, J., & Chen, R. (2022). Risk assessment and maintenance strategies for China's industrial chain and supply chain security. *Reform, (4)*, 12–20.

Zhao, F., & Li, L. (2021). Research on the entrepreneurial effects of intellectual property rights systems: Evidence from the construction of intellectual property demonstration cities in China. *Industrial Economics Research, (6)*, 44–57.

Chapter 7
Optimisation of China's Semiconductor Industry Layout

Tiantian Wang

Abstract Chapter 7 explores strategic approaches to optimising the spatial layout of China's semiconductor industry. It emphasises the importance of aligning with global industrial trends and strengthening regional coordination to foster technological self-reliance and harness regional comparative advantages. The chapter articulates two core strategic objectives: enhancing global competitiveness and safeguarding industrial security, both underpinned by forward-looking planning and policy support. It further outlines several strategic pathways, including enhanced domestic regional coordination, integration of international resources, and the internationalisation of industrial parks and production bases. Through a combination of policy incentives and market-driven technological upgrading, the chapter presents a roadmap for transitioning China's semiconductor sector towards a high-end, resilient, and globally integrated configuration.

Keywords Semiconductor Industry Layout • Regional Coordination • Global Competitiveness • Industrial Security

7.1 Optimisation of Semiconductor Industry Layout and Strategic Goal Setting from a Global Perspective

7.1.1 Follow the Development Laws of the Semiconductor Industry and the Principles of Regional Coordination and Development

In the increasingly globalised semiconductor industry environment, China's semiconductor industry must thoroughly understand the laws of international industrial development and flexibly apply the principles of regional coordination and

© The Author(s) 2026
T. Wang et al., *China's Semiconductor Industry Strategy*,
SpringerBriefs in Economics,
https://doi.org/10.1007/978-981-95-3332-9_7

development when optimising its layout to ensure that the industry can maintain a leading position in global competition. The semiconductor industry is a highly globalised sector, with its technological innovation, market demand, production capacity, and capital flows all significantly influenced by the international industrial landscape. Therefore, China's industrial layout must not only adhere to the universal laws of global industrial development but also leverage the unique advantages of each region through scientific and reasonable optimisation to achieve sustained competitiveness.

First, the development of the semiconductor industry follows the global patterns of technological progress and deepening of the industrial chain. With the continuous development of emerging technologies such as 5G communications, artificial intelligence (AI), and high-performance computing (HPC), the global semiconductor industry's technology cycle is constantly shortening, driving continuous innovation in production processes and product design (Semiconductor Industry Association 2023; Shalf 2020). This technological transformation requires China's semiconductor industry to pay close attention to changes in global technology trends and breakthroughs in cutting-edge technologies during the optimisation of its layout in order to maintain its competitiveness in the global industrial chain. China should increase investment in core technology research and development, especially in the areas of high-end chips, advanced manufacturing processes, and key materials, to ensure that industrial development does not rely on external technology, promote technological self-reliance and control, and further consolidate its position in the global industrial chain.

With the high degree of division of labour and globalisation in the global semiconductor industry, collaboration and cooperation within the industrial chain are crucial. Different regions play different roles in the semiconductor industrial chain and have their own unique technological and resource advantages. For example, Chinese Taiwan and South Korea have strong technical advantages in semiconductor manufacturing, while the United States dominates in chip design and R&D. When optimising industrial layout, China must fully consider the resource endowments and industrial advantages of each region and form complementary effects within the global industrial chain through cross-regional collaboration. Regional coordination should not be limited to domestic cooperation but should also be expanded to international cooperation through technology sharing, capital investment, and strategic partnerships to enhance the innovation capacity and risk-resilience of the entire industrial chain.

The principle of regional coordination requires effective resource allocation and complementary cooperation between different geographical locations and industrial links. China's semiconductor industry should optimise the distribution of its industrial chain based on the characteristics of each region. For example, the eastern region has rich technical accumulation, infrastructure, and capital advantages, making it an ideal base for high-end design, R&D, and manufacturing; while the central and western regions, with their advantages in land and labour costs, are suitable for developing manufacturing, packaging, and testing links. Through reasonable regional layout, it is possible to not only improve resource utilisation efficiency, but also promote technology transfer and talent exchange, thereby enhancing the overall competitiveness of the industrial chain. Furthermore, regional coordination and development should avoid excessive concentration and instead optimise the allocation of resources and advantages to avoid over-reliance on a single region for the industry and enhance the overall stability of the industrial chain.

In addition, in the context of globalisation, regional coordination and development also means that China must establish closer cross-regional strategic cooperation in the international market. For example, relying on the Belt and Road Initiative, China can strengthen cooperation with other countries and regions to promote the global layout of the semiconductor industry chain and ensure its competitive advantage in the global market. By strengthening technical cooperation and market penetration on a global scale, China's semiconductor industry can enhance its technical capabilities and influence in the international market.

In summary, adhering to the laws of global industrial development and the principles of regional coordination and development is the core strategy for optimising the layout of China's semiconductor industry. By deeply understanding global technological and market trends and combining the resource advantages of different regions, China can occupy a favourable position in the global semiconductor industry competition and promote the industry's leapfrog development. This strategy will not only help enhance the independent innovation capabilities of China's semiconductor industry but also further strengthen the stability and overall competitiveness of the industrial chain through regional coordination and cooperation, enabling China to gain strategic initiative in the global industry.

7.1.2 Setting Goals for Enhancing Global Competitiveness and Ensuring Industrial Security

Against the backdrop of intensifying global competition in the semiconductor industry and profound changes in the international landscape, setting strategic goals to enhance global competitiveness and ensure industrial security is of critical importance to the long-term development of China's semiconductor industry. As international markets become increasingly diversified and the global semiconductor industry grows more complex, ensuring the stability and security of the industrial chain has become particularly crucial. Therefore, enhancing global competitiveness and ensuring industrial security have become the core strategic objectives for optimising the layout of China's semiconductor industry.

First, enhancing global competitiveness is the primary goal of China's semiconductor industry development. With rapid technological innovation in semiconductors and surging global demand for high-end chips, AI chips, 5G chips, and other products, competition in the global semiconductor industry is becoming increasingly fierce. To stand out in this competitive environment, China's semiconductor industry must continuously enhance its global competitiveness through technological innovation, brand building, market expansion, and other multi-dimensional measures. Specifically, China should focus on strengthening basic research and technological breakthroughs, achieving major progress in areas such as chip design, advanced manufacturing processes, and materials research and development, gradually reducing its dependence on external technologies, and enhancing its independent innovation capabilities. At the same time, it should promote the high-end and intelligent development of the industry, enhance the added value of its products, and strengthen its competitiveness and influence in the international market.

While enhancing global competitiveness, industrial security is also a strategic goal that cannot be ignored. The globalisation of the semiconductor industry and the high degree of dependence on supply chains pose serious challenges to industrial security (Bown 2021). Especially in the current international political and economic environment, the increase in risk factors such as trade barriers, technology blockades, and supply chain disruptions pose a threat to the stability of China's semiconductor industry (Varas et al. 2020). Therefore, ensuring industrial security must be the top priority in the optimisation of China's semiconductor industry layout. To achieve this goal, China should adopt multiple strategies to ensure the stability of the industrial chain. First, it is essential to strengthen independent research and development and production capabilities for key technologies and core materials to ensure that 'chokepoint' technologies are not constrained by external factors. Second, the global supply chain layout should be optimised to enhance supply chain diversification and flexibility, reduce over-reliance on single markets and suppliers, and improve the resilience and stability of the industrial chain. Finally, cross-border cooperation should be promoted, and active technical cooperation and innovation sharing with global leading companies should be pursued to ensure that China's semiconductor industry maintains a stable position in the global supply chain.

In addition, policy guidance and resource allocation are crucial to achieving these strategic goals. The Chinese government should formulate forward-looking policy frameworks and industry standards, provide necessary financial support and technical guidance to help enterprises innovate and develop. For example, the government can encourage enterprises to increase R&D investment and improve their technological level through policy measures such as tax incentives, R&D funding, and talent training. At the same time, it should strengthen industry supervision and intellectual property protection to create a favourable industrial environment and ensure industrial security and sustainable development. At the same time, the Chinese government should strengthen international exchanges and cooperation to enhance the competitiveness of China's semiconductor industry in the global industrial chain and secure a favourable position in international trade rules to further safeguard industrial security.

In summary, enhancing global competitiveness and ensuring industrial security are key components of the strategic objectives for optimising the layout of China's semiconductor industry. By strengthening independent innovation, enhancing the resilience and security of the industrial chain, and optimising international cooperation, China can secure a favourable position in global semiconductor industry competition, enhance the industry's global influence, and ensure sustainable development in a complex international environment. This strategy is not only crucial for the long-term development of China's semiconductor industry but also an important step towards achieving self-reliance and strength in science and technology.

7.1.3   Aligning with Global Industrial Development Trends and Setting Scientific and Forward-Looking Goals

In the process of optimising the layout of the semiconductor industry, the scientific nature and forward-looking nature of objectives are of critical importance. The development of China's semiconductor industry must not only be grounded in the current technological, market, and policy environment but also closely align with global trends, anticipate future technological and market changes, and establish strategic objectives with a long-term perspective and feasibility. Only by ensuring the scientific and forward-looking nature of these objectives can China's semiconductor industry maintain its leading position in intense international competition while preparing adequately for future challenges.

First, the scientific nature of goal-setting must be based on objective data and the laws of industrial development. Throughout the global semiconductor industry's development, technological innovation has always been the core driving force propelling the industry forward, particularly through continuous breakthroughs in chip design, manufacturing processes, and materials research, which have driven progress across the entire sector (Thompson & Parthasarathy 2006). To ensure the scientific nature of goals, China's semiconductor industry should conduct in-depth analyses of the current technological landscape and industrial chain structure, identify technical bottlenecks and potential breakthrough areas, and establish reasonable objectives aligned with the industry's current technical capabilities and market demands. In addition, changes in policy support and the international competitive environment must also be taken into consideration to ensure that the goals are forward-looking and can be effectively implemented in practice. Policy support, especially policies that encourage innovation and improve the resilience of the industrial chain, should be closely integrated with global technology trends to promote the sustainable development of China's semiconductor industry.

Second, the forward-looking nature of goal setting must keep pace with the future development trends of the global semiconductor industry. With the continuous application of emerging technologies such as artificial intelligence (AI), 5G communications, high-performance computing (HPC), and quantum computing, the global semiconductor industry is facing a wave of rapid technological development. Future semiconductor products will be more intelligent, personalised, and efficient, while traditional production models and product types will gradually fail to meet market demand (Shalf 2020). Therefore, the goals of China's semiconductor industry should be closely aligned with the innovation and application of these emerging technologies and take an early lead in future markets. For example, AI chips are an important direction for the future of the semiconductor field. Major global technology companies have already invested heavily in research and development. With the popularisation of deep learning and big data applications, the demand for high-performance AI chips will increase significantly in the future. China's semiconductor industry should take the lead in AI chip technology research and development, promote independent innovation, and secure a leading position in the global market.

In addition, the trend towards deeper integration and greater complexity in the global supply chain also requires forward-looking goal setting. With the increasing multipolarisation of the international market, geopolitical changes and market demand uncertainties, the stability of the semiconductor industry chain is facing challenges. Therefore, in the process of optimising its layout, China's semiconductor industry should attach greater importance to improving the security and autonomy of the industry chain. In particular, there are still asymmetries and uncertainties in the global market in terms of the supply of high-end manufacturing equipment, advanced packaging technologies and key raw materials (such as rare earth metals).

To address these challenges, the Chinese semiconductor industry should focus on enhancing the integrity of its independent supply chain, particularly in key technologies and materials, through technological innovation and policy support, gradually reducing its reliance on external resources to ensure the autonomy and control of the industrial chain. The forward-looking nature of the goals should not only be reflected in technology and the supply chain, but also in industrial synergy and global cooperation. With the acceleration of global economic integration, it is difficult for individual countries and enterprises to independently cope with global competition.

The goal of China's semiconductor industry should not be limited to improving domestic technology, but should also be committed to strengthening cooperation and competition on a global scale. For example, China can strengthen technical exchanges and investment cooperation with global semiconductor industry clusters (such as Silicon Valley, Chinese Taiwan, and Singapore) to promote the internationalisation of the industry and further increase its share and influence in the global market.

In summary, the scientific nature and forward-looking nature of goal setting are core principles of China's semiconductor industry strategic planning. Only by deeply understanding global industrial development trends, combining domestic and international technological advantages, market demands, and policy orientations, and establishing strategic goals that align with the current industrial landscape while addressing future challenges, can China ensure its semiconductor industry steadily advances in global competition, continuously driving technological breakthroughs and industrial upgrades. Through this process, China will not only enhance its position within the global semiconductor supply chain but also make positive contributions to global scientific and technological innovation.

7.2 Regional Coordination and Global Industrial Chain Integration Strategies

7.2.1 Strengthen Domestic Regional Industrial Cooperation and Enhance the Synergistic Effects of the Industrial Chain

Against the backdrop of accelerating globalisation and technological innovation, the competitiveness of China's semiconductor industry depends not only on breakthroughs in technological research and development, but also on the efficiency of industrial chain collaboration. In order to secure a favourable position in the global market, it is crucial to enhance the overall efficiency of the industrial chain. Strengthening domestic regional industrial collaboration and enhancing the synergistic effects of the industrial chain have become key measures for promoting the high-quality development of China's semiconductor industry.

Regional Collaborative Development: Optimising Resource Allocation. China's semiconductor industry is widely distributed, covering all stages from upstream materials and design to downstream packaging and testing. Different regions possess distinct resource advantages and industrial accumulations. For example, the Yangtze River Delta and Pearl River Delta regions have a large concentration of high-end talent and advanced manufacturing capabilities, while the central and western regions have advantages in terms of land, labour and policy environment. By strengthening collaboration between these regions, resources can be better optimised, avoiding duplication and waste, thereby improving the overall efficiency of the industrial chain.

To better promote domestic regional collaboration, the government should encourage different regions to complement each other's strengths in different links of the industrial chain. In design and R&D-intensive industrial links, the government can guide and incentivise more high-end talent and technology companies to gather in regions with strong technical and innovative capabilities. In manufacturing and packaging and testing links, more production resources can be directed to regions with lower labour and land costs to reduce production costs and increase production capacity. Information sharing and technological coordination.

To enhance the synergy of the industrial chain, it is also necessary to focus on information sharing and technological coordination. The semiconductor industry is highly dependent on the flow of information and technology, and close technological interaction and timely market feedback between different links are key to enhancing overall competitiveness (Dedrick et al. 2010). Domestic enterprises and research institutions in different regions can establish cooperation platforms to strengthen technological exchanges and cooperation, form sharing mechanisms, accelerate the transformation and application of technologies, and promote the enhancement of innovation capabilities. In addition, enterprises across regions should strengthen strategic cooperation and share market intelligence, technological breakthroughs, and production capacity.

In different links of the industrial chain, such as material supply, chip design, and manufacturing processes, enterprises can engage in joint innovation, jointly develop advanced products that meet market demand, promote technological synergy, and enhance the overall efficiency and risk resistance of the industrial chain. Policy support and the role of local governments.

The government plays an indispensable role in promoting domestic regional industrial collaboration. By formulating more flexible regional cooperation policies and providing tax incentives and financial support, local governments can effectively promote cooperation and resource sharing among enterprises within the region (Porter 1998). For example, cross-regional innovation funds can be established to encourage enterprises in different regions to form partnerships in areas such as technology research and development and market development, further promoting vertical and horizontal integration of the industrial chain. At the same time, local governments can also formulate regional industrial development plans, clarify the key development areas of each link in the industrial chain, and guide the coordinated development of industries within the region. This will not only enhance the overall efficiency of the industrial chain, but also help local industries maintain their competitive edge in globalisation.

Promote industrial agglomeration and industrial chain integration. The ultimate goal of regional coordination is to promote industrial agglomeration and industrial chain integration (Feser & Bergman 2000). By strengthening collaboration among different regions within the country, the formation and development of industrial clusters can be enhanced. For example, around core areas of the semiconductor industry, such as Suzhou, Shanghai, and Shenzhen, more closely integrated industrial clusters can be established to form a complete industrial chain from R&D to production, packaging, and testing. Industrial clustering can further improve resource utilisation efficiency, reduce transaction costs, and enhance market competitiveness through economies of scale. In addition, industrial chain integration should not only be reflected in technological innovation and production processes, but also in industrial policies and talent cultivation. For example, through regional technology innovation centres and industry-academia-research collaboration, the industrialisation process of technologies can be accelerated, and the overall technological level and market response speed of the industrial chain can be improved.

In summary, strengthening domestic regional industrial collaboration is an important path to enhancing the synergistic effects of the semiconductor industry chain. By optimising resource allocation, strengthening information sharing, promoting technological collaboration, and providing policy support, different regions within China can complement each other's strengths in different segments of the semiconductor industry chain, thereby improving the overall efficiency and competitiveness of the industry chain. This will not only help enhance the competitiveness of China's semiconductor industry in the global market, but also help form a more stable and flexible industrial ecosystem to ensure the sustainable development of the industry.

7.2.2 Accelerate the Integration of Domestic and International Resources and Optimise the Global Industrial Chain Layout

As global competition in the semiconductor industry intensifies, resource integration has become an important strategy for promoting industrial upgrading and globalisation. To secure a leading position in the international market, China's semiconductor industry must accelerate the integration of domestic and international resources, optimise the industrial chain layout, and enhance global competitiveness. By effectively integrating domestic and international resources and optimising the industrial chain layout, China can not only enhance its position in the global industrial chain but also strengthen the industry's innovation capabilities, flexibility, and risk-resistance capabilities.

Accelerate domestic resource integration and improve industrial chain synergy efficiency. Domestic resource integration is the foundation for enhancing the competitiveness of the semiconductor industry (Varas et al. 2020). Different regions in China possess distinct advantages in industrial development. How to efficiently integrate these advantages and promote efficient synergy within the industrial chain has become the key to optimising industrial chain layout. First, it is necessary to establish a more closely integrated industrial synergy mechanism within the country. The various links in the industrial chain across regions should be precisely aligned based on market demand, technological capabilities, and resource advantages to avoid duplicate construction and inefficient competition. For example, regions such as the Yangtze River Delta and Pearl River Delta have relatively complete semiconductor industry infrastructure, while central and western regions have lower production costs and abundant resources. The advantages of these regions should be optimally allocated through policy guidance and industrial alignment. By establishing regional collaboration platforms and strengthening cooperation in areas such as technology sharing, information exchange, and talent training, the synergy efficiency of the industrial chain can be enhanced, driving the steady growth of China's semiconductor industry.

International resource integration: Deeply participate in the global industrial chain. In addition to domestic resource integration, international resource integration is also crucial for optimising the global industrial chain layout (Varas et al. 2020). The global semiconductor supply chain is highly globalised, with production and technology in every link—from raw material supply to manufacturing processes, product design, and market sales—often spanning national borders. To meet global market demand and competition, China's semiconductor industry must actively participate in the division of labour and collaboration within the global supply chain and fully leverage the resource allocation advantages brought by globalisation. Chinese companies can strengthen cooperation with global leading enterprises through mergers and acquisitions, partnerships, and investments to gain access to advanced technologies, market information, and global resources. For example, in recent years, Chinese companies have acquired advanced semiconductor design technologies and manufacturing capabilities from the United States, Europe, and other regions through mergers and acquisitions, which has played a crucial role in enhancing the global competitiveness of China's semiconductor industry. At the same time, Chinese companies can also leverage the Belt and Road Initiative to strengthen cooperation with emerging market countries around the world, promoting the optimisation of global resource allocation and layout in the semiconductor industry.

Optimise the global industrial chain layout and enhance global competitiveness. The core of optimising the global industrial chain layout is to improve the flexibility and risk resistance of the global industrial chain through resource integration. Faced with a complex and changing international market environment, the stability and flexibility of the industrial chain are of paramount importance. By optimising its global layout, China can better respond to changes in global market demand, geopolitical risks, and uncertainties such as the global pandemic. In the global industrial chain layout, the first step is to enhance the diversification of global production capacity. For example, China can further optimise the production links in the semiconductor industry chain and build manufacturing plants and R&D centres in different countries and regions to avoid over-reliance on resources in a single region. In particular, in terms of the supply of key materials (such as rare earth metals and silicon materials), it is necessary to ensure a diversified supply source to reduce the risk of fluctuations in the international market. Second, enhance the synergy of the supply chain. There are close links between the various links in the semiconductor industry. China should form effective synergies between the upstream raw materials, design, manufacturing, and packaging and testing links through global cooperation to avoid bottlenecks in a single link dragging down overall efficiency. Strengthening the linkage between upstream and downstream industrial chains, especially in terms of technology sharing and production planning, can effectively reduce production costs and improve production efficiency.

Promote innovation and technical cooperation to upgrade the technological level of the industrial chain. Resource integration is not just about the flow of capital; technical cooperation and innovation also play a crucial role. China's semiconductor industry should strengthen international technical cooperation to upgrade the overall technological level of the industrial chain. Introducing advanced global technologies and accelerating independent innovation can effectively enhance the core competitiveness of the industry. Chinese companies can strengthen technological innovation cooperation by establishing research and development centres, cooperating with global semiconductor technology companies, and participating in the formulation of international standards. In particular, in emerging fields such as AI chips, 5G communication chips, and high-performance computing, technical cooperation and joint research and development will help to quickly break through technical bottlenecks and seize market opportunities.

The role of policy support and international cooperation. Optimising the global industrial chain layout requires strong government policy support. In the process of resource integration, the government can help enterprises obtain resources in domestic and foreign markets through policy measures such as financial support, tax incentives, and talent introduction. In addition, the government should promote international trade cooperation and provide strong policy support for domestic enterprises to expand into international markets. For example, the Chinese government can reduce international trade barriers and promote the expansion of the semiconductor industry in the global market through the construction of free trade zones and multilateral trade agreements. In addition, the government should strengthen supervision in areas such as intellectual property protection and anti-monopoly policies to provide a stable environment for international cooperation.

Accelerating the integration of domestic and international resources and optimising the global industrial chain layout are key strategies for enhancing the global competitiveness of China's semiconductor industry. By optimising the allocation of domestic resources and efficiently integrating international resources, China can drive technological innovation, production capacity diversification, and synergistic effects across the global industrial chain. This will enable China to better respond to changes and challenges in the global market and lay a solid foundation for the sustainable development of the industry. Meanwhile, the promotional role of policy support and international cooperation will also provide a more favourable external environment for resource integration.

7.2.3 Promote Coordinated Development Among Different Regions Within the Country and Enhance the Overall Competitiveness of Industries

Against the backdrop of intensifying global competition in the semiconductor industry, the advantages of a single region or a single link in the chain are no longer sufficient to meet complex and changing market demands. In order to enhance the overall competitiveness of China's semiconductor industry, promoting coordinated development among different regions within the country has become critical. By coordinating the industrial layout, resource allocation, and technological cooperation among different regions, it is possible to not only improve the overall efficiency of the domestic industrial chain but also secure a more advantageous position in the global industrial chain.

Regional industrial coordination: fostering complementary advantages. China's semiconductor industry is widely distributed, with different regions possessing distinct characteristics in terms of technological capabilities, industrial foundations, and market demands. For example, the Yangtze River Delta and Pearl River Delta regions, with their strong technical foundations, R&D capabilities, and comprehensive industrial support systems, have become core areas for semiconductor design and high-end manufacturing. In contrast, central and western regions, with their lower land and labour costs, have become important development bases for manufacturing and packaging. Therefore, to promote coordinated development across regions, it is essential to fully leverage each region's strengths and enhance collaboration between regions to achieve complementary advantages across the supply chain and different stages. The government should formulate flexible policies based on the characteristics of each region to guide capital, technology, and talent towards key links in the industrial chain. For example, coastal regions can focus on developing high-end chip design and R&D, while central and western regions can continue to strengthen the manufacturing sector and attract more manufacturing and packaging and testing enterprises through policy support. Through such regional layout, the resource advantages of each region can be maximised, and homogenised competition can be avoided.

Strengthen technological coordination and innovation cooperation within regions. In addition to resource allocation and optimisation, technological coordination and innovation cooperation are another key factor in promoting coordinated regional development. Major domestic semiconductor companies and scientific research institutions should strengthen cross-regional technological cooperation and innovation platform construction to promote the transformation and application of technological achievements. Through cross-regional technological collaboration, innovation in all links such as design, manufacturing, and packaging and testing can be promoted, which not only improves the technological level of the industrial chain but also accelerates the rapid application of technology in different links. In addition, enterprises within the region can also join forces to tackle technical challenges and conduct joint research and development. The state and local governments should promote industry-university-research cooperation through financial support and policy guidance, especially in areas such as advanced manufacturing processes, semiconductor materials, and new packaging technologies, to enhance the overall technical capabilities of the industrial chain through innovation cooperation within and outside the region.

Talent mobility and regional talent cultivation. Talent is the core resource in semiconductor industry competition. Due to differences in industrial foundations and development stages, there are gaps in talent attraction and cultivation across regions. To promote coordinated development across regions, efforts must be intensified to attract and cultivate high-end talent, and facilitate talent mobility between regions. Governments can establish regional talent exchange platforms to promote cross-regional talent mobility, optimising the allocation of technical and human resources during industrial development. At the same time, efforts should be made to strengthen talent cultivation in key areas of the semiconductor industry chain, particularly in chip design, manufacturing processes, and materials science. This can be achieved through the establishment of special funds, cooperative projects, and academic exchanges to accelerate talent cultivation and reserves.

Regional policy coordination and industry chain integration. Government policy support is crucial to promoting coordinated development across regions in China. Local governments should formulate development strategies tailored to their regional characteristics based on the national semiconductor industry development plan and their own industrial foundations and resource endowments. The government should also strengthen policy coordination to avoid policy conflicts or duplication of construction in industrial development between different regions. For example, regional industrial alliances or industrial clusters can be established to promote policy alignment and resource sharing between different regions, thereby improving the integration efficiency of the industrial chain. At the same time, the government can guide capital flows to the weak links in the midstream and downstream of the industrial chain to ensure the development and upgrading of each link, thereby enhancing the overall competitiveness and resilience of the industrial chain.

Optimise regional market expansion and external cooperation. Domestic regions should also strengthen market expansion and external cooperation to further enhance their position in the global semiconductor industry chain. Through cooperation between domestic and foreign enterprises, market development and internationalisation should be promoted, and the transformation of China's semiconductor industry from a 'manufacturing powerhouse' to an 'innovation powerhouse' should be gradually advanced. For example, under the Belt and Road Initiative, China can expand its market share in the semiconductor industry by increasing foreign investment and cooperation, especially in emerging markets such as Asia, Africa, and Latin America. At the same time, domestic enterprises should also strengthen cooperation with leading international semiconductor enterprises to share markets, technologies, and resources and enhance their global competitiveness.

Promoting coordinated development among various regions in China is a key strategy for enhancing the overall competitiveness of China's semiconductor industry. By optimising resource allocation, promoting technological synergy and innovation cooperation, strengthening talent cultivation, implementing policy coordination, and expanding markets, the overall efficiency and competitiveness of the domestic industrial chain can be effectively enhanced. As cooperation and coordination among regions strengthen, China's semiconductor industry will be able to occupy a more important position in the global industrial chain, promote the sustainable development of the industry, form a more robust industrial ecosystem, and ensure that the industry maintains its leading position in future international competition.

7.3 Internationalisation Development Pathways for Key Industrial Parks and Bases

7.3.1 Planning and Construction Benchmarked Against International Advanced Parks: From Park Construction to Operation and Management

Against the backdrop of rapid development in the global semiconductor industry, the planning and construction of industrial parks have become critical factors in enhancing the overall competitiveness of the sector. Drawing on the experience of international leading parks, particularly in terms of planning, construction, and operational management, is of vital importance for the upgrading and internationalisation of

China's semiconductor industry. Successful international parks typically feature well-integrated industrial chains, efficient management models, and global operational systems. How to achieve the 'internationalisation' of China's semiconductor industrial parks is a major challenge currently facing the industry.

The successful experiences and planning elements of international advanced parks. The success of international advanced parks is not accidental; it is typically underpinned by a systematic planning and construction framework. Silicon Valley, TSMC's headquarters park, and the Gyeonggi-do Park in South Korea are representative examples of global semiconductor industrial parks. These parks are not merely collections of production facilities; they integrate R&D, manufacturing, packaging, and testing through precise industrial positioning and planning, forming a deeply integrated full industrial chain. First, industrial positioning and planning are critical. Successful parks typically conduct precise planning based on industry development trends, technological demands, and market dynamics. For example, Silicon Valley positions itself as an innovation and technology development hub, concentrating on R&D and high-tech companies, while Chinese Taiwan's parks focus on semiconductor manufacturing, forming a complete industrial chain ecosystem. China's semiconductor industrial parks need to develop customised planning based on their unique characteristics, clearly define the core industrial direction of the park, promote the R&D and innovation of core technologies, and enhance the global competitiveness of the industry. Second, the construction of infrastructure must be closely aligned with the characteristics of the semiconductor industry. The semiconductor industry has extremely stringent requirements for facilities, necessitating the construction of high-standard cleanrooms, advanced manufacturing equipment, and a comprehensive supply chain logistics system within the park. Additionally, the park must provide an excellent environment for innovation and R&D, ensuring that companies can conduct technological innovation in a relatively closed environment and accelerate the conversion and application of R&D outcomes.

The entire lifecycle of park construction and operational management. Park construction is not merely about building infrastructure; it encompasses the entire lifecycle from planning and design to operational management. During the initial construction phase, scientific planning is essential to ensure the park can adapt to future demands of the semiconductor industry, particularly the rapid changes driven by technological advancements and industrial upgrades. Therefore, park design must be flexible and scalable to swiftly respond to shifts in technological development and market needs. Once operational, park management becomes critical to ensuring efficient operations. Internationally advanced parks typically have modern operational management systems, including intelligent management, digital monitoring, and optimised resource allocation. These management measures not only improve the operational efficiency of the park but also help it maintain flexibility and innovation capabilities in global competition. Chinese semiconductor parks should strengthen the professionalism of their management teams, introduce operational management experience with a global perspective, and use technological means to improve management levels to ensure the rational allocation and utilisation of resources. The core of park operations is how to continuously attract innovative enterprises and high-end talent in global competition. Park management should actively cooperate with universities, research institutions, and domestic and foreign enterprises to establish cross-regional and cross-border technological innovation platforms and industrial alliances. Such platforms can not only accelerate the transformation of technological achievements, but also promote the deep integration of different industrial links and provide more cooperation opportunities for enterprises within the park.

International cooperation and talent introduction in global development. To achieve international development, talent recruitment and international cooperation are key. The success of advanced parks often depends on the aggregation of global top-tier talent. To attract international scientific and technological talent, parks can offer preferential, talent recruitment policies, and startup incubation support to attract global technical elites and entrepreneurial teams to settle in the park. Additionally, parks should host international conferences and technical forums to facilitate global talent and technology exchange and cooperation, enhancing the park's innovative atmosphere and internationalisation level. At the same time, the internationalisation of industrial parks does not only depend on talent, but also requires the strengthening of global cooperation networks. Through cooperation with world-leading semiconductor companies, scientific research institutions, and government departments, industrial parks can integrate more deeply into the global industrial chain. Industrial park management should actively promote international cooperation projects, especially in areas such as technology research and development, standardisation, and supply chain management, and work with international partners to promote the globalisation of industrial technology and markets.

Policy support and adaptation to the external environment. The internationalisation of China's semiconductor industrial parks requires the support and promotion of government policies. National and local governments can encourage enterprises to settle in the park and accelerate the integration of the industrial chain by providing policies such as tax incentives, financial support, and land use. At the same time, the government should adjust policies in line with global industrial development trends, reduce trade barriers, and facilitate park enterprises in expanding into international markets. The park also needs to flexibly adapt to changes in the global economic environment during the process of internationalisation. Internationalisation requires not only that parks have a global perspective, but also that enterprises within the parks have keen market insight and strong market adaptability. Park management should work closely with enterprises to provide innovative solutions that meet international market demand and guide enterprises to actively participate in global market competition.

Benchmarking the planning and construction of advanced international parks is an important way to promote the internationalisation of China's semiconductor industry. By drawing on international best practices, leveraging China's resource advantages and market demands, Chinese semiconductor parks can secure a favourable position in global competition. By optimising park infrastructure, enhancing operational management standards, strengthening international cooperation and talent recruitment, and ensuring efficient operations throughout the entire park development and operation process, the industry can secure more opportunities and development space in the global market. This will lay a solid foundation for the long-term development of China's semiconductor industry.

7.3.2 Pathways for Promoting the Transformation of Industrial Bases into High-End Manufacturing and R&D Innovation Centres

As global competition in the semiconductor industry intensifies, the transformation of industrial bases has become a critical pathway to enhancing the overall competitiveness of the supply chain. China's semiconductor industrial bases, particularly traditional manufacturing hubs, urgently need to transition from low-end manufacturing to high-end manufacturing and R&D innovation centres to adapt to rapidly evolving technological requirements and global market demands. This transformation is not only an inevitable trend in industrial development but also a key factor in strengthening global market competitiveness.

The necessity of transforming into high-end manufacturing and R&D innovation centres. As the global semiconductor industry enters a new phase driven by innovation, traditional manufacturing models can no longer meet the ever-changing market demands. High-end manufacturing not only requires the production of high-performance, low-power, and highly integrated semiconductor products but also demands refined and intelligent production methods throughout the manufacturing process. Therefore, semiconductor industrial bases must transition to high-end manufacturing to improve manufacturing process precision, production line automation, and product value-added.

At the same time, with continuous global technological breakthroughs, R&D innovation has become the focus of global competition. The sustainable development of the semiconductor industry depends on the continuous innovation of new technologies, especially in chip design, new material applications, and advanced manufacturing processes. Industrial bases that wish to occupy an advantageous position in global competition must increase their investment in technology R&D, transform from manufacturing bases to R&D innovation centres, and promote technological breakthroughs and industrial chain upgrades.

Key elements of the transformation path. To drive the transformation of industrial bases into high-end manufacturing and R&D innovation centres, the following key elements must be addressed. Enhancing R&D capabilities: The core of the transformation is to enhance the R&D innovation capabilities of industrial bases. This requires not only increasing investment in R&D for advanced technologies, but also building innovation platforms such as R&D centres and technology incubators to support enterprises in achieving technological breakthroughs. In this process, the government can encourage enterprises to increase R&D investment through policy support and financial assistance, especially in key areas such as advanced manufacturing processes, chip design, and new materials. Smart manufacturing and digital transformation: To achieve high-end manufacturing, industrial bases must upgrade through smart manufacturing and digital technologies. By introducing emerging technologies such as artificial intelligence (AI), big data, and the Internet of Things (IoT), industrial bases can achieve automation and intelligence in the production process, improving production efficiency and product quality. Intelligent manufacturing not only improves production flexibility, but also reduces costs and optimises resource allocation, providing technical support for industrial bases to transform to high-end manufacturing. Introduction and training of high-end talent: The implementation of high-end manufacturing and R&D innovation cannot be separated from top scientific and technological talent. To achieve transformation, industrial bases need to increase their efforts to introduce and train talent. Through industry-university-research cooperation and overseas talent introduction programmes, industrial bases can attract high-end talent from home and abroad to settle in the park, while strengthening the training of local talent. Industrial bases should establish close cooperative relationships with domestic and foreign universities and scientific research institutions to promote the integration of technological research and talent cultivation and ensure a sustainable driving force for innovation. Industrial chain coordination and innovation ecosystem construction: The transformation of industrial bases is not only an internal technological innovation, but also requires strengthening industrial chain coordination and integration. In the semiconductor industry, the upstream material supply and design manufacturing are closely linked to the downstream packaging and testing links. Industrial bases need to build a powerful industrial synergy platform to promote information flow and technology integration between various links and form a complete industrial chain. By gathering leading enterprises and innovative resources in the industrial chain, the synergy of the entire industrial chain can be enhanced to promote rapid response to technology and market changes.

Implementation path for the transformation of high-end manufacturing and R&D innovation centres. The implementation path for the transformation of industrial bases can be divided into the following stages: Stage I: Infrastructure construction and industrial agglomeration. In the initial stage of transformation, industrial bases must first upgrade their infrastructure. This includes introducing facilities that meet the requirements of high-end manufacturing and R&D, such as clean rooms, production equipment, and laboratories. The construction of infrastructure is not only to meet production needs, but also to provide space and conditions for future technological innovation and industrial development. At the same time, industrial bases should increase guidance and support for key enterprises to attract companies in related fields to settle in the area and gradually form an industrial cluster effect. Second stage: Technology R&D and product innovation. Building on the foundation of infrastructure and industrial agglomeration, industrial bases should increase investment in technology R&D, particularly in key areas such as semiconductor process innovation, chip design, and new material applications. By establishing R&D centres, innovation incubators, and corporate laboratories, they should drive technological breakthroughs and product innovation. The core objective of this stage is to gradually enhance the technological capabilities of industrial bases through innovation-driven R&D and break through technical bottlenecks in global markets. Third stage: Internationalisation and supply chain integration. With the continuous advancement of technological R&D and the gradual improvement of the industrial foundation, the industrial base can gradually achieve globalisation, attracting more international enterprises and capital to cooperate. By strengthening cooperation with global leading enterprises, particularly in technological R&D, product design, and market expansion, the industrial base can be transformed into an international R&D centre. At the same time, the integration of all links in the supply chain should be strengthened to promote the industrial base into a globally competitive semiconductor innovation centre.

Policy Support and Industrial Upgrading Guarantees. Government policy support is crucial during the transformation of industrial bases into high-end manufacturing and R&D innovation centres. The government can formulate a series of supportive policies, such as tax incentives, R&D subsidies, and financial support, to help enterprises overcome technical difficulties and funding shortages during the transformation process. At the same time, policies should focus on industrial infrastructure construction, innovation platform development, and talent recruitment, providing comprehensive support. Furthermore, the government should strengthen intellectual property protection to provide legal safeguards for technological innovation and encourage enterprises to increase investment in innovation. Policy support and industry guidance can effectively enhance the overall competitiveness of industrial bases and ensure the smooth progress of industrial upgrading and internationalisation.

Promoting the transformation of industrial bases into high-end manufacturing and R&D innovation centres is an important direction for the future development of China's semiconductor industry. Through measures such as strengthening technological research and development, enhancing smart manufacturing capabilities, optimising industrial chain coordination and innovation ecosystems, and attracting high-end talent, industrial bases can gradually transition from traditional manufacturing to high-end manufacturing and innovation centres. This will not only enhance the position of China's semiconductor industry in the global industrial chain but also contribute more to global scientific and technological innovation. With government policy support, industrial coordination, and international cooperation, China's semiconductor industrial bases can occupy a more advantageous position in global competition and achieve comprehensive upgrading and innovative breakthroughs in the industrial chain.

7.3.3 Challenges and Solutions in the Process of Internationalisation

As China's semiconductor industry continues to advance toward internationalisation, industrial parks and bases are facing increasingly complex challenges. Globalisation has brought more market opportunities, but it has also brought various risks and uncertainties. To achieve industrial internationalisation and help industrial parks and bases gain a competitive edge in the global market, China's semiconductor industry must address a series of challenges and adopt effective solutions. These challenges not only come from technology, markets, and policies, but also involve adapting to changes in the global industrial chain, the complexity of international cooperation, and the adaptation of cross-border regulations.

First, intensifying global market competition is a major challenge facing China's semiconductor industrial parks and bases in their internationalisation process. With the rapid development of the global semiconductor industry, especially the strong competition from countries such as the United States, South Korea, and Japan, China's semiconductor industrial parks and bases are facing increasingly fierce market competition in their internationalisation process. This competition is not only reflected in technological competition but also in the of global market share, industrial resources, and the entry of foreign-invested enterprises. To address this challenge, industrial parks need to enhance their independent innovation capabilities by increasing investment in technology research and development, promoting the construction of high-end manufacturing and R&D innovation centres, and strengthening the overall competitiveness of the industrial chain.

Second, the complexity of international cooperation and cross-border mergers and acquisitions is another major challenge in the internationalisation of industrial parks. In expanding into international markets, semiconductor industrial parks must not only strengthen technical cooperation with international companies but also navigate the complex legal and market access issues associated with cross-border mergers and acquisitions. Cultural differences, political risks, and integration challenges during the merger process can all impact the smooth development of industrial parks. To address this issue, industrial parks should strengthen technical cooperation and strategic alliances with leading international companies, promote post-merger integration management, and prioritise cross-cultural management to ensure the smooth implementation of cooperation.

Regulatory policies and intellectual property protection issues are also challenges in the internationalisation process of semiconductor industrial parks. Policy and regulatory differences among countries and regions worldwide require industrial parks to comply with the laws and regulations of each country when entering global markets, particularly in areas such as trade, investment, and technology transfer. Additionally, intellectual property issues are particularly important in the semiconductor industry, as the protection of technological innovations is crucial for the long-term development of industrial bases. To address these challenges, industrial parks need to strengthen compliance with global market policies while improving their intellectual property protection systems to ensure the legitimate rights and interests of their proprietary technologies.

Another challenge is the shortage of talent and the difficulty of attracting international talent. The semiconductor industry's high-end manufacturing and R&D innovation rely on technical elites and innovative talent, but in the global competition for talent, how to attract top scientific and technological talent has become a challenge for industrial parks. To address this challenge, industrial parks need to increase their efforts to attract talent. In addition to offering attractive compensation and policy support to attract international talent, they should also establish industry-academia-research cooperation platforms and collaborate with domestic and international universities and research institutions to cultivate local technical and management talent to support the development needs of the park.

Additionally, the instability of the global supply chain poses challenges to the internationalisation process of semiconductor industrial parks. The deep integration of the global supply chain means that when facing external risks such as market uncertainty, geopolitical risks, and the global pandemic, parks and enterprises often encounter issues like supply chain disruptions and raw material shortages. To address this challenge, industrial parks should strengthen the diversification of their supply chains by localising production and establishing diversified supply chains to reduce their dependence on single markets and suppliers, thereby enhancing the risk resistance of the industrial chain. At the same time, they should promote the digitalisation and intelligent management of supply chains and leverage big data and artificial intelligence technologies to improve the flexibility and responsiveness of supply chains.

In the process of globalisation, industrial parks also need to face more uncertainties in international markets, such as changes in global trade policies, obstacles to cross-border cooperation, and economic imbalances between regions. How China's semiconductor industrial parks respond to fluctuations in the global market will depend on policy support and the strategic adaptability of industrial parks. The government should provide stable policy support for the internationalisation of industrial parks through cross-border trade agreements, the construction of free trade zones, and other measures to promote the global layout of park enterprises.

Overall, China's semiconductor industrial parks and bases face multifaceted challenges in their internationalisation process. However, through measures such as strengthening technological innovation, optimising global cooperation, enhancing intellectual property protection, strengthening talent recruitment and training, and optimising supply chain management, the parks can effectively address these challenges. As these issues are gradually resolved, China's semiconductor industrial parks will gradually achieve internationalisation, enhance their global competitiveness, and lay a solid foundation for the sustainable development of the industry.

7.4 Policy and Market-Driven Industrial Layout Optimisation Pathways

7.4.1 Policy Guidance: Support the Development of High-Tech Industrial Parks and the Process of Globalisation

In the context of globalisation and rapid technological development, the competitiveness of the semiconductor industry no longer depends solely on technological innovation and changes in market demand; the guiding role of policy has become increasingly important. As core carriers for promoting scientific and technological innovation and industrial upgrading, industrial parks must rely on policy guidance and support for their development. This is especially true in a high-tech, capital-intensive field such as the semiconductor industry, where government policy support can provide parks with the necessary resources, environment, and market opportunities to help them make the leap from domestic to international markets.

Policy guidance in the development of industrial parks is mainly reflected in tax incentives, financial support, infrastructure construction, and market opening. Through these policies, the government can create a favourable innovation ecosystem and provide sufficient development space for enterprises. At the same time, with the acceleration of globalisation, government policies not only need to serve the domestic market but also focus on how to support park enterprises in entering the international market and forming global competitiveness.

First, policies can reduce enterprise operating costs through tax incentives and financial subsidies, especially for start-ups and R&D-oriented enterprises. Policy support can effectively alleviate financial pressure and encourage greater innovation investment. For example, the government can provide tax breaks to semiconductor enterprises entering the park and grant them R&D activity funding to help them accelerate technological R&D and product innovation. This not only incentivises enterprises to increase their technological innovation efforts but also provides a guarantee for the sustainable development of enterprises in the park.

Second, policies can also support park development by promoting infrastructure construction. In the semiconductor industry, infrastructure construction within parks directly affects the production capacity and technological research and development progress of enterprises. The government can provide parks with high-standard production facilities, laboratories, logistics systems, and other support to ensure that enterprises within the park can efficiently carry out production and research and development work. In addition, the government can encourage parks to build facilities by providing land use and financial support, and attract more enterprises to settle in the park by providing advanced infrastructure, thereby promoting industrial agglomeration effects.

In the process of globalisation, the role of policy is not limited to domestic support. As China's semiconductor industry increasingly participates in global competition, the international development of park enterprises faces more challenges and opportunities. Therefore, the government needs to help park enterprises expand into international markets through international cooperation policies and foreign investment introduction policies. Specifically, the government can promote cooperation between park enterprises and global leading enterprises through measures such as cross-border cooperation agreements and free trade zone construction to enhance the international competitiveness of the park. For example, policies can encourage enterprises within the park to introduce advanced technology, capital, and market resources through cross-border mergers and acquisitions or international cooperation, thereby accelerating the globalisation process of the park.

In addition, as technological innovation increasingly becomes the core of industrial competitiveness, policy support should also focus on promoting the construction of an innovation ecosystem in the park. In the operation of high-tech industrial parks, the government can build innovation platforms, such as R&D incubators and technology alliances, to provide enterprises with technical exchanges, talent training, project incubation, and other support. These innovation platforms can effectively aggregate various types of innovation resources, promote technological innovation and the transformation of research results within the park, and accelerate the technological upgrading and transformation of the industrial chain. At the same time, the government can also provide incentives such as innovation rewards and patent protection to encourage enterprises to continue technological research and development and promote the development of the semiconductor industry towards high-end manufacturing and innovative research and development.

The introduction and training of talent is also an important aspect of policy support. With the transformation of the semiconductor industry towards high-end manufacturing and R&D centres, the park needs to attract and train a large number of high-end technical talents. The government can attract top domestic and foreign talents to join the park through talent introduction programmes and overseas high-end talent support policies. In addition, the government can cooperate with domestic and foreign universities and scientific research institutions to establish talent training bases and promote the continuous growth and accumulation of technical talents within the park.

The ultimate goal of policy guidance is to promote the park's development in the global market. The government can formulate policies in line with international standards to promote the globalisation of industrial parks. For example, under the framework of the Belt and Road Initiative, the park can leverage policy support to strengthen cooperation with other countries and regions, expand overseas markets, and export the advantages of China's semiconductor industry to the world. Through international market expansion and technological cooperation, park enterprises can not only increase their market share but also enhance their voice in the global industrial chain.

In summary, policy guidance plays a crucial role in supporting the development and globalisation of high-tech industrial parks. By providing policy support such as tax incentives, financial subsidies, and infrastructure construction, the government can provide parks with a favourable innovation environment and a platform for global development, helping park enterprises enter international markets and enhance the global competitiveness of the industry. With further policy optimisation and the advancement of globalisation strategies, industrial parks will be able to secure a more advantageous position in the global semiconductor industry, driving the Chinese semiconductor industry toward more comprehensive and sustainable development.

7.4.2   Market Demand Changes Drive Industrial Optimisation: The Dual Role of Technological Progress and Market Guidance

In the rapid development of the global semiconductor industry, changes in market demand and technological progress interact with each other, jointly driving the optimisation and upgrading of the industry. Changes in market demand are not only the driving force behind technological innovation, but also an important guiding factor for the optimisation of industrial layout. As a technology-intensive industry, the development of the semiconductor industry is not only driven by technological progress, but also closely dependent on changes in market demand and market trends. How to utilise changes in market demand to guide industrial optimisation and how to respond to market demand through technological progress have become key factors in enhancing the competitiveness of the semiconductor industry in global competition.

The guiding role of changes in market demand in industrial optimisation. With the continuous improvement of global technology levels, changes in market demand are driving the continuous optimisation of the semiconductor industry. Whether in consumer electronics, automotive electronics or industrial control, the market demand for semiconductor products is increasingly leaning towards high performance, low power consumption and miniaturisation. These changes in market demand have forced the semiconductor industry to continuously improve its manufacturing processes and product performance, thereby driving technological progress and guiding the optimisation of the industry's layout. Specifically, with the rise of emerging applications such as artificial intelligence (AI), 5G communications, and the Internet of Things (IoT), the market's demand for high-performance computing, low latency, and high bandwidth has increased dramatically. To meet these demands, the focus of the semiconductor industry has shifted from traditional storage and processing chips to AI chips, 5G baseband chips, and other areas. This shift in demand has driven technological research and development and supply chain integration. For example, the design and manufacturing of AI chips require higher integration and stronger computing capabilities, thereby driving innovation in semiconductor manufacturing processes. Market demand changes not only drive product technology upgrades but also guide the optimisation of the industrial chain layout. As market demand for high-end products continues to grow, semiconductor industrial parks and bases must transition towards high-end manufacturing and R&D innovation. Enterprises within the parks need to strengthen technological innovation and promote collaboration across the industrial chain to enhance the overall competitiveness of the industrial chain.

The role of technological progress in responding to market demand and promoting industrial optimisation. Technological progress is a response to changes in market demand and also an important driving force for industrial optimisation. In the semiconductor industry, technological progress not only affects product performance but also directly drives innovations in production models, manufacturing processes, and product design. Technological innovation continuously meets the increasingly diverse and high-end market demands, driving industrial optimisation and upgrading. For example, with the gradual breakthrough of Moore's Law, semiconductor manufacturing processes are moving towards smaller process nodes, significantly increasing the integration of semiconductor products, reducing power consumption, and enhancing performance. This technological progress responds to market demand for high-performance computing and low-power chips. At the same time, technological progress has also promoted the research and application of new semiconductor materials, driving breakthroughs in technologies such as quantum dots and new semiconductor materials to meet market demand for smaller, higher-performance, and more environmentally friendly products. Technologi-cal progress has also promoted the application of new models such as automated production and smart manufacturing, helping industrial parks improve production efficiency, reduce costs, and flexibly respond to market changes. Through the appli-cation of intelligent production lines and industrial Internet technologies, industrial parks can monitor production data in real time, adjust production plans in a timely manner, and improve production flexibility and response speed. Technological progress has also promoted the overall optimisation of the industrial chain, espe-cially in supply chain management, material innovation, and product customisa-tion. Technological innovation enables the semiconductor industry to better adapt to rapidly changing market demands, improve the overall efficiency of the industrial chain, and accelerate product upgrades.

The interactive dual role: mutual promotion between market demand and tech-nological progress. Market demand and technological progress are not unidirec-tional drivers; there is a two-way interaction between the two. Changes in market demand drive technological innovation, while breakthroughs in technological prog-ress continuously meet new market demands. This interactive relationship drives the rapid development of the semiconductor industry and continuously optimises the industrial layout. For example, market demand for 5G has driven technological innovation in areas such as 5G base station equipment and mobile terminals. These technological breakthroughs, in turn, have driven improvements in the performance of 5G chips and reductions in production costs, further accelerating market demand for 5G products. In addition, market demand for AI technology and big data has prompted semiconductor companies to increase their R&D investment in AI chips, while also driving the development of AI-related technologies such as deep learning and big data processing, thereby providing strong technical support for the overall development of the industry. Through this dual effect, the semiconductor industry is better able to adapt to the rapidly changing market environment. The interac-tion between technological progress and market demand enables industrial parks to adjust their production strategies in a timely manner, optimise their R&D paths, and promote the deep integration of the industrial chain.

Future direction of industrial optimisation: parallel development of technology leadership and market demand. In the future, market demand and technological progress will continue to drive the optimisation and upgrading of the semiconductor industry. With the in-depth application of emerging technologies such as 5G, arti-ficial intelligence, and the Internet of Things, the market demand for semiconduc-tor products will become more diverse and personalised. Semiconductor industrial parks and bases need to optimise multiple aspects, from product design and tech-nology research and development to manufacturing processes and industrial chain coordination, in order to stand out in global competition.

At the same time, with the further popularisation of intelligent manufacturing, automated production, and digital transformation, technological progress will not be limited to improving product performance, but will also involve comprehensive optimisation of production models and supply chain management. These techno-logical breakthroughs will drive the semiconductor industry's transformation from traditional manufacturing to high-end manufacturing and intelligent manufacturing, and promote the transformation of industrial parks into innovation centres and R&D bases. The dual effects of market demand changes and technological progress are the main driving forces behind the optimisation and upgrading of the semiconductor industry.

By closely monitoring changes in market demand and promptly adjusting their technological research and development directions, industrial parks and bases can effectively respond to global market challenges, achieve rapid industrial development, and make technological breakthroughs. At the same time, driven by technological progress, they can not only meet market demand but also provide sustained momentum for the overall optimisation of the industrial chain. In the future, the two-way promotion of market and technology will further facilitate industrial transformation and upgrading, helping China's semiconductor industry secure a more advantageous position in global competition.

References

Bown, C. P. (2021). *How the United States marched the semiconductor industry into its trade war with China* (Peterson Institute for International Economics Working Paper 21–16). Peterson Institute for International Economics. https://www.piie.com/publications/working-papers/how-united-states-marched-semiconductor-industry-its-trade-war-china

Dedrick, J., Kraemer, K. L., & Linden, G. (2010). Who profits from innovation in global value chains? A study of the iPod and notebook PCs. *Industrial and Corporate Change, 19*(1), 81–116. https://doi.org/10.1093/icc/dtp032

Feser, E. J., & Bergman, E. M. (2000). National industry cluster templates: A framework for applied regional cluster analysis. *Regional Studies, 34*(1), 1–19. https://doi.org/10.1080/00343400050005844

Porter, M. E. (1998). Clusters and the new economics of competition. *Harvard Business Review, 76*(6), 77–90.

Semiconductor Industry Association. (2023). *2023 factbook: Semiconductor industry statistics.* Semiconductor Industry Association.

Shalf, J. (2020). The future of computing beyond Moore's law. *Philosophical Transactions of the Royal Society A: Mathematical, Physical and Engineering Sciences, 378*(2166), 20190061. https://doi.org/10.1098/rsta.2019.0061

Thompson, S. E., & Parthasarathy, S. (2006). Moore's law: The future of Si microelectronics. *Materials Today, 9*(6), 20–25. https://doi.org/10.1016/S1369-7021(06)71539-5

Varas, A., Varadarajan, R., Goodrich, A., & Yinug, F. (2020). *Strengthening the global semiconductor supply chain in an uncertain era.* Semiconductor Industry Association & Boston Consulting Group. https://www.semiconductors.org/strengthening-the-global-semiconductor-supply-chain-in-an-uncertain-era

Chapter 8
The Development of the Semiconductor Industry in Fujian Province: A Regional Sample of China's Semiconductor Industry Chain

Jian Zhang

Abstract Chapter 8 examines the development of Fujian Province's semiconductor industry as a representative regional case within China's broader semiconductor supply chain. It outlines the industry's rapid expansion since 2014, marked by investments exceeding 150 billion yuan and the emergence of an integrated industrial ecosystem encompassing design, manufacturing, packaging and testing, equipment, and materials. The chapter discusses key industrial clusters in Xiamen, Jinjiang, and Quanzhou, alongside notable achievements by firms such as Xiamen Lianxin (28 nm foundry), Rockchip (AIoT chips), and Sanan Integration (compound semiconductors). It assesses core strengths—including cross-Strait collaboration and robust materials capabilities—while also identifying persistent structural challenges, such as underdeveloped design capacity, financing constraints, weak policy coordination, and talent shortages. The chapter concludes by outlining strategic priorities: reinforcing key industry segments, promoting government–industry–academia collaboration, strengthening innovation platforms, and accelerating talent cultivation and supply chain integration to enhance regional resilience and drive sustainable growth.

Keywords Fujian Semiconductor Industry • Regional Development • Industrial Ecosystem • Structural Challenges • Innovation and Talent Strategy

8.1 Current Status of Semiconductor Industry Development in Fujian Province

8.1.1 Overall Situation

Since 2014, under the strong leadership of the Fujian Provincial Party Committee and Provincial Government and with the support of the National Industrial Investment Fund, Fujian Province has actively implemented strategies such as 'filling the screen and strengthening the core' and 'building a semiconductor industry cluster in the southeastern coastal region.' The semiconductor industry environment has been continuously improved, industrial layout has become increasingly rational, and industrial scale has continued to expand, laying a solid foundation for leapfrog development. In recent years, Fujian Province has collaborated with the National Integrated Circuit Industry Investment Fund to establish local semiconductor industry investment funds exceeding 150 billion yuan, with new industrial scale ranking among the top in the country. The province has gradually built a complete semiconductor industry chain ecosystem covering design, manufacturing, packaging and testing, equipment and materials, as well as terminal applications. Xiamen and Jinjiang have successively introduced industrial development guidelines and supporting policies, with industrial and talent policies holding certain advantages domestically. The scale and technological level of the semiconductor manufacturing industry have continued to improve, and the industrial supporting environment has been further enhanced.

8.1.2 Overall Status of the Industry

After eight years of development, the semiconductor industry in Fujian Province has achieved a sales revenue of nearly 50 billion yuan, representing an increase of over 400% compared to less than 10 billion yuan in 2014. The overall status of the industry is characterised by the following features:

The overall industrial layout is gradually becoming more rational. Fujian Province has actively promoted the layout of its semiconductor industry, initially forming a coastal semiconductor industry belt centred on Fuzhou, Xiamen, Quanzhou, and Putian. This belt is anchored by Xiamen and Quanzhou as core cities, with specialised industrial parks focusing on compound semiconductors, memory chips, and other niche segments, creating a 'one belt, two cores, multiple parks' industrial structure (Yu 2018). This has attracted companies such as Rockchip, StarChip Technology, Jinjiang Jin Hua, Xiamen Lianxin, Qu Liang Electronics, Xiamen Tongfu, Zhongshi Guangxin, Xinmi, Xintianhong, Xinhua Zhang, Xiamen Unisoc, Sanan Integration, Fujian Fuliang, Xiamen Youxun, and Fujian Yixinyuan, among over 100 semiconductor companies, laying a solid foundation for leapfrog development.

Billions of dollars in investment have driven the initial formation of an industrial chain. Since 2014, Fujian Province, represented by Xiamen and Jinjiang, has established local semiconductor industry investment funds with a total scale exceeding 150 billion yuan, joining cities such as Nanjing, Hefei, and Wuhan as hotspots in this round of domestic industrial development. Xiamen, Jinjiang, and other areas have all issued industrial development guidelines, leveraging both policy guidance and market-driven forces. They focus on creating a favourable policy environment, fostering leading enterprises, and addressing shortcomings. An industrial supply chain covering design, manufacturing, and testing has begun to take shape, with the semiconductor testing industry emerging from scratch and supporting equipment and materials gradually improving.

Key enterprises are driving technological advancement. Currently, Xiamen Lianxin in Fujian Province has achieved 28 nm logic circuit foundry process technology for 12-inch wafers; Fuzhou Rockchip has successfully mass-produced the RK3588 smart terminal AIoT chip using advanced FinFET process technology, reaching leading domestic technical standards; Xiamen Sanan is capable of manufacturing compound semiconductor chips such as gallium arsenide RF chips, gallium nitride RF chips, silicon carbide power devices, optical chips, and silicon-based gallium nitride power devices; Jinjiang Jin Hua has been included in China's 13th Five-Year Plan for major semiconductor production capacity, becoming one of the three major storage bases in the country. The aforementioned key enterprises have already secured a leading position prior to the launch of the second phase of the National Integrated Circuit Industry Investment Fund (the 'Big Fund').

8.1.3 Current Status of the Design Industry

The industry has a solid foundation but growth has slowed. The design industry in Fuzhou and Xiamen has been developing for over a decade. In 2016, Fujian Province's design industry sales reached 3.6 billion yuan, ranking 7th nationally. However, with the rapid rise of design industries in other domestic cities in recent years, Fuzhou's industrial growth has slowed, and Fujian Province's national ranking has slightly declined. According to the latest 'China Statistical Yearbook 2024,' it now ranks 15th.

The industry has a broad product coverage but overall technological levels are lagging behind, though there are notable highlights. Major products include mobile multimedia chips, network communication, video and image processing, automotive electronics, digital television, power management, and household electronics-specific chips. Overall technological levels still lag significantly behind international standards. Rockchip's smart terminal SoC chip technology is at the leading domestic level. In addition to undertaking the National Key Research and Development Program (01 Special Project) in 2009 and the 02 Special Project in 2016, the company has continuously undertaken the Ministry of Industry and Information Technology's semiconductor R&D special project from 2005 to 2013.

Xiamen Youxun holds a steady global top-three market share in the niche segment of medium and low-speed transmission and has applied for IPO in 2024. Xiamen Yixinyuan's 10G optical communication chips have begun to enter the supply chains of domestic mainstream manufacturers.

The industry is dominated by small and medium-sized enterprises, and insufficient investment in technology research and development has led to a decline in competitiveness. Fujian Province is home to nearly 100 semiconductor design companies, including Rockchip, Xiamen Xingchen Technology, Ziguang Zhanrui, Xiamen Yuanshun, Xiamen Youxun, and Yixinyuan, which are mainly small and medium-sized enterprises with a significant technological gap compared to foreign counterparts. Companies in the analogue sector have distinct characteristics but are generally small in scale, facing risks such as fragmented technical routes and weak market competitiveness. In the digital sector, R&D investments for advanced process logic chips amount to tens of millions of yuan, leaving little room for survival for small and medium-sized design companies. Factors such as inadequate financing channels for enterprises and the lack of engineering research institutions within the province have led to insufficient R&D investments in key technologies for upstream and downstream integration, hindering the formation of a healthy ecosystem for vertical integration of the industrial chain and weakening enterprises' ability to sustain development and withstand risks.

8.1.4 Current Status of Manufacturing Development

In recent years, key semiconductor production projects in Fujian Province have been undergoing a new round of construction and expansion, with total investment exceeding 100 billion yuan. Key semiconductor production projects such as Xiamen Lianxin, Jinjiang Jin Hua, Sanan Integrated, Fujian Fuliang, Fushun Wafer, and Xiamen Silan Microelectronics have successively commenced production. The main businesses of these companies cover high-end chip foundry, DRAM memory manufacturing, compound semiconductor chips, and power management chip manufacturing.

Leading enterprises are driving improvements in product technology levels. Xiamen Lianxin's 28 nm mass production process technology and yield rate are both at the leading domestic level;

Jinjiang Jin Hua's advanced DRAM memory technology and processes have been included in China's 13th Five-Year Plan for major semiconductor production capacity layout; Xiamen Sanan Integrated's compound semiconductor process technology has reached domestic leading levels and has successively undertaken national 01 and 03 special projects; Xiamen Sanan Integrated and Fujian Fuliang have both initiated R&D on third-generation compound semiconductor technology processes. Capital expenditures continue to increase, and the long return cycle has led to increased financing pressure for enterprises.

Currently, the total investment in key semiconductor production projects within the province exceeds 100 billion yuan, with equipment investment continuing to grow. These projects have long return cycles, high fixed asset investment expenditures, and significant depreciation costs, making them less attractive to private capital. Existing low-interest loans and industrial fund buyback policies are insufficient to alleviate the growing financing pressures faced by enterprises, which will inevitably weaken the competitiveness of key enterprises in the global oligopoly market structure.

8.1.5   Current Status of the Packaging and Testing Industry

Leading companies have driven the packaging and testing industry from its infancy to its current state. Due to weak foundations, the packaging and testing industry lacks key links in various regions, with significant technological deficits in related fields, resulting in severe development lag.

Since 2016, Jinjiang has actively developed the integrated circuit industry, forming a complete industrial chain ecosystem covering chip design, manufacturing, packaging and testing, equipment, and materials. Currently, over 50 industrial chain projects have been established, with total investments exceeding 100 billion yuan. The city has planned and constructed 'Three Parks and One Zone' as spatial carriers for industrial parks, aiming to build a leading national base for memory production and packaging and testing.

Xiamen has been designated as a key city in the national integrated circuit planning and layout, and its integrated circuit industry has achieved leapfrog development. In 2024, Xiamen hosted the Second Semiconductor Advanced Packaging and Testing Industry Technology Innovation Conference, showcasing cutting-edge packaging and testing technologies such as 2.5D/3D packaging and glass through-via (TGV), and promoting industrial technological innovation and cooperation.

As an important city in Fujian Province, Quanzhou is actively promoting the development of the semiconductor industry. It has formulated the 'Quanzhou Semiconductor Industry Development Plan (2016–2025),' focusing on the development of upstream and downstream industries such as packaging and testing, manufacturing equipment, and key raw materials, and has formed a relatively complete industrial chain layout.

In recent years, under the leadership of leading semiconductor companies, Xiamen and Jinjiang have successively attracted international first-tier packaging companies such as Quliang Electronics and Tongfu Microelectronics, filling the gap in the packaging and testing sector in the China West Coast region. These companies primarily serve the regional markets and key enterprises in the 'Fuzhou-Xiamen-Quanzhou-Putian' area and the southern China region. Quliang Electronics' Phase I project has achieved full production and sales, while the expansion project for Phase II is being accelerated.

8.1.6   Current Development Status of the Equipment and Materials Industry

Supporting equipment and materials are gradually being improved. In terms of semiconductor equipment, Fujian Province has identified the research, development, and manufacturing of key integrated circuit equipment (such as lithography machines, etching machines, and ion implantation machines) and key components as key areas for technological innovation, supporting enterprises in tackling key technological challenges and enhancing the level of equipment self-reliance. Longyan, Nanping, and Ningde leverage their abundant non-ferrous metal resources to focus on the development of ultra-high-purity rare metals and target materials, copper-nickel-silicon, copper-chromium-zirconium lead frame materials, and bonding wires for electronic information materials, providing raw material support for the semiconductor materials industry.

Under the leadership of leading enterprises, upstream semiconductor manufacturing companies have also established operations in Xiamen, Jinjiang, and other areas, with initial signs of industrial agglomeration emerging. In June 2017, Xiamen Meirifengchuang Photomask Co., Ltd., a joint venture between US-based Photronics and Japan's DNP, was established in Xiamen. The company is capable of producing photomasks supporting 14 nm and above processes and plans to develop into the largest commercial photomask production base in mainland China. Bochun Materials is an advanced semiconductor process-enabled ultra-high-purity germanium production base, an Intel-backed company, and China's first special gas company to export to TSMC. Its germanium and other special gas products account for 60% of the Asia-Pacific market; Hengkun Co., Ltd. is capable of mass-producing photoresists and precursors for 12-inch and 28 nm processes, with customers including Intel and SMIC, among other leading domestic and international companies.

Fujian Province's semiconductor equipment and materials industry has achieved significant results in policy guidance, industrial layout, technological innovation, and industrial cluster development, forming an industrial cluster centred around Fuzhou, Xiamen, and Quanzhou. In the future, with continuous technological progress and the improvement of the industrial chain, Fujian Province is expected to occupy an even more important position in China's semiconductor equipment and materials industry.

8.2   Advantages and Disadvantages of Fujian Province's Semiconductor Industry Development

8.2.1   Advantages of Industry Development

Industrial cooperation between Fujian and Chinese Taiwan continues to deepen. Fujian Province is separated from Chinese Taiwan by a narrow strait, with close geographical proximity and deep cultural ties, giving it a distinct advantage in terms of proximity to Taiwan. Leveraging Taiwan's strong position in the semiconductor industry, Fujian is driving the development of its own semiconductor industry. Xiamen Lianxin, a subsidiary of Taiwan Semiconductor Manufacturing Company (TSMC), has filled the gap in Fujian Province's 12-inch logic chip wafer foundry production lines. It has also partnered with local enterprises to establish the Xiamen United Semiconductor Industry Equity Investment Fund Partnership, which has helped attract a number of companies to settle in Fujian Province. Jinhua Innovation's Fujian-Taiwan technology and talent cooperation model is dedicated to developing a domestic memory chip industry and has successfully attracted Taiwanese packaging and testing giant Quliang Company to enhance supporting facilities. YouShun Semiconductor has invested in the construction of a 6-inch wafer foundry production line and packaging and testing production lines in Fujian Province and is actively planning for the listing of Fushun Semiconductor on the STAR Market. Fujian and Chinese Taiwan have achieved effective collaboration across multiple dimensions, including technology, talent, capital, markets, and raw materials. Meanwhile, universities in Fujian Province have begun to actively establish semiconductor-related disciplines and seek master's and doctoral degree authorisation points to cultivate the talent needed for the industry. A number of specialised platforms, including the Fujian Semiconductor Industry-Education Integration and Innovative Development Alliance, the 6·18 Collaborative Innovation Institute Microelectronics Branch, and the Intellectual Property Centre Quanzhou Branch, have been established to provide specialised services such as talent training, intellectual property, and project incubation for enterprises inside and outside the province.

8.2.2   Insufficient Industrial Development

Compared with advanced regions in China such as the Yangtze River Delta, the Beijing-Tianjin-Hebei region, and the Pearl River Delta (excluding Fujian), Fujian Province has a relatively weak semiconductor industry foundation and faces the following issues:

The industrial policy environment needs improvement. Currently, while industrial policies in places like Xiamen and Jinjiang are robust, they are limited to local areas. Provincial-level departments cannot track and monitor the overall dynamics of the semiconductor industry across the province, making it difficult to achieve coordinated development and mutual benefits on a provincial scale. Existing policies have not prioritised enterprises and talent, and issues such as significant policy disparities between regions, lack of targeted industrial policies, and difficulties in implementing cross-departmental policy coordination remain.

The industrial structure remains unbalanced. The province's industrial structure is unbalanced, with insufficient investment in the design industry and the rapid development of manufacturing coexisting with a slowdown in the growth of the design industry. At the same time, due to a weak foundation, supporting packaging and testing, equipment, and materials companies in various regions are still in the introduction phase, with significant technical deficits in related fields and severe development lag. Preferential policies in various regions cannot be shared across regions, making it difficult to promote the integration of upstream and downstream industries across provinces.

An industrial ecosystem has not yet been formed. The lack of key technologies and coordination mechanisms between upstream chip design companies and downstream equipment manufacturers within the province has resulted in weak value chain integration capabilities and an unclear industrial driving role for regionally advantageous and emerging industries. There is a lack of investment in key process technologies for upstream and downstream coordination, and the development cycle is long. The lack of an IP library in advanced wafer factories makes it difficult to respond quickly to upstream companies' demands and effectively utilise existing production capacity.

Severe shortage of technology and talent. Global policy adjustments have increased the difficulty for China to acquire advanced overseas technology and engage in mergers and acquisitions. Fujian Province currently lacks high-level microelectronics research institutes, and the core technologies and key processes of Fujian's advanced manufacturing enterprises are dependent on foreign imports, resulting in weak independent R&D capabilities and poor ability to withstand market risks. Fujian Province faces a significant shortage of industry talent, particularly in terms of composite leading talent with both market and technical experience. Intensified domestic competition has eroded the comparative advantages of Fujian Province's talent policies, and the training capacity of existing microelectronics colleges such as Fuzhou University and Xiamen University is insufficient to meet the short-term demand for mid-to-high-end talent in the industry (Wang et al. 2022).

8.3 Key Directions and Main Tasks

8.3.1 Key Directions for Industrial Development

In terms of the semiconductor design industry, Fujian Province will actively respond to national policies and the 'Big Fund' initiative, focusing on promoting the application of artificial intelligence technology in 4K/8K ultra-high-definition video, industrial intelligent gateways, and other fields; it will provide key support to Fuzhou to develop smart terminal SoC chips, smart wearable device chips, MEMS devices, IoT sensor chips, optical communication chips, high-definition image sensors, and information processing chips with a focus on digital chips; provide key support to Xiamen to develop network communication chips, automotive electronic chips, and sensor chips with a focus on analogue chips; and provide key support to Quanzhou to develop memory-related chips and application chips for smart wearables and digital walkie-talkies.

In terms of semiconductor manufacturing, Fujian will focus on supporting the construction of an internationally advanced semiconductor and related product packaging and testing base in Jinjiang to carry out storage chip and logic chip packaging and testing services for the whole country and even the world; and promote Xiamen to cooperate with Tongfu Microelectronics to invest in the construction of an advanced packaging and testing industrialisation base for logic chips and compound semiconductor chips. The semiconductor equipment and materials industry will vigorously develop advanced photomask technology compatible with 20, 25, 28, and 40 nm wafer foundry services and achieve mass production; it will continue to encourage various regions to introduce equipment, technology, and material manufacturers compatible with leading enterprises to settle in Fujian.

8.3.2   Main Tasks for Industrial Development

In accordance with the requirements of 'focusing on leading enterprises and building industrial chains,' we will focus on Fujian's leading industries, traditional advantage industries, and strategic emerging industrial chains, with an eye toward filling gaps in the industrial chain and improving upstream and downstream support, and we will sort out and form a roadmap for extending and expanding the industrial chain. We will identify industrial chain needs and potential owner units and generate a number of key projects.

Support leading enterprises to take the lead in piloting new initiatives. Vigorous support will be provided to provincial leading enterprises such as Jin Hua to pilot domestically produced EDA software, equipment, and raw materials, and to establish a multi-regional, multi-enterprise supply chain system both domestically and internationally, as well as within and outside the province, to help build a domestic demonstration enterprise for the production of domestically produced memory chips. Strengthen the supply of insurance products suitable for the integrated circuit industry, explore the establishment of a joint insurance mechanism for integrated circuits and a mechanism for dispersing major disaster risks, and provide comprehensive insurance support for enterprise property, cargo transportation, scientific and technological research and development, and achievement transformation. Focus on supporting the development and verification of domestically produced and controlled equipment, materials, and EDA, and study and formulate insurance premium subsidy support policies for key areas and key projects.

Optimise the layout of key projects. Fully implement the specific work arrangements of the Fujian Province Integrated Circuit Industry Special Coordination Group, and conduct a comprehensive review of the current state of the industry in Fujian Province. Strengthen the concept of 'one province, one plan, with differentiated approaches in various regions,' and explore the establishment of corresponding guidance mechanisms. Encourage cities and counties to leverage their resource advantages, develop targeted investment attraction plans, explore joint investment attraction models, and pursue complementary development with 'sister' cities and counties. For major integrated circuit-related projects in cities and counties, support the formation of expert teams to assist in project evaluations.

Achieve breakthroughs in multiple areas of the industrial chain. Focus on developing chip design, specialised manufacturing processes, packaging and testing, materials, equipment, and components. First, strengthen chip design. Continue to attract high-quality design companies to settle in the province, support existing leading enterprises, and promote the research and development of core chips. Second, expand wafer manufacturing. Accelerate the construction of ongoing projects and provide support in terms of land, approvals, and other factors. Actively guide and assist key projects in applying for national 'window guidance.' Third, improve packaging and testing. Accelerate the construction of key projects such as Xiamen Tongfu and Quliang Electronics, encourage the establishment of R&D centres, and attract and cultivate high-quality packaging and testing projects to build a leading national packaging and testing base. Fourth, develop specialised materials, equipment, and components. Support Fujian's advantageous material and equipment companies, such as photoresist, germanium-based special gases, coating machines, and coating and developing machines, to continuously improve product performance and expand production capacity. Increase the localisation rate of the supply chain for Fujian's integrated circuit manufacturing and packaging and testing companies, further ensure the supply chain security of local companies, create national-level specialised, refined, and innovative companies, and cultivate a batch of listed companies. Explore the construction of provincial-level specialised zones for electronic gases and wet chemical materials, and plan major industrial projects in the integrated circuit materials sector, while establishing public warehousing facilities for integrated circuit-specific materials.

Enhance the synergy between government, industry, academia, and research. Take multiple measures to cultivate local high-end talent and continuously increase the 'localisation rate' and 'indigenisation rate' of high-end talent. First, strengthen cooperation between universities and enterprises. Leverage the advantages of universities such as Xiamen University and Fuzhou University in gathering high-end talent, and establish deep cooperation with leading enterprises such as Jin Hua, Qu Liang, and Sanan Optoelectronics. Adopt methods such as 'order-based training' and 'dual mentors' to smooth the channels for the cultivation and circulation of high-end talent. Implement the spirit of the Ministry of Education and the Ministry of Industry and Information Technology on the construction of modern industrial colleges, promote the 'new engineering' training model of Putian University, and support universities such as Fuzhou University, Fuzhou Normal University, Hua University, and Putian University in establishing integrated circuit industry colleges, opening experimental classes, and hiring industry experts as part-time mentors. Support Xiamen University and Fuzhou University in sharing experimental platforms with other universities within the province to enhance trainees' practical skills. Second, strengthen discipline construction. Support Fuzhou University in establishing a doctoral degree programme in integrated circuit science and engineering, actively connect with leading integrated circuit disciplines at universities outside the province such as Tsinghua University, Zhejiang University, Xi'an Jiaotong University, and Chengdu University of Electronic Science and Technology for academic and talent exchange, and establish a number of joint master's and doctoral programmes. Third, strengthen platform construction. Continue to promote the construction of the National Demonstration Microelectronics College of Fuzhou University and Xiamen University, the Fuzhou University-Jinjiang Microelectronics Research Institute, and the National Integrated Circuit Industry-Education Integration Innovation Platform. Flexibly introduce high-end talent in key fields strategically prioritised by Fujian Province to promote complementary technological advantages and collaborative innovation. Continuously improve and optimise platform management mechanisms, establish evaluation criteria and methods oriented towards innovation quality, contribution, and performance, and streamline procedures for the reimbursement of research funds and submission of data and materials to reduce the administrative burden on researchers.

Create a provincial-level integrated circuit collaborative innovation platform. Focus on key sub-industries in Fujian Province, attract domestic and international innovative resources, and support the construction of provincial-level innovation platforms. First, accelerate the construction of laboratories. Focusing on the proposed innovation laboratories for 'high-performance chip design and next-generation independent innovation architecture DRAM storage research and development,' accelerate the mass production and expansion of storage chip manufacturing projects, promote domestic substitution, establish a goal of building major national equipment, and refine key research tasks. Second, actively plan for future technologies.

Research and develop next-generation core chips such as high-speed optical chips and silicon optical chips, and achieve the development and production of high-speed chip DFB, EML, VCSEL, and 800Gbps and 1.6Tbps silicon-based optical chips to fill domestic gaps and break international monopolies. Actively build application demonstration scenarios. Seize market opportunities brought about by new technologies, new applications, and domestic production, and deepen applications in 5G communications, automotive electronics, image sensing, data centres, photovoltaics, and energy storage.

Design and release a list of integrated circuit application scenarios for public access, encouraging Fujian Province's integrated circuit companies to adopt them first. Encourage terminal manufacturers, component suppliers, and system solution integrators to actively test, trial, and procure products and services developed by local integrated circuit companies, promoting synergy between 'chip and machine' to accelerate the growth and strength of local design companies.

Strengthen financial support for key projects. First, explore the establishment of a coordination mechanism between fiscal funds and annual plans for key projects. Develop funding 保障 schemes, using key project construction plans as the basis and priority for allocating fiscal construction funds. Coordinate various government funding sources, including budget funds, idle funds and assets, debt funds, policy-based funds contributed by the government, and government equity assets, to ensure adequate funding for key projects and monitor implementation. For national-level projects, actively seek central government policies and funds to further meet project needs. Second, strengthen project evaluation. Flexibly utilise expert teams from within and outside the province to implement the project proposal review system, strictly review the necessity, urgency, construction scale, and investment estimates of projects, and guide the orderly and reasonable construction of projects. Third, explore the establishment of industrial guidance funds. Establish a provincial-level industrial investment guidance fund for integrated circuits, and encourage cities with the necessary conditions to establish industrial guidance funds. Coordinate with the National Integrated Circuit Industry Investment Fund to secure support from the National Integrated Circuit Industry Investment Fund for the development of enterprises in the province.

8.4 Insights into the Development of Fujian Province's Semiconductor Industry

During his first term, Trump initiated sanctions against China's semiconductor industry, implementing large-scale measures such as the Entity List. Unlike the Biden administration's sanctions targeting advanced processes (7 nm), memory (18 nm DRAM, 128-layer or higher NAND), and artificial intelligence, Trump sought to establish a US-dominated, 'de-Chinaised' global semiconductor supply chain, encompassing manufacturing, materials, and equipment. Semiconductor materials provide chemicals and materials for the front-end manufacturing and back-end packaging and testing stages, serving as the cornerstone of industry development. According to research institutions, the market growth rate for domestic substitution of semiconductor materials is expected to exceed 10% from 2024 to 2027, with the market size expanding to 58.6 billion US dollars by 2027. Currently, China remains highly dependent on imports from the United States, Japan, and the European Union for certain critical materials, with domestic production rates below 10%. Trump's re-election has once again sounded the clarion call for China to accelerate the domestic production of semiconductor materials. Provinces such as Guangdong, Jiangsu, and Zhejiang are seizing the window of opportunity for domestic substitution to expand their market share. It is recommended that Fujian Province leverage its development foundation and address its bottlenecks to accelerate the establishment of a semiconductor materials innovation ecosystem with Fujian characteristics, strengthen the resilience of the semiconductor industry chain and supply chain along the southeastern coast, and strive to chart a 'Fujian-specific' map of the semiconductor industry within the national industrial development landscape.

8.4.1 Accelerate the Development of the Upstream Industry Chain and Leverage the Industrial Foundation to Develop the Semiconductor Materials Segment

8.4.1.1 Lessons from Japan: Mastering Upstream High-End Materials to Control Key Links in the Global Semiconductor Industry

Japan's semiconductor industry has undergone four stages: rise in the 1970s, peak in the 1980s, decline in the 1990s, and transformation in the 2000s, transitioning from the world's leading chip manufacturing nation to a global semiconductor materials powerhouse. Among the 19 essential materials for semiconductor manufacturing, Japanese companies hold over 50% of the market share for 14 of them, maintaining an absolute advantage globally for an extended period. This was driven by four key factors: (1) robust domestic downstream demand; (2) a strong foundation in basic materials industries; (3) the transformation and upgrading of traditional raw material industries; and (4) the collaborative R&D ecosystem between government, industry, and academia.

The development environment and current stage of China's semiconductor industry bear significant similarities to Japan's situation three to four decades ago. In 1985, the United States initiated the US-Japan trade war with the signing of the Plaza Accord. Subsequently, the 1986 and 1991 US-Japan Semiconductor Agreements forced Japan to relinquish its global dominance in the semiconductor industry. Similarly, in 2018, the Trump administration abruptly imposed 'Section 301 tariffs' on China, officially launching the first shot in the US-China trade war. In 2022, the Biden administration enacted the 'Chips and Science Act,' intensifying structural suppression of China's semiconductor and other high-tech industries. With the recent re-election of Trump, who enjoys the support of both chambers of Congress, more extreme suppression policies may be introduced. The development model of Japan's semiconductor industry, which has shifted from manufacturing to upstream materials, is worth studying and learning from.

8.4.1.2 The State Has Increased Support for the Upstream Segment of the Industrial Chain, and Fujian Province Also Possesses the Four Key Elements for the Development of Japan's Semiconductor Materials Industry

According to the '2024 Global Wafer Capacity Report,' as of the end of 2023, mainland China's monthly wafer production capacity accounted for 19.1% of the global total, trailing only South Korea's 22.2% and Chinese Taiwan's 22.0%, ranking third globally. It is projected that by 2026, mainland China will become the world's largest source of integrated circuit wafer production capacity. Unlike the first and second phases of the National Integrated Circuit Industry Investment Fund, which allocated 50% to 70% of its funds to the manufacturing sector, the newly established third phase explicitly prioritises investments in upstream supply chain equipment and materials. Through research into the development trajectory of Japan's semiconductor industry, Fujian Province has identified that it possesses all four key elements necessary for the development of semiconductor materials. First, through the implementation of the 'Enhancing Semiconductor Chips and Strengthening Display Screens' strategy over the past decade, Fujian Province has formed a relatively complete production chain and sales chain for semiconductor-related industries, with strong domestic downstream demand driving growth. Second, Fujian Province has firmly implemented the 'less oil, more chemicals' development strategy, extending its industrial chain towards chemical new materials and high-end specialty chemicals, laying a solid foundation for upgrading to semiconductor materials and high-end specialty chemicals. Third, Fujian Province is part of the first tier of the 'Eastern Coastal Industrial Agglomeration Zone' alongside provinces and municipalities such as Jiangsu, Guangdong, Zhejiang, and Shandong in the new materials sector. It leads in traditional raw material fields such as textile materials, chemical materials, and metal new materials. Fuzhou, Xiamen, and Putian's new functional materials have been selected as the first batch of national strategic emerging industrial clusters, providing both technological support for the development of high-value-added products such as semiconductor materials and driving force for transformation and upgrading to seek new growth points. Fourth, Fujian's universities have strong disciplines in chemistry, chemical engineering, and materials science. The School of Chemical Engineering at Xiamen University ranks among the top 0.005% globally in the ESI subject rankings, while the chemistry and materials science disciplines at Fuzhou University rank among the top 3 in the university and enter the top 0.1% globally in the ESI rankings. The three provincial-level innovation laboratories—Mindu, Qingyuan, and Jiageng—have all commenced cutting-edge research and technology transfer in the field of semiconductor materials.

8.4.1.3 Fujian Province Lacks a Comparative Advantage in the Design, Manufacturing, Packaging and Testing, and Equipment Segments of the Semiconductor Industry Chain and Should Accelerate Its in Semiconductor Materials

The distribution of China's integrated circuit industry overall presents a 'one dominant, multiple strong' pattern. The 'one dominant' refers to the Yangtze River Delta region represented by Shanghai, Jiangsu, Zhejiang, and Hubei. In terms of the industrial chain segments such as chip design, wafer manufacturing, and packaging and testing, Fujian Province lags significantly behind the aforementioned provinces and municipalities. However, in the semiconductor materials sector, Fujian Province has 'many highlights,' having cultivated a significant number of material companies (over 30) and exhibiting characteristics of differentiated and regional specialised development, with a relatively diverse range of products. These include ultra-high-purity germanium, photoresist, developer, cleaning agents, target materials, bonding wires, lead frames, flexible substrates, and SiC substrate epitaxial materials.

Fujian Del Technology is a 'super unicorn' in the electronic specialty gases sector, with recent progress in its IPO, aiming to raise 3 billion yuan to achieve full-grade coverage of electronic-grade hydrogen fluoride products from G1 to G5. Bochun Materials is an advanced semiconductor process-enabled ultra-high-purity germanium hydride production base, an Intel-backed company, and China's first special gas supplier to TSMC, with its germanium hydride and other special gas products holding a 60% market share in the Asia-Pacific region; Hengkun Co., Ltd. can mass-produce photoresists and precursors for 12-inch and 28 nm processes, serving leading global companies such as Intel and SMIC; Meirifengchuang can produce photomasks supporting 14 nm and above processes, establishing a world-class photomask R&D centre, and plans to build the largest integrated circuit commercial photomask production base in mainland China; Quanzhou Sanan can produce 4/6-inch lithium tantalate polishing wafers and other filter front-end materials, supporting filter manufacturing; Beidian New Materials and Hantiancheng can produce SiC substrates and epitaxial materials. Additionally, Fujian Province has introduced and cultivated a number of high-quality projects, including Shenyuan New Materials, Nanping Huiyi San'ai Fu, Sanming Haifu, and Tianfu Electronics Semiconductor Chemicals.

8.4.2   Addressing Development Bottlenecks to Accelerate the High-Quality Development of the Semiconductor Materials Industry

8.4.2.1   Bottleneck 1: Lack of Enterprises with Core Technologies in Key Areas in Fujian Province

Although Fujian Province has achieved localisation of supply chains in areas such as photomasks, photoresists, glass substrates, target materials, electronic specialty gases, and wet chemicals in recent years, most semiconductor material companies remain in the early stages of development. Only one listed company, Aishengchuang, and one company, Del Technology, selected for the '2024 China New Materials Enterprise Top 100 List,' are present in the sector. Fujian Province still has no domestic production capacity for silicon wafer slices, CMP materials, FMM, and OLED functional materials.

Recommendations: First, cultivate core product lines suited to Fujian Province's resource endowments. Utilise the two national-level petrochemical bases in Quanzhou and Zhangzhou, as well as chemical industrial parks in Fuzhou Jiangyin, Nanping Shaowu, Sanming Qingliu, and Longyan Shanghang, to extend the industrial chain. Leverage Fujian Province's advantages in fluorite mines, rare metal niobium-tantalum mines, barite mines, tungsten ore, and other resources. Classify and categorise industries based on their development stage, and prioritise the development of key materials in high-end fluorinated polymers, electronic specialty gases, sputtering targets, optical base films, and other key areas to form a specialised industrial cluster centred on "fine chemicals—wafer manufacturing materials, packaging materials manufacturing—chip, panel manufacturing/packaging and testing—electronic products and applications' specialised industrial chain cluster, connecting Fujian Province's two trillion-yuan-level industries and generating a '1+1>2" cluster effect.

Second, increase the proportion of production lines and capacity in new fields of semiconductor materials. Relying on the good cooperation foundation between Wanhua Chemical, Huayi and Fujian, promote the increase of investment by the group's electronic materials companies in Fujian, focusing on Shanghai Silicon Co., Ltd., HuaTe Gas, Shanghai Xinyang, Nanjing University of Science and Technology Optoelectronics, and other national-level manufacturing champions in semiconductor silicon wafers, electronic specialty gases, wafer-level chemicals, photoresists, and other semiconductor material segments. We will track their needs to expand production scale and increase capacity, and support them in raising capital through private placements to establish new production bases in Fujian Province.

Third, leverage third-party system integrators to overcome barriers to introducing core technologies. Target the core technologies and technology sources of semiconductor materials, leverage existing technology transfer and conversion platforms or technology introduction service centres to first introduce them to third-party solution providers or integrators, and after comprehensive use of intellectual property rights to analyse or redevelop them, then authorise or transfer them to Fujian-based companies with demand (Chen & Chen 2022).

8.4.2.2 Bottleneck 2: Lack of a Collaborative Ecosystem for Material Verification and Production Application in Fujian Province

The semiconductor materials industry requires collaboration among upstream and downstream enterprises in all links of the industrial chain to overcome issues such as lengthy verification cycles and difficulties in promoting application. To this end, the Ministry of Industry and Information Technology (MIIT) has led the establishment of 18 national new materials production and application demonstration platforms, 13 testing and evaluation platforms, and 1 resource-sharing platform by new materials production enterprises and application enterprises. These platforms aim to achieve synergistic collaboration between new materials and end-products, but Fujian Province has limited participation.

Among these, only two companies from Fujian Province are involved in the production and application demonstration platforms, which have a total of 159 participating companies nationwide. No companies from Fujian Province are involved in the testing and evaluation platforms.

Suggestions: First, draw on Dongguan's full industrial chain business model to strengthen collaboration across the material-chip-integration-application segments. Referring to the provincial-municipal joint construction approach of Guangdong Province and Dongguan City, encourage enterprises in the midstream and downstream of Fujian's new display and wafer manufacturing/packaging and testing industries to actively participate and jointly invest in the establishment of semiconductor material companies, and build comprehensive platforms for scientific research, pilot testing, inspection and testing, and technical services. This will gather the development elements of the entire industrial chain, including specialised materials, specialised chips, device modules, and power electronic devices, and break the situation of 'scattered resources' and 'disconnected upstream and downstream'.

Second, introduce provincial-level comprehensive insurance policies for key new materials pilot production and first-batch application insurance compensation to overcome market bottlenecks during the initial application phase. Fully implement the national key new materials first-batch application insurance compensation policy, draw on the experiences of Shanghai, Zhejiang, and other provinces and municipalities, actively coordinate with the China Integrated Circuit Co-insurance Consortium, and guide provincial insurance institutions to innovate products such as liability insurance for domestically produced supply materials. Provide appropriate support and subsidies to semiconductor material companies that purchase insurance, and use market-based mechanisms to share the risks associated with the use of domestically produced new materials by integrated circuit and new display companies, thereby eliminating concerns about 'good materials not being used.'

Third, promote close collaboration between the competent authorities for the semiconductor materials industry and fund management institutions to aggregate innovative resources in the industrial chain through equity investment. The competent authorities should compile an industry map, combine local resource endowments, industrial foundations, and fund types, and formulate a list of tasks for attracting investment for funds to provide information support for the investment decisions of government-guided funds and social fund management teams. Jointly establish sub-funds with fund management institutions in other provinces in the semiconductor field, connect with the National Integrated Circuit Industry Innovation Fund, and leverage its strength to strengthen cooperation and collaboration with leading enterprises in the industry and upstream and downstream small and medium-sized enterprises in other provinces.

8.4.2.3   Bottleneck 3: Lack of Organisational Guidance for Innovation-Driven Development in Fujian's Government, Industry, Academia and Research

The semiconductor materials industry is characterised by high technical barriers and high industry concentration, which requires organised collaborative innovation consortia to strengthen the development of common technologies. According to patent database searches, enterprises account for over 56.2% of total patent applications in Fujian's new materials industry, but each enterprise holds few patents. Among the top 10 applicants, seven are universities and research institutions, which control most of the preliminary research results. However, research areas are scattered, and there is a lot of low-level repetitive research. As a result, among the 163 national-level innovation platforms in the new materials sector, Fujian Province has only three.

Recommendation: Explore three organisational forms of collaborative innovation consortia.

First, explore the 'chain leader department + chain leader enterprise' promotion model. Incorporate the semiconductor materials industry chain into Fujian Province's integrated circuit task force, establish a high-end new materials cluster construction working group, and refer to the hydrogen energy industry joint research institute model, with relevant provincial departments serving as chain leaders with relevant provincial state-owned enterprises as chain leaders, to form the Fujian Semiconductor Industry Joint Research Institute led by the 'chain leader + chain leader' model. This would coordinate relevant provincial departments and industrial clusters to form a collaborative effort, avoid the dispersion of innovation resources and duplicate construction of innovation platforms in the semiconductor materials field, establish a research and development and industrialisation technology roadmap for semiconductor materials, and build an innovation ecosystem of 'symbiotic integration and coordinated development' spanning the entire industrial chain from materials, devices, terminals to final applications.

Second, explore a fusion innovation model driven by terminal application enterprises. Led by application-end enterprises such as the Fujian Electronics Information Group, in collaboration with semiconductor material enterprises, Fuzhou University, Xiamen University, and the Fujian Institute of Structure of Matter of the Chinese Academy of Sciences, establish a National Technology Innovation Centre (NTIC) or a National Manufacturing Innovation Centre for Semiconductor Materials. This centre will establish a four-tier testing and analysis service platform covering frontier basic research, technology development, pilot production and evaluation, and matching manufacturing/testing and packaging, to integrate the entire chain from scientific research to technology transfer.

Third, explore a frontier breakthrough model led by research institutions. Support Xiamen University, Fuzhou University, and the Fujian Institute of Structure of Matter of the Chinese Academy of Sciences to coordinate the construction of new material collaborative research institutions, restructure and establish high-level innovation platforms such as the National Engineering Research Centre for Advanced Electronic Chemicals, actively undertake national key projects for semiconductor materials, address common technical challenges and 'chokepoint' issues across industries, and intensify technological breakthroughs and product upgrades in key areas such as advanced electronic chemicals, electronic specialty gases, and sputtering target materials.

8.4.2.4 Bottleneck 4: Fujian Province Lacks Methods for Attracting, Cultivating, and Retaining Talent

In the semiconductor field, Fujian Province has only one national-level innovation platform established by a company, Xiamen Tungsten Industry, There are few national-level new materials research platforms/projects, and young researchers in Fujian Province lack career development opportunities, resulting in an almost zero retention rate of locally trained postgraduates in related disciplines, let alone attracting domestic and international new materials innovation talent. Additionally, existing chemical materials talent primarily focuses on traditional petrochemical fields, while the semiconductor materials industry spans chemistry, physics, electronics, and materials science—a multidisciplinary and cross-sectoral field—making it difficult to cultivate talent through the 'master-apprentice' model and unable to establish a sustainable talent supply chain for the industry.

Suggestions: First, conduct integrated circuit professional title evaluations. Commission provincial-level think tanks, industry associations, industrial alliances, and other institutions to investigate the talent institutions and distribution in Fujian's semiconductor industry to provide guidance on identifying talent gaps and technological sources. Learn from the practices of Jiangsu, Beijing, Shandong, Shanghai, and other places, and rely on Fujian's electronic professional title evaluation committee to promote integrated circuit and new materials professional title evaluations throughout the province (city) to accelerate the gathering and training of integrated circuit materials engineering and technical personnel.

Second, launch activities to attract high-level overseas industrial talent. Seize the opportunity presented by the Trump administration's anti-China policies, which have prompted overseas talent to return to China, and monitor the dynamics of high-end Chinese talent in the US semiconductor industry. Utilise platforms such as the 'China Overseas Talent Conference' and the 'Digital China Summit' to invite overseas high-level entrepreneurial talent who have returned to China and achieved entrepreneurial success, academicians and experts with overseas experience, and leading talent in the semiconductor materials industry to invest and start businesses in Fujian through project cooperation, part-time employment with additional compensation, or special appointment positions.

Third, strengthen the cultivation and retention of semiconductor materials talent in Fujian Province. Support domestic universities to collaborate with new display companies and wafer manufacturing/packaging and testing companies to establish semiconductor materials industry colleges or interdisciplinary programmes in cutting-edge semiconductor materials fields, accelerate the integration of industry and education, and cultivate innovative, application-oriented talent with cross-disciplinary expertise in semiconductors and materials.

References

Chen, R., & Chen, Z. (2022). Research on countermeasures for modernizing the integrated circuit industry chain in Fujian Province [In Chinese]. *Journal of Minnan Normal University (Philosophy and Social Sciences Edition), 36*(4), 20–26.

Wang, S., Zeng, Y., Shi, L., & others. (2022). An analysis of the current supply and demand situation for integrated circuit talent in Fujian Province [In Chinese]. *China Integrated Circuit, 31*(5), 18–21.

Yu, X. (2018). Strategies and recommendations for promoting the development of the integrated circuit industry in Fujian Province [In Chinese]. *Strait Science, 2018*(11), 92–94.